MUSIC AND ETHICS

Music and Ethics

MARCEL COBUSSEN
Leiden University, The Netherlands

NANETTE NIELSEN
University of Nottingham, UK

ASHGATE

© Marcel Cobussen and Nanette Nielsen 2012

All rights reserved. No part of this publication may be reproduced, stored in a retrieval system or transmitted in any form or by any means, electronic, mechanical, photocopying, recording or otherwise without the prior permission of the publisher.

Marcel Cobussen and Nanette Nielsen have asserted their right under the Copyright, Designs and Patents Act, 1988, to be identified as the authors of this work.

Published by
Ashgate Publishing Limited
Wey Court East
Union Road
Farnham
Surrey, GU9 7PT
England

Ashgate Publishing Company
Suite 420
101 Cherry Street
Burlington
VT 05401-4405
USA

www.ashgate.com

British Library Cataloguing in Publication Data
Cobussen, Marcel, 1962–
  Music and ethics.
  1. Music – Psychological aspects. 2. Music, Influence of.
  3. Ethics.
  I. Title II. Nielsen, Nanette.
  781.1'1–dc23

Library of Congress Cataloging-in-Publication Data
Cobussen, Marcel, 1962–
  Music and ethics / Marcel Cobussen and Nanette Nielsen.
    p. cm.
  Includes bibliographical references and index.
  ISBN 978-1-4094-3496-2 (hardcover)—ISBN 978-1-4094-3497-9 (ebook)
  1. Music—Philosophy and aesthetics. 2. Music—Moral and ethical aspects 3. Music—Psychological aspects. 4. Music, Influence of. 5. Ethics. I. Nielsen, Nanette. II. Title.

ML3820.C72 2012
780'.017—dc23

ISBN 9781409434962 (hbk)
ISBN 9781409434979 (ebk – PDF)
ISBN 9781409484172 (ebk – ePUB)

Printed and bound in Great Britain by the MPG Books Group, UK.

Contents

List of Music Examples		*vii*
Acknowledgements		*ix*
Introduction *Nanette Nielsen and Marcel Cobussen*		1
1	Listening *Marcel Cobussen*	13
2	Discourse *Nanette Nielsen*	37
3	Interaction *Marcel Cobussen*	59
4	Affect *Marcel Cobussen*	91
5	Voice *Nanette Nielsen*	117
6	Engagement *Marcel Cobussen and Nanette Nielsen*	155
Bibliography		*167*
Index		*177*

List of Music Examples

5.1 Alban Berg, *Wozzeck*, bars 136–142. Full score © 1926 by Universal Edition A.G. Wien, English Translation 1952 by Alfred Kalmus London. Full score copyright renewed 1954 by Helene Berg, Pocket Score © 1955 Universal Edition A.G. Wein.   136

5.2 Alban Berg, *Wozzeck*, bars 381–385. Full score © 1926 by Universal Edition A.G. Wien, English Translation 1952 by Alfred Kalmus London. Full score copyright renewed 1954 by Helene Berg, Pocket Score © 1955 Universal Edition A.G. Wein.   143

5.3 Alban Berg, *Wozzeck*, bars 85–96. Full score © 1926 by Universal Edition A.G. Wien, English Translation 1952 by Alfred Kalmus London. Full score copyright renewed 1954 by Helene Berg, Pocket Score © 1955 Universal Edition A.G. Wein.   145

5.4 Alban Berg, *Wozzeck*, bar 106. Full score © 1926 by Universal Edition A.G. Wien, English Translation 1952 by Alfred Kalmus London. Full score copyright renewed 1954 by Helene Berg, Pocket Score © 1955 Universal Edition A.G. Wein.   147

Acknowledgements

For a book in which aspects of ethics and morality are rethought, re-evaluated and transformed it is almost impossible to imagine that the acknowledgements – usually considered as a *hors d'oeuvre*, a *par-ergon*, a non-essential supplement – would not also be affected. What about the ethicality of the acknowledgements, of thanking people who contributed in some way or another to our book's materialization?

Nanette's contributions were made possible by her institutional research leave at the University of Nottingham in the spring of 2011. She would like to thank her colleagues in the Department of Music in particular for having provided this window of opportunity for valuable research and writing time. Marcel's input could never have been effectuated without the support of Frans de Ruiter, Director of the Academy of Creative and Performing Arts at Leiden University, who created a stimulating environment in which Marcel's research on music and ethics could take place.

We have benefited from numerous and various interactions with colleagues, conference audiences and students: there have been conversations with far too many people to name all of them here, but you know who you are! At different stages during the process of thinking and writing, a few people in particular have offered stimulating dialogue, advice, and/or comments on drafts of chapters. We would like to thank Robert Adlington, Nicholas Baragwanath, Michael Beckerman, Richard Bell, Bruce Ellis Benson, Andrew Bowie, Darla Crispin, John Deathridge, Lydia Goehr, Garry Hagberg, Björn Heile, Sarah Hibberd, Kathleen Higgins, Julian Johnson, Jerrold Levinson, Susan McClary, Vincent Meelberg, Stephen Mumford, Richard Taruskin, Lucy Walker, Ruud Welten and Peter Wright. The team at Ashgate, especially Heidi Bishop and Laura Macy, should receive special thanks for their support at every step in the process towards completion. Finally, an enormous debt of gratitude is owed to Nathan Seinen, who edited the entire book, correcting in detail the language of two non-native English speakers and offering many useful comments and criticisms. Of course, the authors take full responsibility for the final text.

Having said our thanks, however, we also recall that thinkers such as Jacques Derrida and Emmanuel Levinas, who play such important roles in this book, have taught us that in order to create an ethical work, one should receive gifts – comments, advices, dialogues, which in themselves can be called ethical works – *ungratefully*, in order to suppress any presumption of reciprocity. If the giver expects something in return, the gift is not a true gift and therefore not ethical. As a result, this book should *not* be given back to the individuals named above.

Does this mean that acknowledgements are unethical by nature? And is it possible to escape this unethicality? In this book we propose a (musical) ethics that implies an engagement which can only be achieved through an open listening attitude, an openness towards other voices and the voices of others. It is precisely this kind of open attitude from those we thank above that has made it possible for us to create something which can only be given but never be given back. So, we thank them – ungratefully…

Introduction

Nanette Nielsen and Marcel Cobussen

> Music is, first of all, an experience.
> Kathleen Higgins, *The Music of Our Lives*, p. 113.

The relationship between ethics and music is one of the oldest topics in philosophical discussions of music, dating at least as far back as Plato, who warned against the morally corrupting power that music could have on the soul while also recognizing that it could engender grace and harmony.[1] Music and ethics is, at the same time, one of the most recent topics attracting attention within both music studies and philosophy, in that it is only within the last twenty-five years that critical developments have begun to open up this sphere of inquiry. This book is an attempt to respond, and add something, to these developments. Our exploration is by no means intended to be exhaustive in scope. We seek, rather, to unravel various 'ethical moments', which involve, on the one hand, ethical issues that warrant musical discussion and, on the other, examples of music that invite ethical explication. Of course, these issues and examples often overlap and interact across fluid borders; ethical moments can be profoundly musical, and evade straightforward discussion or translation, but nevertheless (or therefore) add to ethical discourses within philosophical and critical disciplines. In addition to providing a new angle within music studies, our study accords with recent attempts to demonstrate how music can contribute to the study of philosophy. We would argue that philosophy should not be considered merely a tool with which music can be theorized and explained, and that 'the ethics of music' should not be regarded as a problem that needs to be solved by philosophical discourse. Our primary aim is instead to examine music in ways that lead to critical and philosophical reflections on ethics. To this extent we answer Andrew Bowie's exhortation, 'to regard the "philosophy of music", not as the philosophy whose job is conceptually to determine the object "music", but rather as the philosophy that emerges from music.'[2]

One major challenge encountered in scholarly developments relates to the intersection between ethics and aesthetics. Many twentieth-century philosophers of art have not only neglected this intersection, but in fact presented it as

---

[1] See, for example, Plato, *The Republic*, Book III, trans. Benjamin Jowett (Charleston, SC: BiblioBazaar, 2007), p. 115 and pp. 124–26.

[2] Andrew Bowie, *Music, Philosophy, and Modernity* (Cambridge: Cambridge University Press, 2007), p. 11.

irrelevant, or conceptually invalid. This has been due in particular to the Kantian legacy, and to formalism and aestheticism ('art for art's sake'), for which it would make little sense to include discussions of ethics in relation to art. By the mid-twentieth century, many analytic philosophers were still relying on Kant's second edition of the *Kritik der Reinen Vernunft* (*Critique of Pure Reason*) from 1787, including its stern critique of aesthetics, which Kant claimed was not a philosophical discipline at all.[3] He radically altered this view with his writings on aesthetics in the *Kritik der Urteilskraft* (*Critique of Judgement*) in 1790, but this was not fully acknowledged or pursued. In recent years this state of affairs has changed, however, and analytical philosophy has added a great deal to the study of aesthetics, including its relationship to ethics.[4] Nevertheless, certain limitations still hinder this branch of philosophy's deeper engagement with music and ethics, as we shall see in Chapter 2, 'Discourse'.

The area of music and ethics has also been opening up in music studies and within other philosophical approaches. Two works should be mentioned here. Kathleen Higgins published a book in 1991 entitled *The Music of Our Lives*, in which she presents as ethically significant the affective character of music that makes listeners aware of their connection with others.[5] Music contributes to a better understanding of one's place within the world, and (thus) to an ethical sensibility. Higgins's work can be seen as complementary to our own, in that there is some similarity between our perspectives, including the exploration of music and ethics in light of (human) interaction, and the wish to ground music and ethics in intersubjective relations (not least from the perspective of listening). We argue, as Higgins does, for contextual understanding and engagement rather than Platonic or other universalist approaches to 'music as object'. Another 'precursor' of the present book is the November 2002 issue of the *Dutch Journal of Music Theory* (henceforth *DJMT*), devoted to the theme 'Music & Ethics'.[6] The articles in this issue addressed ethical issues related to authority, responsibility and

---

[3] Analytic (or Anglo-American) philosophers at this time dismissed aesthetics as unworthy of study. One example is John Passmore's article 'The Dreariness of Aesthetics', *Mind*, 60/239 (1951), pp. 318–35. Peter Kivy (ed.), *The Blackwell Guide to Aesthetics* (Oxford: Blackwell Publishing Ltd., 2004), p. 3.

[4] See especially Jerrold Levinson (ed.), *Ethics and Aesthetics: Essays at the Intersection* (Cambridge: Cambridge University Press, 1998); Garry Hagberg, (ed), *Art and Ethical Criticism* (New York: Blackwell Publishing, 2008); and Peter Kivy, *Antithetical Arts: On the Ancient Quarrel between Literature and Music* (Oxford: Oxford University Press, 2009).

[5] Kathleen Higgins, *The Music of Our Lives* (Lanham, MD: Lexington Books, 2011). Previously published by Temple University Press (1991).

[6] *Dutch Journal of Music Theory*, 7/3 (November 2002). (The journal has two official titles: the Dutch title is *Tijdschrift voor Muziektheorie*.) The articles in the volume emerged from a meeting held in Rotterdam on 11 January 2002 entitled 'The Future of Musicology: Towards Music(ology) and Ethics'. This meeting was directly linked to Marcel Cobussen's defence of his PhD thesis, 'Deconstruction in Music', held the previous day.

openness. Many of the contributors to *DJMT* refer to Emmanuel Levinas as their inspiration for a new conceptual framework with which to shape musicological discourse. However, in very few of the articles is 'ethics' examined as a concept; rather, it is approached primarily in general terms, without attention to particular circumstances and therefore to any specific ethics that would relate to the music in question.

'Music' and 'ethics' are both indeterminate concepts, capable of referring to a variety of practices. If 'music' can denote anything from the potato music of the Andes through Cage's aleatoric ventures to Beethoven's Ninth Symphony, 'ethics' can relate to viewpoints as different as Christian morality, Nietzschean celebration of free individuality, or limitless hedonistic pleasure. A satisfying and workable definition cannot easily be constructed for either music or ethics, and once we begin exploring the area of music *and* ethics, the complexity increases exponentially. For ethics, the realization of the challenge of generality has led Bernard Williams to argue that 'philosophy should not try to produce ethical theory, though this does not mean that philosophy cannot offer any critique of ethical beliefs and ideas'.[7] In line with this view, we avoid a reduction of 'the ethics of music' to a universal theory and instead seek to open up more fruitful avenues of critical investigation. For ethics and music, a related call for particularity and contextual considerations has been made by Andrew Bowie in a paper entitled 'Prolegomena to Any Future Ethics of Music',[8] in which he points out that it would be very difficult and, indeed, undesirable to achieve a 'general' relation of ethics to music, due to the fact that philosophy offers such a vast array of ethical theories. Although we may be able to relate music broadly to, for example, Aristotelian ethics and music's relation to the 'good life', this would not be sufficient if we venture to ask and answer more probing and relevant questions: '"Which music in which ethical context?" is surely the issue', Bowie concludes, 'not generalisations about aesthetics and ethics.'[9]

Therefore, while acknowledging the complexity and breadth of both concepts, and avoiding *a priori* theoretical propositions about what ethics and music might be and how they can be linked abstractly and generally, our approach attempts to unravel interconnections between music and ethics in particular social, cultural and political contexts. The question of whether we can talk about 'a specifically musical ethics'[10] will depend on the extent to which a musical work, performance or listening practice can be linked to such a context. Crucially, we consider music

---

[7] Bernard Williams, *Ethics and the Limits of Philosophy* (London and New York: Routledge 2006, reprinted 2007), p. 17.

[8] Paper given at the Society for Music Analysis Winter Study Day on 'Music and Ethics', held at the University of East Anglia on 23 February 2002. We are grateful to the author for providing us with a typescript of this (unpublished) paper.

[9] Ibid., p. 2.

[10] This is Lawrence Kramer's expression. See *Dutch Journal of Music Theory* 7/3, p. 167.

as *process*, and music-making as interaction. Fundamental to our understanding is music's association with *activity* ('Interaction'), including contact with music through the act of listening ('Listening' and 'Voice'), music as an immanent critical process that possesses profound cultural and historical significance ('Discourse'), and as an art form that can be world-disclosive, formative of subjectivity, and contributive to intersubjective relations ('Interaction', 'Affect', and 'Voice').

Art and morality

Although philosophy has long neglected to pay adequate attention to the various relations between art, ethics and morality,[11] this has been of little consequence for artists who endeavour to address ethical principles or moral dilemmas and taboos through their work. If the connection between music and ethics is at first perhaps not a very obvious one, it might help our investigation to start here with a little detour to the domain of the visual arts.

In 2011 the Dutch artist Katinka Simonse, alias Tinkebell, was charged with animal abuse. She had participated in an art project called *Save the Pets*, creating a work consisting of ninety-five transparent plastic balls, each containing a hamster, which rolled through a gallery space (Masters) in Amsterdam. The animals were exhausted and stressed because they had been kept in the balls for four hours without food or drink, and were filthy because of their internment in an undersized cage for the remainder of the day. The Dierenbescherming (Animal Protection Society) decided that it was absolutely necessary to take action, and so the exhibition was closed, and Tinkebell and the gallery owner were taken to court.[12] Prior to this event, Tinkebell had already caused quite a stir with her idea to grind sixty chicks in a shredder during an art fair, and her actual strangling of her own cat in order to make a purse out of its fur.[13]

Of course, art can be even more repulsive than this. The most famous work of the Beijing-based performance artist Zhu Yu, entitled *Eating People*, was

---

[11] The common distinction between ethics and morality is that the first is mainly focused on 'the good' and 'the good life', whereas the latter pays more attention to 'the right' and to 'justice'. However, it needs to be recognized that a stable opposition is hard to maintain (cf. Nancy Fraser, 'Recognition without Ethics?' in M. Garber *et al.* (eds), *The Turn to Ethics*. (New York: Routledge, 2000), esp. pp. 97–99). We use ethics and morality interchangeably throughout this book, without distinguishing between them, unless this is required by a specific context or discussion.

[12] Both Tinkebell and the gallery owner were discharged as the court could not determine whether the hamsters' health had indeed been damaged by the project. In general, their condition appeared much better than had been claimed by the Animal Protection Society.

[13] 'Tinkebell. My Dearest Cat Pinkeltje', at: http://looovetinkebell.com/pages/my-dearest-cat-pinkeltje.

performed at a Shanghai arts festival in 2000. It consisted of a series of photographs of him cooking and eating what is alleged to be a human foetus. The UK television channel, Channel 4, defended a documentary about this 'baby-eating' artist by claiming that Yu merely makes the point that, in the end, humans are but a piece of meat. Equally laconically, the artist himself proclaims that no religion forbids cannibalism, nor could he find any law which proscribes it. So his art takes advantage of the space between morality and the law.[14]

Both of these examples – and it would be easy to add dozens more, from Maurizio Cattelan's figure *Him*, a devoutly kneeling Adolf Hitler, to Andres Serrano's *Piss Christ*, a small plastic crucifix submerged in a glass of the artist's urine – confront us with questions about the relation between art and ethics. A frequently expressed notion is that certain objects or events can escape prosecution when they are presented as artworks or artistic occurrences; that which would probably be forbidden in a non-artistic context is permitted when it occurs within the (rather vague) boundaries of what Howard Becker once coined 'the art world'.[15] Opinions about this alleged ethical freedom with regard to art range from radical moralism on the one side to radical autonomism on the other. Radical moralism asserts that every moral violation by or through an artwork should result in a condemnation of that work. Radical autonomism sets forth the exact opposite: art is autonomous and should be judged only according to aesthetic (and not social or ethical) norms. The basis of this autonomism is formed by the presupposition (which also prevails in the juridical world) that artists aspire to recognition of their work only as art. In between these two extremes one can find, for example, Noël Carroll's 'moderate moralism',[16] which states that an artwork can be called immoral when its content prevents a spectator from aesthetic pleasure, Berys Gaut's 'ethicism',[17] for which ethical flaws can be aesthetically relevant, depending on the particular work or context under consideration, and the 'ethical autonomism' of Rob van Gerwen,[18] who claims that a work is morally good when it requires us to relinquish an ordinary moral attitude in favour of a purely aesthetic one.

In addition to exploring artworks that would arguably be immediately repulsive to the recipient, we can equally uncover ethical–aesthetic tensions resulting from our engagement with art that is not necessarily immediately

---

[14] 'Baby-eating Art Show Sparks Upset', BBC News, 3 January 2003, at: http://news.bbc.co.uk/2/hi/entertainment/2624797.stm.

[15] Howard S. Becker, *Art Worlds* (Berkeley: University of California Press, 1982).

[16] Noël Carroll, 'Moderate Moralism', *British Journal of Aesthetics*, 36 (1996), pp. 223–38.

[17] Berys Gaut, 'The Ethical Criticism of Art', in Jerrold Levinson (ed.), *Aesthetics and Ethics: Essays at the Intersection* (Cambridge: Cambridge University Press, 1998), pp. 182–203.

[18] Rob van Gerwen, 'Ethical Autonomism: The Work of Art as a Moral Agent', *Contemporary Aesthetics*, 2 (2004), online at: http://www.phil.uu.nl/~rob/PF_oud/s_inlcolleges/s_inlteksten/ea.pdf.

shocking, but nevertheless stirs our moral consciousness. Here something may be added to the ethical dimension of art by the context in which it is created and/or received. Political art is an obvious example of this, and a famous example is Leni Riefenstahl's film *Triumph des Willens* (*Triumph of the Will*), a documentary of the 1934 Nüremberg Rally of the NSDAP, the National Socialist German Workers' Party. The film received the highest awards for artistic achievement, including a gold medal at the Venice Biennale in 1936 and the Grand Prix at the World Exhibition in Paris in 1937. After the war, however, it was condemned as National Socialist propaganda, and its status as art was called into question. For today's viewers, it is entirely possible to recognize the aesthetic qualities of the film, which contains some beautiful images and sequences. It nevertheless remains impossible to ignore the film's promotion of National Socialism: it is precisely the positive vision of the Nazis that is offered *as* beautiful. So if it is possible to recognize the aspects of *Triumph of the Will* that would arguably link it to the category of 'high art', deserving of aesthetic appreciation, our judgement is challenged because we need to decide not only whether our response is still appropriate in ethical terms, but also whether our moral response must necessarily have an impact on our aesthetic interpretation. As the philosopher Mary Devereaux argues, the conjunction of beauty and 'evil' makes the film disturbing, but it is also this conjunction that, along with our critical reflection, provides us with a reason to watch and engage with it.[19]

From the example of *Triumph of the Will* we can deduce two points relevant to the methodology we propose for the study of music and ethics. First, art that is normally recognized as 'high art' can also be caught in ethical dilemmas that are due to the context of its creation or reception. Second, from the possibility for a variety of responses inevitably follows responsibility: agency is an important element within ethical–aesthetic tensions, and therefore, while considering the many possible contexts for art, we also attempt to address the scope of agents' ethical choices. The issues that emerge with political art correspond to one notable aspect of *Music and Ethics*. We examine ethical–aesthetic tensions that are initiated through various processes and forms of engagement, and this requires an understanding that reaches beyond art 'as an object' into the ever-changing situatedness of art where the relationship between art and recipient is key.

One further example from the visual arts will help to illustrate this essential interactive and contextual aspect of our methodology. In the immediate aftermath of the killings in Norway on 22 July 2011, *The Sunday Times* published a drawing by the political cartoonist Gerald Scarfe that was a play on Edvard Munch's 1893 painting *The Scream*, arguably Norway's most famous artwork.[20] The cartoon was

---

[19] For a detailed discussion of this dilemma, see Mary Devereaux 'Beauty and Evil: The Case of Leni Riefenstahl's *Triumph of the Will*, in Levinson, *Ethics and Aesthetics*, pp. 227–56 at p. 251.

[20] The attacks by a right-wing Norwegian extremist included a mass shooting at a summer youth camp for the Norwegian Labour Party on the island of Utøya. The victims

a close copy of the Munch painting, depicting in the foreground the famous face distorted in a scream, holding his/her hands up to the cheeks, except that in the background, Scarfe had placed just one person (in the original there are two), and this figure holds a gun. It requires little capacity for interpretation to recognize the representation of the real gunman (Anders Behring Breivik), while the screaming face is that of one of his potential victims. Regardless of Scarfe's actual intentions, the cartoon clearly confronts us with an ethical challenge. What concerns us here is the multiplicity of possible ethical responses in its reception.[21] Many commentators on *The Times*' website were shocked by the extreme insensitivity of the cartoon, pointing out that it was both inappropriate and tasteless (this was linked to the presumed low intellectual level of *The Times* itself). At the opposite end of the spectrum, it was claimed that the cartoon was not intended as either a parody or funny, but could be seen instead to represent the angst of the Norwegian people, and thereby served as an expression of sympathy towards the victims and the nation as a whole.

The variety of responses to Scarfe's knowing play on well-known cultural motifs and current events within the form of a cartoon serves as an example of the potent yet often ambiguous force of humour, which is particularly evident when igniting ethical controversy. This is useful in that it suggests a comparative link between humour and ethics, and between music and ethics. Humour, like music, can generate powerful responses and can carry a multiplicity of meaning. Interpretation, affectivity and understanding often depend on context and framing, on cultural references and on vagaries of 'taste'. Scarfe's cartoon could elicit powerful moral responses because of its obvious associations and references; in order to provide an adequate explanation, meaningful interpretation and criticism, a recipient would need to be informed of a range of topics, including the fact of the Norwegian attacks themselves, the cultural context of the original Munch painting, the nature and meaning of cartoon parody, the possible reference in the cartoon to the spoof horror film *Scream*, Scarfe's other work, the nature of the newspaper in which the cartoon was published and its intended readership, and so on. Only then would the relevant ethical–aesthetic tensions emerge – for example, between high and low art (for instance, what happens when we understand Munch's painting in the context of *Scream*), between sincerity and banality (whether and how a newspaper cartoon in this case trivializes a serious matter), and how this cartoon – given the circumstances – could be seen in some way to cause harm to its audience or to others.

---

of the massacre were mostly teenagers, and 77 were killed in all (in addition to 96 injured). Scarfe's cartoon was published on Sunday 24 July, before all missing teenagers and victims had been accounted for.

[21] It was briefly given attention by one Channel 4 reporter and by another newspaper, the *Guardian*, resulting in a number of comments from the public. See especially Benjamin Cohen at: https://plus.google.com/100441642353694045036/posts/WeQV18n3KVZ.

From the visual to the sonic

The examples given above to introduce the often problematic relation between aesthetics and ethics are taken from the domain of the visual arts. Can the same kind of ethical challenges be found in (Western) auditory culture? Understanding music in terms of its potential ethical import similarly depends to a great extent on consideration of its contexts and cultural references, and its different effects on a range of listeners. Furthermore, we may feel a responsibility to *explain* our responses and associations in addressing ethical dilemmas (we turn to this in Chapter 2). Awareness of, reflection on, and explanation of our responses is crucial. Music may have a tendency to work also on an unconscious level (unnoticed, perhaps, in the background) and is thus able to affect us even more directly than the visual arts: we can close our eyes, but we cannot shut our ears. Sound and music have the capacity to reach very directly into the innermost core of our being, both physically and mentally (as we discuss in Chapter 4, 'Affect').

If we accept that violence is one possible manifestation of unethical behaviour, Bruce Johnson and Martin Cloonan's book *Dark Side of the Tune* is one study that can be highly instructive. Through references to numerous examples, Johnson and Cloonan demonstrate the ways in which music can be physically or aesthetically painful, although they do also stress the fact that negative reactions to music are usually due to the listener's lack of control of the sound source: it may be played by an inconsiderate neighbour, or by torturers conducting an interrogation.[22] They do not pass explicit judgement on the tensions between music and ethics that they uncover, but simply ascertain the potential roles that music can play in the enactment of power and violence. The same approach is taken by Steve Goodman in his monograph *Sonic Warfare*,[23] in which he investigates the use of (musical) sound in wars, in social disciplining and controlling through sound (for example, the application of Muzak to entice people, or 'sonic weapons' to chase away undesirable persons) and in marketing strategies that deploy sound in 'sonic branding'. These instances are presented as *faits accomplis*, rather than being assessed according to the measuring rod of either autonomism or moralism.

Within the context of the relation between art and ethics, these books demonstrate several things. As with the examples from the visual arts offered above, it is clear that the roles that music plays in societies can also transgress ethical norms and limits. Here, it is not music's content but its usage that creates a connection with ethics. More than any other art form, music has the potential to invade personal spaces and can be employed in behaviour that could qualify

---

[22] Bruce Johnson and Martin Cloonan, *Dark Side of the Tune. Popular Music and Violence* (Farnham: Ashgate, 2009), p. 24.

[23] Steve Goodman, *Sonic Warfare: Sound, Affect, and the Ecology of Fear* (Cambridge, MA: MIT Press, 2009).

as unethical, torture being the most extreme example.[24] However, music can also be used as an auditory tool to thwart unethical behaviour as is the case with Muzak, which is often used to induce customers to buy while also solving loitering problems in shopping malls. Music can prevent unrest in prisons, and classical music played in planes appears to calm its passengers before take-off or landing. However, here we arrive at a tricky problem. Music can, in some ways, contribute to the structuring of the world, of civilization and of a culture in order to prevent it from chaos and disorder; but a striving for order can itself display unethical traits, as in the case of overtly or covertly repressive state interventions.[25] The powers-that-be can decide whether (certain) music should be allowed or advocated, or regarded as subversive and banned. In any case, it is evident that it is difficult to maintain an absolute autonomous position for music in the light of ethical and moral questions and attitudes. Often, music is – more or less directly – involved in various complicated ethical situations, either supporting certain ethical norms or challenging them. The role, function and position of music in contemporary society exceed the aesthetical realm; music has more to offer to humanity than various kinds of aural entertainment, or of beauty for beauty's sake. Alongside its social, religious, political and economic roles, music is also an active participant in ethical concerns.

Does our rejection of music's still often proclaimed (radical) autonomy mean that we are forced to embrace either a radical or a more moderate moralism – one of the alternatives sketched above? We do not think so. These theories present the ethical content or effects of art products in relation to existing ethical principles or moral norms. In other words, ideas about ethics and morality precede here the artwork under consideration and provide, in advance, arguments with which to evaluate its ethical and moral qualities. These arguments, these principles and norms are often pre-established, deriving primarily from political, philosophical and juridical discourses.

In our view, this is only one side of the story. Of course, judging music according to ethical standards means entering into juridical–political–ethical discourses and accepting certain norms and values developed in and through those discourses. But we also propose and try to test another option. It is our claim that these discourses can benefit from the recognition of certain *experiences* encountered in and through music. Music offers much more to the topic than just adjustment to, or transgression of, prevailing ethical standards or moral laws; through music, aspects of ethical and moral discourses and behaviours can be rethought, revisited

---

[24] See, for example, Suzanne Cusick, "'You are in a Place That is Out of the World …": Music in the Detention Camps of the "Global War on Terror"', *Journal of the Society for American Music*, 2/1 (2008), pp. 1–26.

[25] The positive and negative consequences of structuring with the help of music or sound are also the main topics of Jacques Attali's famous book *Bruits* (Paris, 1981); English translation *Noise. The Political Economy of Music*, trans. B. Massumi (Minneapolis: University of Minnesota Press, 2003).

and revised. Instead of a mere reactive role, music can proactively contribute to debates around ethical and moral issues.[26] At the centre of this is the idea that the *responses* elicited by music in particular historical, political and cultural circumstances matter. Ethical issues are revealed more fully if we avoid the tendency to turn to the 'music itself', as an object, for insights on this issue, and instead explore the ways in which music engages with its listeners.

One of the ideas we develop in this book is that music's contribution to ethical issues can be useful and fruitful *because* music operates, at least partially, outside the domain of language, outside the restraints of discursivity. The specific role that music can play in and around ethics or morality is a musical one: via encounters with music, prevalent ideas about ethics and morality can be challenged, transgressed, changed or deepened. It is here that the relevance of *Music and Ethics* is most conspicuous. Music always already plays a role in the (de)(con)struction of our society, a fundamental but also very specific role, which might in turn influence the ways in which we deal with ethical and moral matters. Furthermore, music also (de)(con)structs our sonic, as well as our social, environments, and musical *discourses* have the power to shape our (moral) imaginations. We want to explore ways of doing justice to music and musical discourse: we hope that the following pages will convincingly demonstrate a few useful avenues.

Summary of the book

The opening chapter, 'Listening', provides a first sketch of a possible connection between music and ethics. In order to avoid presenting a musical ethics as 'ethical music' – that is, assigning ethical features to (certain) music, thereby creating a kind of essentialism – the idea is offered of an *aural ethics*, emerging in the encounter between music and listener. The act of listening (or at least *attentive* listening) requires both openness and curiosity. Drawing on a variety of theorists, including Badiou, Bauman, Derrida, Levinas and Scarry, ethics is clarified as adherence to singularity and otherness, in an aim to uncover a particular musical ethics in the concept of hospitality. We argue that the attentiveness inherent in adopting a hospitable, caring attitude creates a space between music and listener where ethics can happen.

---

[26] We acknowledge that such a proactive role is not completely absent in the theories proposed by Gaut *et al*. Nevertheless the differences between our approach and 'ethicism' and 'moderate moralism' will become clear throughout this book. Whereas these theories seem to suggest a focus on the inherent ethical dimensions of an artwork, we would rather position ethics in a space between artwork and recipient. Furthermore, we do not share Carroll's presupposition of cultural cohesion and homogeneity, which then leads to the potential achievement of a right and correct reading of a work. Instead, the ambiguity and uncontrollable aspects of artistic productions and perceptions need to be discussed: it is precisely here that an ethical potential of music might be traced.

Chapter 2, 'Discourse', explores recent attempts to carry out ethical criticisms of music and identifies some of the ethically charged layers within discourses on music. We assess approaches from both philosophy and musicology, and point to those avenues which we believe are likely to take us furthest for the area of music and ethics. Pointing to how music as aesthetic experience carries with it a variety of possible associations, we argue that in order to do justice – in an ethical sense – to music and musical discourse, the roles of agency and responsibility will need to be taken into consideration.

Returning to listening, the starting-point of 'Interaction' is the question of how the concept of non-listening, as suggested by improvising guitar player Keith Rowe, can undermine, or, conversely, deepen an aural ethics. Chapter 3 deals with the collaboration of improvising musicians on stage, focusing on the way in which improvisers interact during performance and critiquing the (principally Western) idea that ethics is a matter of individual responsibility. We also consider communitarianism – a mainly American alternative, which assumes that successful interaction within a community can only take place on the basis of some pre-established and shared ethical principles – but this also appears unadaptable to improvised music. With the help of Rowe's non-listening and, in particular, the philosophy of Jean-Luc Nancy, a 'third stream' is developed, summarized by Gary Peters as 'collective, yes, communal, no'.

Thus far, we have tried to argue that music can contribute positively to existing ethical discourses and concrete ethical behaviour. Chapter 4, 'Affect', however, concentrates on what should not be forgotten, namely that music often plays a dubious role in affairs that relate directly to ethics and morality. Football songs, Muzak and the playing of loud music as a method of torture are just three examples in which music is used to exclude and eliminate otherness from what Levinas calls 'the order of the Same'. Music often operates as a tool to control and discipline people in order to create a homogeneous community of obedient bodies. However, this more or less *un*ethical function of music is at the same time a demonstration of music's unique potential to contribute to current philosophical thought on ethics. Music's effect on human beings, its ability to penetrate bodies, allows man to appear not as an autonomous, self-consistent, rational Self, but as a *relational* subject, thereby opening the possibility to think a de-individualized ethics.

Chapter 5, 'Voice', explores relationships between the musical voice and ethics, and examines how music can be regarded ethical (or unethical) through a theoretical framework focusing on voice. While discussing the active interplay between phenomenology and hermeneutics from a variety of angles, we show how voice allows us to move beyond language and into a sphere where ethics has an important role to play: we argue that music and voice are crucial to the ways in which individuals articulate their being in the world. As a case study, in which we again turn to the important role of listening, we offer a new reading of Alban Berg's opera *Wozzeck* based on the proposed framework, and show how a focus on intersubjectivity and voice brings out important ethical layers that can have an impact on our moral perception of the opera as a whole.

Finally, in conclusion, Chapter 6, 'Engagement', brings together some of the themes explored in the previous chapters. Built around a close reading of *Appassionata*, a novel by Eva Hoffman, it shows once again music's potential to influence and contribute to ethical thinking and concrete moral behaviour in its own way. Likewise, 'Engagement' demonstrates that the possibility to relate music productively and creatively to ethics has to start from the only way humans can encounter music and sounds: by listening to it. It is a listening engagement and a resulting sonic sensibility that motivates and grounds this book. Working beyond composers' intentions, or stable registrations of a musical work with predetermined modes of analysis, this engagement continually re-produces the work in its perceptual moments: an ethics of music implies, first of all, a strategy of (attentive) listening. That is why so many pages in this book are dedicated to meditations and reflections around the process of listening (to sounds, voices, discourses), not as a scientific endeavour to reach 'the Truth' about music, but as an experiential adventure offering important strategies for imagining and interpreting, giving music a voice to speak, to speak differently, to speak differently each time again. In that sense the form and content of *Music and Ethics* coincide.

Chapter 1
Listening

Marcel Cobussen

> There will come a time when music alone will provide a way of slipping through the tight meshes of functions; leaving music as a powerful and uninfluenced reservoir of freedom must be accounted the most important task of intellectual life in the future. Music is the truly living history of humanity, of which otherwise we only have dead parts. One does not need to draw from music for it is always within us; all we have to do is listen simply, otherwise we would learn in vain.
>
> Elias Canetti, The Human Province, p. 17.

The power of music

Did the events of 11 September 2001 come as a gift from the gods for (Western) discourse on music? Did Al-Qaeda bring about a certain transition in the way we approach music, a shifting towards an increasing interest in the topic of ethicality in relation to music, manifested in an increased number of publications on this topic? Did these terrorist attacks and their far-reaching consequences also knock cracks in the formalist bastion, still powerful in some musicological landscapes? Valery Gergiev's scornful reply, 'I am interested in Prokofiev, not in Stalin', when asked whether Prokofiev's late works somehow reflected the political context in which they were composed, seems an echo from an ancient world where music was still considered immune to ethic-political influences. Granted, certain discourses surrounding music have stressed the relationship between music on the one hand and politics, morality and social behaviour on the other, years before Al-Qaeda attacked the icons of Western capitalist society. And, granted, thinking about the relationship between music and morality goes as far back as Pythagoras and Plato, and thus belongs to the core of Western cultural history. Nevertheless, questions related to the role music plays, can play, or should play in the formation of political, moral and/or ethical standpoints seemed to become all the more urgent (again) after Osama Bin Laden & Co. shocked the (Western) world. Even music could no longer shut itself up in its ivory tower, as if far removed from day-to-day worries.

Authoritative in this transition towards rethinking the connection between music and moral politics was an admonishing essay by Richard Taruskin in *The New York Times* in December 2001.[1] The immediate cause of this publication

---

[1] Richard Taruskin, 'Music's Danger and the Case for Control', *The New York Times*, Sunday, 9 December 2001, AR1. The article is reprinted in Taruskin's collection *The*

was a cancelled performance of three choruses from John Adam's 1991 opera *The Death of Klinghoffer* by the management of the Boston Symphony Orchestra (BSO), two months after the terrorist attacks. The opera dramatizes the hijacking of the passenger liner *Achille Lauro* in 1985 by four members of the Palestine Liberation Front. During the incident, the hijackers executed a disabled American Jewish tourist, Leon Klinghoffer, and tossed his body from its wheelchair into the sea. BSO managing director Mark Volpe explained that, given the proximity of the events of 11 September, they decided 'to err on the side of being sensitive' in order to spare their listeners.

The BSO's decision elicited a variety of responses. Music critic David Wiegrand wrote in the *San Francisco Chronicle* that people should not be spared reminders of recent personal and collective pain when they attend a concert. Others pointed out that perhaps the opera will encourage its audience to think about the situation in the world by revealing certain motives for terrorist actions – for example, the human despair that ultimately leaves no alternative but to take up arms. Maybe this music can perform the function of catharsis, confronting and assuaging the national pain by arousing it once more.

In his article Taruskin takes an opposite view. He acknowledges that the regulation of music is a basic feature of totalitarian politics. Censorship, he writes, is always deplorable. But to take music seriously, to recognize its potential, is (also) to recognize its uncanny power on, for example (or especially), morals and beliefs. Here, Taruskin takes up a standpoint that has already been formulated in more or less the same way by Plato. Music is not merely a source of harmless entertainment and diversion, Plato argues; it has exceptional power to move and stir the emotions, thereby disrupting the harmonious balance of the virtuous soul, undermining self-control, and even posing a dangerous risk to national security. Music threatens to cause people to believe that sensual and hedonic pleasures are higher values than rational or moral ones. Therefore, the persuasiveness of music must be controlled at any cost.[2] Taruskin does not argue in favour of the Taliban who, for reasons related to those of Plato, banned music during their rule of Afghanistan from 1995 until 2001, although he admits that, unlike

---

Danger of Music and Other Anti-Utopian Essays (Berkeley: University of California Press, 2008), pp. 168–80.

[2] The history of Western thought contains many examples of the conflict between the sensuous character of music and a morality that insists on the human mind's freedom from sensible determination. It is known that Leo Tolstoy was ambivalent about music because of its power to induce in him 'fictitious' states of mind, emotions and images that were not his own and not under his control. Immanuel Kant saw in music a poor candidate for moral symbolism because of its appeal to the senses. Augustine insisted that melody employed in worship should be simple, so that the intellect could stay in control. And Eduard Hanslick believed music to be potentially harmful, since it could obstruct the moral independence of the intellectually enlightened will. Music can either incite disruption of moral norms – for example, as an erotic force – or encourage inappropriate ideas.

most Westerners, they at least take its powers seriously.[3] Instead, he calls for self-control or the exercise of forbearance with regard to the performance of Adams' opera. Cancelling the performance attests to empathy and is therefore ethically legitimizable. Implicitly, he accuses Adams of failing to grasp the ethical character of his medium. 'Not to be able to distinguish the noble from the deplorable is morally obtuse.' With that, Taruskin ends his article.

Taruskin's contribution serves to raise several questions directly related to the main concern of this book: how to think about the relationship between music and ethics. Or more specifically, does something like musical ethics exist? In this context, three considerations might cautiously be proposed. First, Lawrence Kramer correctly notices that 'the ethical failings of which [*The Death of Klinghoffer*] stands accused may take musical form, but the basis of their meaning is determined by the narrative'.[4] Although Taruskin also attacks Adams' musical choices – he detects a strong resemblance between the music accompanying Jesus' words in Bach's *Matthäus Passion* and the 'numinous, timeless tones [that] accompany virtually all the utterances of the choral Palestinians or the terrorists', something he considers tasteless as it might be heard as an advocacy by Adams of terrorism – his concerns are mainly based on the plot. In that sense, the ethics involved are not a specifically musical ethics. So, instead of following Taruskin's line of thought, the question should be raised as to if and how an ethics can be located in music, in the sounds of music, independent of the text.

Second, the decision taken by the BSO management might have been prompted by personal considerations. Kramer writes that the final decision was influenced by the fact that the husband of a member of the choir had been aboard the plane that was flown into the World Trade Centre's north tower.[5] This makes relevant the question of when and how personal considerations might sway the political and/or religious issuing of rules, under the guise of educating the people, for example.

Third, can Taruskin admit a case of subjective autonomy or special circumstances and thereby accept that *The Death of Klinghoffer* is performed after all? Or does Taruskin ultimately postulate some general ethical principles, a

---

[3] In Frank Zappa's musical triptych *Joe's Garage* from 1979, one can find a musical example testifying to the recognition of music's uncontrollable powers. *Joe's Garage* tells the story of how Joe and some other characters are driven to noise pollution, crimes and sexual perversities by that 'horrible force called music'. The government of Zappa's imagined society finally decides to make music illegal in order to be better able to control its citizens. From that moment on, Joe can only dream imaginary guitar notes.

In a short comment in the CD leaflet, Zappa writes: 'If the plot of the story seems just a little bit preposterous … just be glad you don't live in one of the cheerful little countries where, at this very moment, music is either severely restricted or … totally illegal.' Zappa was referring to the Iran of the Ayatollah Khomeini. In 2005 Iranian Prime Minister Mahmoud Ahmadinejad attempted to reinstate a certain ban on Western (popular) music.

[4] Kramer, 'A Prelude', p. 167.

[5] Ibid., p. 166.

universal idea of ethics, and is there an ideal that should be enforced, a conviction that cannot be further legitimated?

However, before addressing these specific issues, we take a step back in order to address that enormous and unanswerable question: what are we in fact talking about when we discuss ethics? What is ethics?

Ethics as hospitality

By and large, acting ethically means doing the good thing, doing the right thing. But right according to what? What is 'the Good'? These are not easy questions to answer, as the search for a universal and eternal Good seems to have been unsuccessful. There is no generally acknowledged agreement on what the Good is. For French philosopher Alain Badiou, 'the unrestrained pursuit of self-interest, the disappearance or extreme fragility of emancipatory politics, the multiplication of "ethnic" conflicts, and the universality of unbridled competition' are all clear indications that there are no existing, self-evident principles capable of cementing a global ethical consensus.[6] Or, to put it another way, what is good in certain situations can become evil in others: good and evil change places according to the circumstances. This means that we cannot know in advance what is good and what is bad. There is no natural definition possible, no rule, no law, no formal imperative. It always comes down to a particular state of affairs, to singularity. So, for Badiou, there can be no ethics in general, but only *an ethic* relative to a specific situation.

With this point of departure, Badiou sides with a 'movement' in philosophy that contests the idea of a universal ethics based on the moral decisions of an autonomous and rational individual.[7] Basically, the criticism is directed against the (Socratic) assumption that ethical behaviour can and should be based on knowledge and understanding: virtue is knowledge, and to know oneself leads to morally acceptable behaviour. Moral knowledge is reachable through debate and discussion and, even more auspiciously, through discovery of one's real self. But throughout Western history, philosophers have also argued against this founding of ethics upon rationality. Already in the mid-eighteenth century, David Hume states, in *A Treatise of Human Nature*, that we cannot use logic or reason to identify, justify or verify moral beliefs. We cannot extrapolate moral knowledge

---

[6] Alain Badiou, *Ethics. An Essay on the Understanding of Evil*, trans. P. Hallward (New York: Verso, 2001), p. 10.

[7] The quotation marks should indicate that this is not a movement in the narrow sense – that is, a movement with basic principles shared by its members. Rather, the criticasters of the desirability and possibility to establish a universal and eternal ethics (in fact, of course, a Eurological ethics) are so heterogeneous that it is impossible to lump them together.

from empirical facts.[8] Instead, moral beliefs are psychological rather than logical or empirical in nature.

But where Hume, like most other philosophers, still assumes that one can somehow be responsible for one's ethical behaviour (the premise of the free will), Sigmund Freud discards the idea that we always have control of our (ethical) choices. Freud observes that the (ethical) behaviour of an individual is based on two opposite forces: the censoring and controlling forces of civilization, on the one hand, and the instinctual and unconscious desires of the individual, on the other. The latter obstruct a total control of one's behaviour and therefore subvert the ability to be completely responsible for it. Freud's thesis is adapted by his disciple Jacques Lacan, who regards the 'self' as a linguistic category. Since language exists as a structure before the human subject enters into it, the 'self' becomes a (linguistic) fiction, and morality, based on rational choices by an autonomous individual, becomes untenable. For other, understandable reasons, a consideration of the effects of World War II led to more or less the same conclusion, causing a deep ethical disillusionment: rational progress appeared as absolutely no guarantee for ethical development. What that war demonstrated was the extremely important role of reason in planning and creating inconceivable human suffering. This gave rise to the devaluation of faith in an ethics based on transcendent reason, rationality and universal truth.

In *Postmodern Ethics*, Polish-born sociologist Zygmunt Bauman connects this (superseded) faith to modernism.[9] Modernism responds to moral challenges with 'coercive normative regulation in political practice, and the philosophical search for absolutes, universals, and foundations in theory', Bauman claims.[10] Modernistic moral thought and practice is furthermore animated by the belief in the possibility of a non-ambivalent, non-aporetic ethical code; it admits of no contradictions apart from conflicts amenable to and awaiting resolution. But the fate of modern societies is precisely this aporetic situation in which the autonomy of rational individuals clashes and struggles with the heteronomy of rational management, with no real prospect of lasting peace.[11] Bauman is sceptical of the political agenda of modernism, its dream of progress, reason and unambiguity with regard to ethical behaviour. Precisely because modern societies tend to believe in the objectivity and

---

[8] According to Hume, it is impossible to prove that stealing is wrong, for example. If we start from the premises that someone is stealing something and that society is against theft, the conclusion that therefore one ought not to steal is based on a false argument because there is a gap between the factual and moral statements, between 'is' and 'ought'. The argument is invalid because it jumps too easily to conclusions. See Dave Robinson and Chris Garrett, *Introducing Ethics* (Thriplow: Icon Books, 1996), p. 89.

[9] Like postmodernism, modernism is not a univocal term. There is absolutely no consensus as to what modernism is, when it came into being, and if we are still living in/with it. It is beyond the scope of this book to deal with this issue in greater detail.

[10] Zygmunt Bauman, *Postmodern Ethics* (Oxford: Blackwell, 1993), p. 4.

[11] Ibid., p. 7.

universality of their own moral utopias, they become authoritative and absolutistic. Universalism and uniformization disclaim the social multiformity as well as the particularity of the individual members of a society. They are a cultural crusade against local customs and a disavowal of the temporal and territorially bound. While appealing to universal rights, modern nation-states homogenize their citizens, constructing an unambiguous identity, a 'self', or an inside, while simultaneously creating a clear outside, an 'other(ness)', thereby violating the selfsame principle of universalism.[12] According to Bauman, the idea of so-called universal and eternal moral values is, in fact, no more than an instrument of the dominant (Western) classes to relieve the individual of his responsibilities.

Bauman advocates the end of objective, translocal moral truths. It is not only the historical perspective of globalization that leads to his disbelief in universal moral values; the moral identity of an individual is plural and fragmented, as there are many networks which appeal, simultaneously and contradictorily, to his loyalty. The ethics that Bauman is supporting is not universalizable. It is furthermore non-rational, understood as preceding the consideration of purpose and the calculation of gains and losses. Therefore, ethical behaviour is not a means of self-preservation and not reciprocal: it is not a gift that is expected to be repaid. (Following Levinas, Bauman calls an ethical relationship 'non-symmetrical'.) In this sense, it is without motives (for example, charity). Nor is it contractual, since in a contract one's duties are enforceable because they have been negotiated, defined and agreed upon before any action is undertaken. For Bauman, the responsibility involved in ethics is unconditional and insecure.

What unites purposefulness, reciprocity and contractuality is that all three imply calculability of action. They all assume that rationality precedes ethical acting. Bauman proffers, on the contrary, an ethics that is endemically and irredeemably non-rational, and hence not describable as following rules that are in principle universalizable.[13] Ethics is that which resists codification, formalization, socialization and universalization. One is ethical *before* one thinks, because thinking always means generalizing – concepts, standards and rules are always somehow general.[14] Bauman draws on Levinas in affirming that real ethical behaviour is denied the comfort of already-existing norms and already-followed rules as guidance. Ethics is not about living together (being *with* others) – that is possible and regulable with the help of rules and codes; ethics is defined by Bauman as being *for* the other, a thorough personal and singular call, appealing to an individual sense of responsibility which can only be felt rather than known.[15] I am for the other whether the other is for me or not. What this 'being for' implies

---

[12] Ibid., p. 40–41.

[13] Ibid., p. 60.

[14] Implicitly, Bauman is arguing here against (for example) Aristotle and Hanslick, for whom moral life depends on the free moral choice of an ethical agent.

[15] In Chapter 3, 'Interaction', we will develop an ethics that is based on a 'being *with* others'.

cannot be decided or thought in advance. This question is decided before thinking, in the solitude of one's personal freedom.

Bauman's thoughts on ethics clearly echo Levinas's philosophy. Levinas finds the meaning of ethics in the relation that someone has with the other and in the unique demand that is placed upon him or her by the other.[16] In Levinas, too, ethics is prior to ontological or logocentric metaphysics, 'preceding' moral rules and maxims. 'Being for the other' implies a radically singular relationship between me (not subsumable under the universal concept of the ego, as something belonging in common to all human beings) and the other (a singular other who does not lose him- or herself in a crowd of others). It is a singular self who is responding to a particular other.[17] Directly resounding in Levinas's call for attention for the 'other' are the horrors of World War II (Levinas was a Lithuanian Jew who lost most of his family in the German concentration camps) and, consequently, an aversion to the universalizing and unifying principles permeating Western civilization and its discourses. It is a call demanding that the powerless and vulnerable – particular peoples, realities, histories, experiences, knowledges, values, and truths that are excluded – be heard.

Levinas's thoughts on ethics and otherness are further developed by Jacques Derrida. In *Cosmopolites de tous les pays, encore un effort!* (*On Cosmopolitanism and Forgiveness*), Derrida describes ethics as the act of being hospitable to the other, the stranger, the foreigner:

> Insofar as it has to do with the *ethos*, that is, the residence, one's home, the familiar place of dwelling, inasmuch as it is a matter of being there, the manner in which we relate to ourselves and to others, to others as our own or as foreigners, *ethics is hospitality*; ethics is so thoroughly coextensive with the experience of hospitality.[18]

Derrida, however, asks himself: which foreigner are we talking about here? Is it the foreigner from whom we require that he understands us and speaks our language before we are able to welcome him? And suppose he already speaks our language. Would he still be a foreigner, and, in that case, would our acceptance of him still be a manifestation of hospitality?[19] Derrida distinguishes between two types of foreigners here. On the one hand is the foreigner 'with a name' – that is, the one who claims our hospitality on the basis of a legitimate motive, a good reason. This is the foreigner who speaks our language, whose situation is understandable

---

[16] Simon Critchley, *The Ethics of Deconstruction: Derrida and Levinas* (Oxford: Blackwell, 1992), p. 17.

[17] Ibid., pp. 17–18.

[18] Jacques Derrida, *On Cosmopolitanism and Forgiveness*, trans. M. Dooley and M. Hughes (London: Routledge, 2001), p. 17.

[19] Jacques Derrida, *Of Hospitality*, trans. R. Bowlby (Stanford, CA: Stanford University Press, 2000), p. 15.

to those of us already on the inside. On the other hand, one is confronted with the absolute stranger, the one without a name, the one whose motives and reasons for knocking on our door remain concealed. His discourse is not ours; we can only hear his cry for help. According to Derrida, this distinction corresponds to two types of hospitality: the conditional laws of hospitality by right, offered to the 'rightful' foreigner, and the Law of an unconditional hospitality, offered *a priori* to every other, to all foreigners, whoever they may be. For Derrida, ethics always oscillates between the laws and the Law. The unconditional Law of hospitality needs the laws; it requires them although they, concurrently, deny it, or at any rate threaten it. The Law would not be effectively unconditional if it did not need to become effective, concrete, determined. On the other hand, the conditional laws would cease to be laws of hospitality if they were not guided, required, even, by the Law:

> These two regimes of law, of the Law and the laws, are thus both contradictory, antinomic, and inseparable. They both imply and exclude each other, simultaneously. They incorporate one another, they are dissociated at the moment of enveloping one another.[20]

Especially interesting in Levinas's and Derrida's thoughts on ethics – interesting in light of the relationship between music and ethics – is their emphasis on a more or less unconditional recognition of 'the other' or 'otherness'. Unlike Bauman's strict socio-political contribution, their ideas open a space to think 'the other' (and therefore ethics) also outside the mere social domain; for them, the other is not only recognized in and as a human being. Both philosophers endeavour to acknowledge the alterity in the heart of Western discourses, in Western logocentrism, in Western philosophical thinking and language, thereby opening another space to 'conceptualize' the other.

In *Autrement qu'être ou au-delà de l'essence* (*Otherwise than Being*), Levinas attempts to trace the possibility of an ethical form of language by articulating a point of exteriority to the philosophical logos or ontological discourse.[21] He is looking for the other of a statement, assertion, or proposition – the other of a language in which all entities are disclosed and comprehended in the light of Being. Such otherness – being otherwise than being – should escape logos. However, as the resources of ontological discourse are the only ones available, one has no choice but to use them, while, at the same time, seeking to promote their displacement. Therefore, Levinas's otherness is not of the same order as the language he is criticizing; it is not a simple alternative alongside or opposite the existing order. The other of logos cannot be caught in constative propositions; it is the non-thematizable *ethical* residue that escapes comprehension and thus

---

[20] Ibid., p. 81.

[21] Emmanuel Levinas, *Otherwise Than Being: Or Beyond Essence*, trans. Alphonso Lingis (Dordrecht: Kluwer Academic Publishers, 1991), esp. chs 1 and 2.

interrupts philosophy; the other is only traceable beyond the categorical imperatives of regulated institutionalized thought. Simon Critchley summarizes Levinas's rethinking of ethics not as 'the simple overcoming or abandonment of ontology, but rather the deconstruction of the latter's limits and its comprehensive claims to mastery'.[22] In other words, 'the other' is not just an entity or quantity opposed to 'the Same', but a deconstructive power always already functioning within the same system; 'the other' is of a different order, a power that disrupts ontology and logocentrism from the inside, a power that traverses any oppositional thinking – including Same–Other contrasts – beyond or between the categories that obscure it and obfuscate its possibilities.[23]

In *Mille plateaux* (*A Thousand Plateaus*), Gilles Deleuze and Félix Guattari refer to this as 'minority'; not the minority as opposed to a majority but a force offering resistance. Minority refers to the incalculable and unpredictable, the 'and' that cannot be governed by a code, a law, a rule: a power outside everything that can be determined as Being, One or Whole – the 'and' as extra-being, or being between. The power of these minorities does not lie in their capability to become a majority, but in their unpredictable actions and subverting influences on existing models.[24]

For Derrida, too, otherness may be regarded as that which remains unthought, that which escapes the grip of every conceptualization. The other is whatever resists definition whenever definition is put in place. Ethics, regarded as the recognition of, and hospitality for, the other, comes into being through opening and destabilizing foreclusionary structures so as to allow passage towards the other. Derrida's philosophy can be thought of as an ethical reading and writing strategy that locates traces of the other within the order of the same. In his work he endeavours to take notice of the other, of the unthought, the invisible, the unheard, without absorbing, assimilating or reducing it to the same - that is, to the cognitive grasp of the knowing subject or self-consciousness. Ethics for Derrida is thus the act of preserving the space of the other as other, but within the order of the same.

Towards a musical hospitality

The appeal of thinkers such as Levinas, Bauman, Derrida and Badiou is to accept and appreciate differences and to refuse 'monological' certainties. Their contributions argue for the necessity of abandoning encompassing moral truths, calling instead for a more modest approach, for ethical *suggestions*, because

---

[22] Critchley, *Ethics of Deconstruction*, p. 8.

[23] This is also the main reason why we, unlike Levinas and Derrida, refuse to write 'the other' with a capital 'O'. It seems to us that capitalizing 'the other' means decapitating this other otherness by converting it again into a metaphysical category.

[24] Gilles Deleuze and Félix Guattari, *A Thousand Plateaus: Capitalism and Schizophrenia*, trans. B. Massumi (Minneapolis: University of Minnesota Press, 1987), pp. 489 ff.

conscientious choices can no longer be made on clear, univocal philosophical grounds. Ethics, as Badiou refers to it, does not say what my duty is, but simply that I should do my duty: act in the service of the good without conclusively defining it. This means that one must constantly redetermine and reconsider one's position, that ongoing dialogues and debates should prevent one from remaining fixed to rooted and undisputable principles.

What part can music play in ethical discussions, in dialogues and debates concerning ethical issues? How can music contribute to ethical position-finding, to encountering the other? Can music confront us with ethical questions and teach us something about hospitality? How ethical is music? In other words, how can we (re)think the relation between music and ethics?

At this point we do not desire to go more deeply into the appropriate and fundamental objections Lawrence Kramer makes against Richard Taruskin's article, in which the ethical dimensions of music are mostly traced in a texted and programmatic narrative. The first step must be to refute the still-prevailing idea that music is an autonomous art form, functioning independently from social, political, economic, technological and ethical developments. As this matter is discussed in many existing publications, we will not allocate too many words to it here. The 'myth of aesthetic autonomy', as Janet Wolff calls it in her contribution to *Music and Society* (1987), is essentially a product of nineteenth-century ideology, although traces can already be found in the late Renaissance with the rise of the conception of the artist as distinct from the craftsperson. In some ways following a Marxist tradition, Wolff seeks to deconstruct the still-existing remnants of this myth by showing that social processes are always involved in the production, distribution and reception of music. In other words, the musical text always already bears the traces of the social contexts from which it originates. Aside from this basic premise, two of Wolff's remarks are even more relevant here. First, she defends the idea that music does not just simply reflect social reality, but also plays an active part in its production. Second, she makes the rather obvious statement that the meaning of non-representational art forms like music cannot be grasped by analyses which focus mainly on textual components. Musical meaning is constructed on a variety of other levels: rhythm, melody, harmony and timbre are but a few parameters that convey meaning, albeit differently from text.[25] Susan McClary's 1991 book *Feminine Endings* is based predominantly on the same two arguments. She, too, challenges the thought that music merely passively represents society; music does much more than 'depict' or embody values. Music is active and dynamic, constitutive not merely of values, but of trajectories and styles of conduct. It thus plays an important role in constructing a society:

---

[25] Janet Wolff, 'The Ideology of Autonomous Art', in R. Leppert and S. McClary (eds.), *Music and Society: The Politics of Composition, Performance and Reception* (Cambridge: Cambridge University Press, 1987), pp. 1–12.

This is not to suggest that music is nothing but an epiphenomenon that can be explained by way of social determinism. Music and other discourses do not simply reflect a social reality that exists immutably on the outside; rather, social reality itself is constituted within such discursive practices.[26]

Music's contribution to prevailing thoughts is furthermore not restricted to discursive narratives, to the choices made with regard to any text it may set: 'This narrative schema is played out quite explicitly in opera. But it is no less crucial to the formal conventions of 'absolute' music.'[27] At the risk of becoming an essentialist (attributing certain meanings to the music 'itself', is in itself the result of a mediating discourse), McClary challenges the assumption that formal aspects of music are intrinsically non-normative and value-free. Musical materials provide parameters that can be used to frame certain experiences, certain perceptions, feelings and comportments.

Following Wolff and McClary, our cautious claim here would be, first, that music is not only capable of representing certain ethical and moral values; moreover, in and through music – to the same extent as in written and spoken texts – ethics sets itself to work, as Heidegger might have put it. Music is not simply an aural depiction of ethical opinions; music might be capable of opening up the ethical, of confronting us with ethics, with concepts like hospitality and alterity. Better yet, through music (and, of course, not only through music), ethics, hospitality and alterity come into existence and receive (specific) meaning. Music is not merely a transparent medium exposing these concepts; rather, it is a substantial means of interacting with them, of letting them appear, of making them experienceable, and of transforming them. The relation between ethics and music affects and thus changes both.

In other words, what interests us here is the possibility of tracing an ethic that can only be summoned by/in/through music. What interests us is an encounter with a musical ethic that avoids the trap of essentialism and which at the same time is not reducible to its textual component (titles or lyrics referring to ethical issues) or to the context in which the music is presented (programme notes, specific places and/or occasions where music is presented in an ethical or moral context).[28] Of course, we know all too well that (con)text is unavoidable. But what we are looking for is an encounter with music which might open a space to discuss

---

[26] Susan McClary, *Feminine Endings: Music, Gender, and Sexuality* (Minnesota: University of Minnesota Press, 1991), p. 21.

[27] Ibid., p. 14.

[28] In that sense, we are less interested in the pop concerts organized soon after 9/11. We don't want to dispute the aptness and relevance of songs like 'Yesterday', 'Bridge over Troubled Water', 'Imagine' and 'We Can Work It Out', performed at those cathartic shows, encompassing the sadness after the attacks though composed in another time; in our opinion, this simply cannot and should not be the only result while rethinking the relation between music and ethics.

music in ethical terms. Put differently, investigating the relationship between music and ethics might call upon an approach towards music that cannot primarily be propagated within an aesthetical, political, economic, and/or music–technical discourse.

The German musicologist Annette Kreutziger-Herr, in her book *Das Andere: Eine Spurensuche in der Musikgeschichte des 19. und 20. Jahrhunderts* (*The Other. A Quest in the Music History of the Nineteenth and Twentieth Centuries*), begins with three examples of three possible relations music might have with ethics – relations wherein ethics is (implicitly) considered as being hospitable to the other.[29] We present these three possible relations here in more general terms. First, she mentions attention for the female, in particular the necessity to emancipate the role of female composers in Western classical music. The second relation is what she calls a 'musical apologetics' of the cultural, ethnic, or religious other, something that should take place through an exclusively musical articulation. Third, she brings up the other of music – that is, the development in musical history towards incorporating sounds and/or techniques previously excluded from the musical domain.[30]

It is perhaps especially in this last example that an opening towards a specific musical ethics becomes best traceable. Whereas the musical emancipation of the cultural and gendered other cannot be effectuated without discursive clarifications, music's invitation to welcome its aural others – noise and silence – within its own territory provides an opportunity to consider a certain, specifically musical, hospitality. Perhaps here we meet with an *aural ethics*, the attention for an alterity that can only be approached through the aural domain, through the sounds of music. However, in order to remain in sync with the ethical proposals of Levinas and Derrida, noise and silence should not be considered as the opposites of music, as powers acting on the same plane. Noise and silence should be regarded as minorities, always already permeating and traversing the musical domain (and perhaps we should also reverse this: there is always music in noise and silence). For this, an emancipation of sound has perhaps been necessary, but not sufficient. In order to evade reducing them to the order of the same, noise and silence should not be presented as 'the Others' of music. I have discussed elsewhere the ways in which the danger of reducing this noisy or silent other to the order of the same (the

---

[29] Annette Kreutziger-Herr, Das Andere: Eine Spurensuche in der Musikgeschichte des 19. und 20. Jahrhunderts (Frankfurt am Main: Peter Lang, 1998), pp. 11–12.

[30] Especially in this last relation, musical sounds are presented as being within the order of 'the same', while other sounds function on the outside and are excluded. However, historically speaking, music as a whole is often considered to be an alterity. In *Classical Music and Postmodern Knowledge* (Berkeley: University of California Press, 1996), Lawrence Kramer shows that, especially in the eighteenth and nineteenth centuries, music has almost exclusively been regarded as a representation of the subversive, the irrational and disorder, thereby opposing many modernistic virtues. See also Richard Leppert, *The Sight of Sound* (Berkeley: University of California Press, 1995), ch. 7.

musical) is or can be avoided.[31] Here, however, we would like to follow a different course. What interests us here is how, through a divergent encounter with music, it might give us the opportunity to experience traces of something that could be called ethical.

Kreutziger-Herr's contribution has as its motto a poem by Rainer Maria Rilke, 'Ich fürchte mich so vor der Menschen Wort' ('I so much feared the human word'), implicitly referring to Levinas's and Derrida's (not to forget Heidegger's) warning as to how easily metaphysical language can assault its objects of thinking, thereby reducing the other to the same. Kreutziger-Herr seems aware of the paradox that as soon as the other is thematized, brought within the horizon of the observer, integrated into his way of thinking, he disappears as other. But she also mentions a possible alternative: the postmodern attempt to recognize the other as the irrational, the passive and the regressive (in opposition to key modernistic concepts such as the rational, the active and the progressive) and the suggestion to (re)think the other as that which has remained in Western thought, a residue bogged down in the violence of the self. Furthermore, she acknowledges an otherness acting in a space between the binary opposition self–other, once the ideas of clear-cut identities are abandoned and deconstructed.[32] Paying attention to the other – that is, attempting to contact a space before or beyond metaphysical thinking (a space that can only be approached *through* metaphysical thinking) – therefore means regaining a certain astonishment and wonder. If ethics has a connection with being hospitable to the other, we must learn not to equate the unknown with disturbance and disruption, with that which causes discomfort and distrust. Welcoming the other means to be led by curiosity, to adopt an expectant attitude, to spare so much world space that in it each thing – a tree, a mountain, a house, the cry of a bird – loses all indifference and commonplaceness, as Heidegger teaches us in his *Einführung in die Metaphysik* (*Introduction To Metaphysics*).[33] For this openness to happen, Heidegger devotes a great deal of attention to art. In art, things lose their ordinariness and triteness. According to Heidegger, it is part of art's innermost being to present a world in which everything is different from normal. To put it differently, art is a creative human activity which puts one in another relation to reality, which generates a different connection to being, and which opens up new areas of play.

Although emerging from a different discourse, a more or less similar thought can be encountered in the philosophy of Alain Badiou. Badiou divides the sphere

---

[31] See Cobussen's online PhD dissertation 'Deconstruction in Music' at: http://www.cobussen.com (especially the text 'Silence, Noise, and Ethics'). See also Cobussen, 'Noise and Ethics: On Evan Parker and Alain Badiou', *Culture, Theory and Critique*, 46/1 (April 2005); and 'Ethics and/in/as Silence', Ephemera, 3/4 (November 2003).

[32] Annette Kreutziger-Herr, 'Das Andere und das Eigene. Zur Einführung', in *Das Andere*, pp. 11–21.

[33] Martin Heidegger, *Introduction to Metaphysics*, trans. G. Fried and R. Polt (New Haven, CT: Yale University Press, 2000).

of human action into two sub-spheres. On the one hand, the ordinary realm of established namings, classifications, divisions and consolidated identities makes up the *state of the situation*. On the other hand, Badiou recognizes what he calls an *event*, a break with the ordinary situation, innovation *en acte*, singular in its location and occasion but universal in its address and import.[34] The event is both situated – it is the event of a particular situation – and supplementary – that is, detached from, and unrelated to, all the rules of the situation. If a situation is composed of the knowledges circulating within it, the event names the void inasmuch as it names the not-known of that situation.[35] Simplifying things considerably, Badiou understands ethics as having the courage to fight against the situation, swim against the current, recognize the void. Doing the Good means being open for 'something to happen' instead of being satisfied with 'what there is'. The Good is the internal norm of a prolonged disorganization. Behaving ethically means resisting the various forms of corruption or exhaustion that can cause a relapse into the known of a situation, into regulated and predetermined moral norms and customs (Badiou calls this 'betrayal').[36]

Art/music is one of the specific realms mentioned by Badiou where events take place and where an ethic is thus traceable. Examples of events appear in Haydn's invention of the classical musical style and Schoenberg's development of the dodecaphonic technique. Haydn's music effects a break with a situation then governed by the predominance of the baroque style. This Haydn-event was not comprehensible from within the plenitude achieved by the baroque style. However, at its heart was a situated void, and the Haydn-event occurs as a kind of musical 'naming' of this absence. What constituted the event was nothing less than a wholly new architectonic and thematic principle, a new way of composing music.[37] It is not difficult to conceive that the same goes, *mutatis mutandis*, for Schoenberg's 12-tone method, the articulation of the void of tonality.

The connection between aesthetics and ethics

It is in the philosophy of Alain Badiou that aesthetics and ethics become interrelated: revolutionary musical developments are not only of aesthetical importance; they achieve an explicit ethical value as well. By revealing the blind spots of a particular situation, the (musical) event opens a space for new experiences, for encountering another other: an other that cannot be perceived through the conventions of the situation, an other that therefore cannot be reduced to the same order as the situation. Being ethical for Badiou seems to mean first of

---

[34] Badiou, *Ethics*, pp. viii–ix.
[35] Ibid., pp. 68–69.
[36] Ibid., pp. 78–80.
[37] Ibid., p. 68.

all being sensitive to voids, being able to perceive and act in a way that deviates from the norm, and also from musical norms.

In this section we will examine this idea of sensitivity. Is (certain) music able to contribute towards a fostering of a general sensitivity or responsiveness – and thereby a hospitality towards otherness? And is music able to invoke a specific sensitivity or responsiveness, one that can only be experienced through/in/during an encounter with music, thereby opening a space for a particular musical ethics?

It will not come as a great surprise that we situate such a musical ethics within the domain of the ear, within the realm of hearing, of the auditory. We therefore think of musical ethics as an *aural ethics*. And, beginning from the idea that music's possible ethical value is not to be found in the music 'itself', but comes into existence instead within a musical encounter – that is, in the space between sender and receiver – it will be our proposal here to look for an aural ethics in the act of listening, a listening attitude that might be described as sensitive, responsive or hospitable.

In her book *On Beauty and Being Just,* Elaine Scarry investigates a possible relation between an aesthetical and an ethical attitude. Setting aside her suggestion that beauty is an intrinsic quality of an object and her rather naive thought that encountering beauty will incite us to produce more beauty, we welcome Scarry's basic idea that by encountering and dwelling on objects or events we consider beautiful, a certain sensibility becomes possible that exceeds mere aesthetical gratification. In her words:

> It seems as if beautiful things have been placed here and there throughout the world to serve as small wake-up calls to perception, spurring lapsed alertness back to its most acute level. Through its beauty, the world continually recommits us to a rigorous standard of perceptual care.[38]

What precisely does one hope to effectuate in oneself when one opens oneself to, or even actively pursues, beauty, Scarry asks. Her answer is that perceiving beauty assists us in the work of addressing injustice, not only by requiring of us continual perceptual acuity – high dives of seeing, hearing, touching – but also

---

[38] Elaine Scarry, *On Beauty and Being Just* (London: Duckworth, 2006), p. 81. First, as stated above, we have great difficulties with the idea that things can be beautiful in and of themselves. Beauty is a (vague, undefinable) quality attributed by people to objects and events. In other words, beauty is one concept by which we relate to the world, with which we order and classify the world, and with which we make sense of the world. Second, the adjective 'beautiful' runs the risk of being too narrowly defined. It is not only 'beautiful things' that attract our attention and demand 'perceptual care'; therefore, less (aesthetically) loaded words as 'conspicuous', 'marked' or 'notable' would perhaps be more appropriate here.

by increasing the possibility that things will be carefully handled and protected.[39] The concept she presents is that the attentiveness demanded by something that we consider beautiful (a vase, a god, a person, a poem, a tree) very likely impels us to a standard of care which we then begin to extend to more ordinary objects.[40] So, according to Scarry, the sensibility and hospitality which characterize the way in which we encounter the world while acting in relation to 'things' which we aesthetically identify as beautiful also positively affects beings from whom or from which the attribution of beauty has been (at least initially) withheld. By relating a perceived being to other beings previously established or experienced as beautiful, our mind not only discovers the limits of its own preconceptions, but may also prompt us to uncover, rediscover and recover those experiences of the beautiful in other beings surrounding us. Furthermore, the desire for beauty might incite us to move forward into new acts of creation, to make conceptual shifts, to bring things into relation. In this sense, beauty and our responses to beauty are life-affirming, life-giving.

It is exactly this aesthetic sensibility that Scarry sees as a prerequisite for ethical behaviour. With a touch of drama she rhetorically asks how one will ever hear the bias and manipulations in a political debate 'unless one has also attended, with full acuity, to a debate that is itself a beautiful object, full of arguments, counterarguments, wit, spirit, ripostes, ironies, testing, contesting'. And, conversely, how will one ever notice the nuances in certain debates 'unless one also makes oneself available to the songs of birds or poets?'[41]

What interests us here is the reversal that has taken place. What Scarry seems to suggest is that the aesthetical domain is not simply an arena where ethical controversies are played off; it is through an aesthetical encounter with a being or object that we can (learn to) act ethically – that is, respectfully and open-mindedly. Importantly, this is an encounter that requires active engagement, not passive spectatorship.

Without making explicit references, Scarry's writings echo those of Heidegger and Derrida. Describing what we coined as the aesthetical encounter, she seems to rely on Heidegger's plea for restraint and Derrida's idea of hospitality when she writes that:

> At the moment one comes into the presence of something beautiful, it greets you.
> It lifts away from the neutral background as though coming forward to welcome

---

[39] 'There are certainly two signs of the genius of great painters, as well as of their humility: the respect, almost dread, with which they approach and enter into color; and the care with which they join together the sections or planes on which the type of depth depends. Without this respect and care painting is nothing, lacking work and thought.' (Gilles Deleuze and Félix Guattari, *What Is Philosophy?*, trans. H. Tomlinson and G. Burchell (New York: Columbia University Press), p. 179).

[40] Scarry, *On Beauty*, pp. 62–66.

[41] Ibid., both p. 61.

you ... It is as though the welcoming thing has entered into, and consented to, your being in its midst. Your arrival seems contractual, not just something you want, but something the world you are now joining wants.[42]

Heidegger would probably call this *inter-esse*: to be among (material and non-material) beings instead of rising above them, (ab)using them and attempting to subdue them. Instead of presiding as a ruler, man should consider himself (once again) as being admitted into the world. It is then that beings can and will show themselves to him.

Following Simone Weil, Scarry argues in favour of a radical decentring, of giving up our imaginary position as the centre. According to her, a transformation then takes place at the very roots of our sensibility:

> It is that we cease to stand even at the center of our own world. We willingly cede our ground to the thing that stands before us ... All the space formerly in the service of protecting, guarding, advancing the self (or its 'prestige') is now free to be in the service of something else.[43]

Attentive listening

From these more general ideas on the interrelations between ethics and aesthetics, let us go back to music, to listening to music, simultaneously endeavouring to tie together some loose ends. Scarry's 'perceptual care', exercised while encountering an event that we consider beautiful, is perhaps not so difficult to transmit to the musical domain; we propose to link her sensory-neutral term with 'attentive listening'.

What is attentive listening? Perhaps surprisingly, it is Theodor W. Adorno who can offer the first clues. He emphasizes repeatedly that the act of reception must meet music's immanent demands; a musical work should be understood on its own terms. When Adorno speaks of recognizing formally organized musical material through the act of listening, he does not mean a certain objectification – the deployment of externally imposed laws in order to understand music – but a particular attitude that is receptive to the intrinsic and specifically systematic development of a musical piece. 'Reflection on style must not be permitted to suppress the concrete musical content and to settle complacently into the pose of transcendent Being', he writes in 'Bach Defended Against his Devotees'.[44] And in 'On the Problem of Musical Analysis' he attacks the Schenkerian form of analysis for reducing music to its most generalized structures, while treating as

---

[42] Ibid., pp. 25–26.
[43] Ibid., pp. 112–13.
[44] Theodor W. Adorno, 'Bach Defended against his Devotees', in *Prisms*, trans. S. Weber and S. Weber (Cambridge, MA: MIT Press, 1981) p. 145.

merely incidental and fortuitous that which is, in fact, most essential.[45] Analysis in Adorno's thinking has to come to terms precisely with the individual moments of a work.

> It may have become plain to you just how much any particular kind of analysis and its legitimacy are actually themselves dependent upon the particular music which is being analyzed. It goes without saying that radical serial and aleatory music cannot be grasped by traditional analytical approaches ... Analysis serves to pinpoint that which I call the 'problem' of a particular composition – the paradox, so to speak, or the 'impossible' that every piece of music wants to make possible.[46]

Encountering music through general terms is not completely rejected by Adorno, but in his opinion this is never sufficient to enable a particular piece of music to speak to us in its singularity. Analysis, which Adorno connected explicitly to (attentive) listening, would essentially need to be derived anew from every (musical) work.

So, attentive listening should at least be described as having an ear for the singular in music, for which there can be no rules, no codes and no principles beyond and between prescribed and predetermined musical concepts.[47] Paraphrasing Derrida, one could say that attentive listening occurs between the laws and the Law of listening. It oscillates between the recognition of compositional principles, formal characteristics and stylistic organization, on the one hand, and the discovery of what escapes this 'order of the same', on the other. Attentive listening makes it possible to relate to a piece of music in a unique way, different each time – that is, each time beyond the familiar frames within which we often try to enclose music. Attentive listening focuses on the unheard in music. Following Badiou's remarks, we might add that this unheard is not absolute but is always relative to the situation, to the listening conventions put into action in order to encounter a specific piece of music.

---

[45] Theodor Adorno, 'On the Problem of Musical Analysis', in Theodor Adorno, *Essays on Music*, ed. Richard Leppert (Berkeley and Los Angeles: University of California Press, 2002), p. 165.

[46] Ibid., pp. 172–73.

[47] It is obvious that we regard listening and hearing here as two separate modes of perceiving, of being attentive to sounds, somewhat following Roland Barthes' line of reasoning. For Barthes, hearing is primarily a physiological condition, whereas listening is, first of all, a psychological act, an attitude.

We also see similarities between our interpretation of attentive listening and what Pauline Oliveros describes as 'deep listening', an openness and sensitivity to the field of sound/music. See Pauline Oliveros, *Deep Listening: A Composer's Sound Practice* (New York: iUniverse, Inc., 2005).

It seems obvious to connect attentive listening to what is often subsumed under experimental or not easily accessible music. These adjectives refer to something that exceeds clear-cut borders, conventions and tradition and thus to a transformative conception of the past; they guarantee, as it were, a surprise, an invitation 'to invent the message at the same time as the language'.[48] Stability is called into question. Instead, this music makes a strong appeal to tolerance (Attali), hospitality (Derrida) and courage (Badiou). In experimental music, the outcome is not known in advance; it opens onto the unforeseen and refuses potential borders. However, we would like to stress here that these kinds of music (free improvised music, contemporary electronic music, aleatoric music, noise music – to name just a few examples) are absolutely not the only 'styles' that require such an attentive listening. 'Listen, if you can, to Beethoven and get something out of it that's not what he put in it.'[49] This statement was made by John Cage, an allegedly notorious adversary of Beethoven's music. This quote, however, seems to make clear that Cage disliked the conventional ways of performing and listening to this music. Locked up in history, Beethoven has been turned into a neutralized cultural monument. According to Cage (and he approaches Adorno here), justice is done to Beethoven not through musicological usurpation, but through a performance practice and listening attitude that reveals the unheard or makes hearable the musical other within his music.

It is not unlikely that Cage would have appreciated Dieter Schnebel's 1998 project *Re-Visionen I*, seven rearrangements of famous classical works. According to Schnebel, this cycle meant

> ... not only a chipping away at the calcification of conventions, but also an attempt to tap into the potential of the past, to carve out its perhaps still undiscovered possibilities ... So the task would be to drill through to layers which we are only now in a position to appreciate or which seem to us contemporary.[50]

Writing about his rearrangement of the first movement of Beethoven's Fifth, entitled 'Again(st) Beethoven', Schnebel states that, with the means available in new music, he is attempting to make audible the idea that Beethoven is not only a master of musical construction but also a sentimental composer. Behind, beyond, but also within the musical structure (all the material develops out of the 'fate' motif), these simmering feelings, as well as subtle humour, seethe.[51]

Schnebel invites us to encounter Beethoven's most famous music differently. Thus performed, the music begins to differ from itself, saying something it has

---

[48] Jacques Attali, *Noise: The Political Economy of Music*, trans. B. Massumi (Minneapolis: University of Minnesota Press, 1985), p. 134.

[49] Quoted in Richard Kostelanetz, *The Theatre of Mixed Means* (London: Pitman, 1970), p. 58.

[50] Dieter Schnebel, *Re-Visionen CD-booklet* (Wergo/Harmonia Mundi, 1998), p. 12.

[51] Ibid., pp. 13–14.

never said before. We could think of Schnebel's project in Levinasian terms: he reveals a musical saying or interruption within the musical said, a residue unable to allow itself to be heard within the state of the situation – that is, through conventional performance and listening practices.

What we would like to emphasize is that attentive listening can address the saying in the said in many different ways and in many different musics. We will limit ourselves here to one more rudimentary example, which may reveal an other otherness within the order of the same. Analysing the music of Bob Dylan with traditional tools, examining melody, harmony, rhythm and structure, will most likely leave a professional musicologist with a feeling of disappointment. Accustomed to exuberant late-romantic symphonies or sophisticated serial music, s/he will qualify this music as uninteresting (though perhaps worth listening to for other, personal or sentimental reasons). However, attentive listening might perhaps bring Dylan's music in line with electronic music experimentation. Both may not serve as fascinating material for melodic or harmonic analysis, but reveal instead the importance of another musical parameter: timbre or sound. 'The closest I ever got to the sound I hear in my mind was on individual bands in the *Blonde on Blonde* album. It's that thin, that wild mercury sound. It's metallic and bright gold ... That's my particular sound,' Dylan says in an interview.[52] The timbre of his nasal, drawling singing, the phrasing, the sound of his voice on a particular recording or performance are all as much a part of the musical work as the melody or the structure. So when Dylan straps on an electric guitar to play 'Like a Rolling Stone', it is because he has something to say that cannot be said with an acoustic guitar.

Timbre and nuance: according to Jean-François Lyotard, these two properties are precisely what escapes definition in terms of vibrations, through specification of pitch, duration and frequency. Nuance and timbre are scarcely perceptible differences between sounds which are otherwise identical in terms of the determination of their physical parameters. They name a sort of infinity and indeterminacy of the harmonics within the frame determined by the identity of the note. Nuance and timbre are the distress and despair of the exact division and thus work against the clear composition of sounds according to graded scales and harmonic temperaments.[53] It is in this context that Lyotard advocates a sensitivity otherwise than Being:

> And yet, if we suspend the activity of comparing and grasping, the aggressivity, the 'hands-on' [*mancipium*] and the negotiation that are the regime of mind, then, through this ascesis (Adorno), it is perhaps not impossible to become open to the invasion of nuances, passible to timbre.[54]

---

[52] Theodore Gracyk, *Rhythm and Noise* (Durham, NC: Duke University Press, 1996), p. 11.

[53] Jean-François Lyotard, *The Inhuman: Reflections on Time*, trans. G. Bennington and R. Bowlby (Cambridge: Polity Press, 1991), p. 140.

[54] Ibid., p. 139.

Listening to Dylan's 'Like a Rolling Stone' as it appeared on the album *Highway 61 Revisited* asks for dealing with nuances. With the moment between the snare drum and the kick drum at the opening (longer than the space between the kick and the band's entrance), the uncertain timing of both piano and tambourine, Dylan's peculiar phrasing of the lyrics, 'Like a Rolling Stone' is, as Seth Kim-Cohen puts it,

> ... [an] abdication of any responsibility to mimesis, verisimilitude, or fidelity to a preceding model of form or content. It is always leaking out of its own seams, never quite what it seems ... [Dylan] turned his back on the values of virtuosity, fidelity, and authenticity.[55]

One should listen, listen carefully, attentively and repeatedly in order to be able to receive the otherness within the order of the same. Hospitable listening. Sensitive listening. Listening beyond the regimes of the (rational) mind. 'What secret is at stake when one truly listens, that is, when one tries to capture or surprise the sonority rather than the message? What secret is yielded – hence also made public – when we listen to a voice, an instrument, or a sound just for itself?' asks Jean-Luc Nancy.[56]

Il faut écouter

We have investigated a first possibility to become more sensitive to a relationship between music and ethics. The quest has led us to the idea that one might seek this ethicality in the contact between music and listener – that is, in listening. In other words, it is in the act of listening to music that the musical domain becomes able to contribute in a very specific way to certain ideas concerning ethics. Through attentive listening, with an attitude that at least endeavours to encounter music with respect, with openness, with responsiveness, a listener can meet an otherness without reducing it to the order of the same. In our opinion, the musical domain is pre-eminently the space where such an attentive listening, an *ethical listening*, can be learned and practised. Attentive listening means informed listening, perhaps even structural listening. However, it remains a bit like Wittgenstein's ladder: once climbed it must be left behind. In that sense, attentive listening is (also) a *post-structural listening*.[57]

---

[55] Seth Kim-Cohen, *In the Blink of an Ear: Toward a Non-Cochlear Sonic Art* (New York: Continuum, 2009), pp. 199 and 206.

[56] Jean-Luc Nancy, *Listening*, trans. C. Mandell (New York: Fordham University Press, 2007), p. 5.

[57] We understand the prefix 'post' here in the same way Lyotard does when addressing the term 'post-modern' – that is, as a moment of instability beyond or before the concretization of rules.

One possible contribution of music to ethics is its call to listen, to listen carefully and intensively, without too many preconceptions and predetermined values.[58] Perhaps it is good to suspend, as much as possible, and at least for a moment, ideas of genre, category, purpose and art-historical context, to achieve a listening that is now, contingently and singular. Music calls for a listening engagement, for a responsibility of perception through exploration, interpretation and imagination, for practical experience.[59] As such, it can also have an impact on our orientation outside a particularly musical context.

In *Wahrheit und Methode* (*Truth and Method*), Hans-Georg Gadamer states that 'anyone who listens is fundamentally open. Without this kind of openness to one another there is no genuine human relationship. Belonging together always also means being able to listen to one another.'[60] Ethics begins with the ability and willingness to listen, to listen unconditionally. The silence in listening seems actually to mediate true communication. (And, on the other end of the communication spectrum, the attentive speaker lets himself be interrupted because there are calls demanding a response even before he proceeds to say what was about to be said. This speaker is commanded to listen.) So, instead of becoming masters of discourse, we should be apprentices of listening. *Response-ability* to the other's call precedes the freedom to speak. I am compelled to answer to this alterity – before any social contract.

In *The Other Side of Language*, Gemma Corradi Fiumara contributes wise words on this topic. True or attentive listening creates a defence against any form of what she calls 'logocratic terrorism', which may enslave the mind. Fiumara presents listening as a possible complement, conjugation or coexistent interaction to the tradition of Western logocentrism, which attempts to excommunicate anything that 'normal' rationality is unable to grasp, thus keeping us within the same theoretical framework. Listening is different from the sort of cognitive endeavours that result in further production of the very knowledge that warrants them; it is 'the de-stitution of the defining'.[61] Fiumara writes, towards the end of

---

[58] This does not mean that attentive listening should always be enacted deadly seriously, straight-faced and immobile, while tied to a chair. Listening carefully can also incite dancing, laughing, enjoyment and, of course, music-making and singing.

[59] These thoughts are informed by Salomé Voegelin's book *Listening to Noise and Silence: Towards a Philosophy of Sound Art* (New York: Continuum, 2010). See also Chapter 6, 'Engagement'.

[60] Hans-Georg Gadamer, *Truth and Method*, trans. G. Barden and J. Cumming (London: Sheed and Ward, 1979), p. 324. Consistent with Gadamer's thoughts, Kathleen Higgins remarks that, first, ethics is essentially social and, second, music has the potential to develop ethically valuable capacities, such as openness to other human beings (*The Music of Our Lives* (Lanham, MD: Lexington Books, 2011), pp. xix–xx). Throughout this book we emphasize the idea that music's potential to address ethical issues can only be achieved through listening experiences.

[61] Gemma Corradi Fiumara, *The Other Side of Language* (London and New York: Routledge, 1990), pp. 19–21.

her book, that '[u]nless we are ready, receptive – and also, possibly, vulnerable – the experience of listening appears to be impossible'.[62] We cannot read her book as anything less than a plea for ethical behaviour founded on the capacity to listen to the other and to otherness. And although she hardly mentions music, we think music can and should play an important role in this undertaking. Perhaps it becomes possible and even necessary to rethink and reverse the relationship between language and music. No matter how intangibly and metaphorically, the musical becomes a non-linguistic indicator, opens a space and becomes a playing field, for the domain of the saying in the said, the Law within the laws, the event of the situation. The play with sounds, with timbre and rhythm, this *non-discursive sonority*, becomes a structural facet of a discourse – a facet resisting the repression of the musical and the sonic by discursivity and rationality.

'Music, if there is any and if it happens in the text, mine or that of others, if there is any music, first of all I listen to it. It is the experience itself of impossible appropriation. The most joyous and the most tragic.'[63] Derrida's deconstructive strategies are aimed at listening to the non-discursive sonorities of a text, impossible to become enclosed in pre-established schemes and forms. That is why it might be necessary to rephrase Derrida's own famous statement '*il faut parler*' ('one must speak') by '*il faut écouter*' ('one must listen').

However, if one of music's possible contributions to ethics can be found in its call to listen, to listen carefully and attentively, to others and otherness, the question can be restated: how can we listen carefully? How can we listen carefully to music? And how can we render account of this attentive listening in our discourses about music? How can we do justice to music in our linguistic reports of our listening experiences? These questions are the points of departure of Chapter 2, 'Discourse'.

---

[62] Ibid., p. 191.
[63] Jacques Derrida, *Points. Interviews 1974–1994*, trans. P. Kamuf et al., ed. E. Weber (Stanford, CA: Stanford University Press, 1995), pp. 394–95.

Chapter 2
Discourse

Nanette Nielsen

> Music is world-disclosive: the world itself can take on new aspects because of it, and an adequate approach to music must be able to respond to this.
>
> Andrew Bowie, *Music, Philosophy, and Modernity*, p. 27.

Ethical criticism

Discourses on music and art more generally are frequently ethically laden. Discussions of 'good' and 'bad' in terms of style, technique, skill, usage of materials, characters, plots and so on are often not solely aesthetic judgements, but merge easily with considerations of ethics. Needless to say there are reasons for recognizing the ethical dilemmas posed by artworks, and there are various consequences resulting from different perspectives on ethical questions. Consideration of these reasons and consequences can offer insight into the scope and possibilities of ethical criticism. This chapter aims to identify some ethically charged discourses on music. We will evaluate certain approaches, and suggest ways that we believe are most likely to take us furthest in searches for ethical insights into music, understood both in broad terms and as applied in particular contexts. The focus of this chapter is on material drawn from two academic areas that have, in recent years, offered ethical criticisms of music – analytical philosophy and musicology. As we shall see, scholars in these fields disagree on what it is 'about' music that warrants attention from an ethical perspective. The examples reveal that an issue at the heart of this criticism is the sense of 'doing justice', but this prompts the question: doing justice to what and to whom? As the opening quotation suggests, a just and proper response to music requires an acknowledgement of music's capacity to reveal, as well as influence, the world around us. While we do not offer a theory in this chapter, we propose a methodology, or rather invite an awareness, that will be applicable to music–philosophical approaches to ethics. We hope that the reflections developed here will inspire further thoughts on the limitations and potentials for ethical engagement within musical discourse.

Although definitions can be both limited and limiting, three different clarifications of 'ethical criticism' can serve as a useful starting-point:

1. The 'issue of ethical criticism' is 'the question of whether an ethical dimension can be essential to a work of art qua work of art, so that an

ethical criticism of the work is also an aesthetic criticism of it, ... thus whether the ethical makes a contribution to the aesthetic.'[1]
2. '"Ethical criticism" refers to the inclusion of an ethical component in the interpretation and evaluation of art. The two traditional opposing positions taken with respect to ethical criticism are "autonomism" and "moralism". The former claims that ethical criticism is never legitimate since moral and aesthetic values are autonomous, while the latter reduces aesthetic value to moral value.'[2]
3. 'Ethical criticism [is] the task of elucidating the ethical content of the arts, the character and viability of our ethical responses to them, and the nature of the moral benefit provided by a serious engagement with literature, the visual arts, and music.'[3]

As with our examples in this chapter, these three definitions reveal some of the possible differences in outlook and methodology that may govern the activity of ethical criticism. The second definition mentions 'interpretation' and 'evaluation'; the third definition refers to the issue of 'our ethical responses' and 'engagement'. For both these definitions, ethical criticism is not focused on the aesthetic object alone, but also includes a consideration of the consequences of our encounter and interaction with the artwork in question. The third definition also mentions the 'content' of the arts and the role of the critic in responding to inherent properties of an artwork, as well as its effects. When dealing with music, pinning down content can be a difficult task, however. The first definition introduces the question of whether ethics can contribute to aesthetics, which is answered in opposite ways by the two extreme positions of 'autonomism' and 'moralism' mentioned in the second definition; but none of the sources quoted here considers the possibility that the aesthetic can also have consequences for the ethical. We begin by scrutinizing some of the factors involved in ethical criticism, turning first to analytical philosophy, and then to musicology. We limit our discussion primarily to instrumental music, but there is no reason why similar approaches could not be applied to a variety of musical styles and genres.

The 'moral character' of music

In recent years there has been a slow but steady development of interest within philosophy in the intersections between ethics and aesthetics. The last decade or

---

[1] Paul Guyer in Garry Hagberg (ed.), *Art and Ethical Criticism* (New York: Blackwell, 2008), p. 4.
[2] Ella Peek, 'Ethical Criticism of Art', *Internet Encyclopedia of Philosophy*, ed. James Fieser and Bradley Dowden, at: http://www.iep.utm.edu/art-eth/ (accessed 3 December 2011).
[3] Hagberg, *Art and Ethical Criticism*, p. xi.

so has also seen a large volume of philosophical research dealing with music, especially from analytical philosophers writing on music's expressiveness, musical ontology and relationships between music and emotion. Studies bringing music and ethics together have, however, been few and far between. Jerrold Levinson's 1998 collection *Aesthetics and Ethics: Essays at the Intersection* did not contain a single chapter on music, while two out of twelve chapters were devoted to music in Garry Hagberg's edited book of 2008, *Art and Ethical Criticism*; perhaps on the basis of this simple numerical comparison, interest could be said to have increased in the interim. Our discussion here focuses on a chapter by Peter Kivy entitled 'Musical Morality', from his book *Antithetical Arts: On the Ancient Quarrel Between Literature and Music* (2009). As we shall see, while it is undoubtedly welcome as a growing area of research, the ethical criticism of music provided by analytical philosophy has both strengths and weaknesses.

As Kivy sets out in *Antithetical Arts* to explore relationships between music and morality, he asks 'whether the music of such great composers as Bach, Mozart, and Chopin is a "moral force" in the world: a moral force, that is to say, for the good'.[4] He has therefore limited the scope of his inquiry to a tiny selection of 'great' composers (although no warrant is provided for this term of approbation). Kivy examines what he calls the 'moral claims of absolute music' in order to unravel the extent to which absolute music can be a 'conveyor of moral beliefs, and purveyor of moral influence'.[5] The advantage of such a restricted framework is that it enables the construction of arguments possessing internal consistency, but at the same time it is unlikely that much insight will be gained into the ethics of music, not least because the uncritical application of the adjective 'great' itself belies an ethical approach; a connection between 'great' and 'moral force' seems to be assumed or implied. Almost any musicologist would be well aware of how problematic such associations have become. The same applies more generally to Kivy's logocentric privileging of Western art music. The terms 'great' and 'moral force' appear to be vague references to universal constructs, but we would instead be interested in asking 'great for whom, when, how, in what ways?'. For Kivy, greatness is presupposed and so, to some extent, is 'moral force', since the two are bound together in his argument. Nevertheless there may be something to gain from so narrow a focus, so let us leave our initial objection to one side for the moment and explore his ethical criticism further.

In the chapter 'Musical Morality', in order to compare literature and music (the aim of his book overall), Kivy distinguishes between three kinds of moral force and asks whether music might be said to possess them.[6] The first is 'epistemic moral force' – that is, the power to convey moral insights and theoretical knowledge in a way that philosophical texts like Aristotle's *Nichomachean Ethics* can. The

---

[4] Peter Kivy, *Antithetical Arts: On the Ancient Quarrel between Literature and Music* (Oxford: Oxford University Press, 2009), p. 218.
[5] Ibid., p. 215.
[6] Ibid., p. 219.

second is 'behavioural moral force' – the power to make people act in a moral way, to get them 'to do the right thing', like that involved in good parenting or moral indoctrination. The third kind is 'character-building moral force', which can make people better human beings ('better' in a moral sense) in one way or another. The question Kivy asks is: '[D]oes absolute music, that is to say music alone, absolute music, possess moral force in any of these three senses?'[7] This reveals a focus on properties that are inherent in the object, or, as Kivy puts it, 'features that absolute music can possess'.[8]

Because music cannot express and communicate moral propositions as literary texts can, the idea that music might possess 'epistemic moral force' is easily refuted.[9] With regard to the second moral force, and the question of whether absolute music is capable of *influencing* moral behaviour, Kivy turns to two possible avenues, which he calls an *emotive* account and a *recognition* account.

For the emotive account, he introduces examples of his familiar concept of 'garden-variety emotions', such as love, fear, happiness and sadness.[10] For Kivy, who is inspired by Hanslick and argues for an 'enhanced formalism',[11] these are 'perceived properties' of the music. Music can *express*, but not *arouse* these emotions or moods (or affective states in general): 'moods are in the music, not the man'.[12] In other words there is no *necessary* link between the particular expression and its effect on the listener (he draws here on the language of philosophical logic). Kivy accepts that his claims are based on a very specific argument and that in general (in real life) it is possible, for example, that music can lift our mood; indeed, he concedes that this frequently happens.[13]

> I am arguing for the *specific* thesis that there is no evidence somber music can engender a somber mood in virtue of its being *somber*, upbeat music and upbeat mood in virtue of being *upbeat* and so on: in other words, there is no evidence absolute music has specific magic bullets for specific mood arousals.[14]

The reason for this is that there is not '"enough information" in absolute music expressive of ... garden-variety emotions' to arouse these emotions in us.[15] Kivy's example is that if I hear an angry voice, I need to know why the person is angry, what he or she is angry *about*, and *then* I may get angry as well. When listening to a piece of music, we cannot perceive specific causes, beliefs,

---

[7] Ibid., p. 220.
[8] Ibid., p. 228.
[9] Ibid., p. 223.
[10] Ibid., p. 224. See also ibid., pp. 80–81.
[11] He introduces this term on p. 60.
[12] Ibid., p. 89.
[13] Ibid., p. 90.
[14] Ibid.
[15] Ibid., p. 91.

emotions or actions. This argument is applied to both emotion and morality, so Kivy dismisses the possibility that music can influence moral behaviour, for music 'simply does not have the resources to do this sort of thing'.[16] As a second option, the *recognition* account, Kivy asks whether we might recognize some feature in absolute music that could potentially influence and improve our moral behaviour. His candidate is 'harmoniousness' (offered without explication or examples), with the suggestion that if we were to recognize this aesthetic feature, we might be motivated to seek harmony in our interactions with other people, be more tolerant and behave in a morally improved manner.[17] 'Well, this is a very nice idea,' Kivy says, and concludes, 'The problem is: *there is absolutely no evidence that listening to music possessing harmoniousness makes people behave in the way stated, or improve their behaviour in any other way*.'[18] Referring to a scene in the Steven Spielberg film *Schindler's List*, where a German soldier plays the Prelude from Bach's English Suite in A minor during the killing of Jews hiding in the Kraków ghetto, Kivy claims that there is evidence instead of music having the opposite effect.[19] Of course, we need to remember that Kivy is searching for a logically necessary condition, so if there is only one counterexample, the universal cannot apply. We return to this specific example from *Schindler's List* below.

Philosophical discussions of musical expression and emotion are plenty,[20] and we have no wish to revisit this well-trodden territory here. We focus on how far Kivy's approach can take us in understanding and furthering ethical criticism of music. If one problem with his argument is its narrow compass, another is the troubling gap between subject and object. Take the proposal that music can express emotions or moods, but cannot arouse them. One weakness of this argument is

---

[16] Ibid., p. 226. Elsewhere – as Kivy (ibid., p. 229) points out – other analytic philosophers, Stephen Davies and Jerrold Levinson, have attempted to argue that music *can* nevertheless arouse the garden-variety emotions, but both have had had to concede that those aroused emotions are empty of *motivational force* and cannot motivate action, so – again – cannot influence moral behaviour. See Stephen Davies, *Musical Meaning and Expression* (Ithaca, NY: Cornell University Press, 1994), p. 307; and Jerrold Levinson, 'Music and Negative Emotions', in *Music, Art and Metaphysics: Essays in Philosophical Aesthetics* (Ithaca, NY: Cornell University Press, 1990), p. 313.

[17] On this, see also Elaine Scarry, *On Beauty and Being Just* (London: Duckworth, 2006) and the discussion in Chapter 1, 'Listening', above.

[18] Kivy, *Antithetical Arts*, p. 229, emphasis in original.

[19] Ibid. Like the soldier's comrades, Kivy is not sure if it is Bach or Mozart, but notes that it 'sounds to [him] like Bach' (ibid., p. 216).

[20] For just three examples, we might mention Jenefer Robinson, *Deeper than Reason: Emotion and its Role in Literature, Music, and Art* (Oxford: Oxford University Press, 2007); Stephen Davies, 'Artistic Expression and the Hard Case of Pure Music', in Matthew Kieran (ed.), *Contemporary Debates in Aesthetics and the Philosophy of Art* (Malden, MA.: Blackwell Publishing, 2006), pp. 179–91; Michael Spitzer (ed.), 'Special Issue: Music and Emotion', *Music Analysis*, 29/1–3 (March–October 2010).

that Kivy presupposes the existence of both objective properties and subjective perception, but does not succeed in creating a bridge between the two. On the objective side he considers those features the music can (according to him) be said to 'possess', assigns them specific 'properties' and states that these 'garden-variety emotions' 'are part of the musical fabric and we perceive them *in* it'.[21] Although he claims that these are 'aesthetic properties of the music',[22] he does not explain how they might be so. Furthermore, they are at the same time *perceived* properties and, to that extent, are not independent of our subjective apprehension of them. The relationship between the objective and the subjective spheres is vague because neither is explained in depth – for example, by reference to either music–theoretical insights or empirical evidence of psychological responses to music. Of course, these disciplinary areas lie outside of Kivy's purview,[23] but the gap between subject and object can also be dealt with philosophically, by drawing on phenomenology, for example. This point has been made well by Andrew Bowie in his criticism of Kivy's idea of the relationship between music and emotion:

> The point Kivy should be making is made by Merleau-Ponty (1945), who rejects the objectifying language of perceived properties in favour of the idea that the perceived world, including music, is already full of meanings. These are of a kind which cannot be reduced to being 'perceived properties' because what they are depends both on the context in which they are encountered and on those encountering them.[24]

This point is easily transferred to our focus on ethics and the possibilities inherent in a phenomenological approach to the ethical criticism of music. In Kivy's search for objective 'properties', his framework for establishing a connection between music and morality reveals a striving for universality based on logical argument – that is, that something would be true for 'all' absolute music. Although he would not deny that we can relate to music in a variety of ways, he does not find this enlightening or valuable for his own purposes.[25] Instead, his intention to refute the possibility for a *necessary* connection between musical expression and the emotional arousal is based, as he readily admits, on 'parameters I have set for myself'. The limitations of his logical system and striving for universality therefore also undermine his ethical criticism.[26]

---

[21] Kivy, *Antithetical Arts*, p. 98, emphasis in original.
[22] Ibid.
[23] As he acknowledges: see, for example, ibid., p. 93.
[24] Andrew Bowie, *Music, Philosophy, and Modernity* (Cambridge: Cambridge University Press, 2007), p. 24. The Maurice Merleau-Ponty work referred to here is *Phénomenologie de la perception* (Paris: Gallimard, 1945).
[25] Kivy, *Antithetical Arts*, p. 92.
[26] Ibid., p. 229.

The final sense of moral force Kivy explores is that of *character-building*, and in this case he believes that we *can* claim that music has a moral force. However, this is merely asserted, for Kivy sees no point in trying to argue for or *explain* musical effects or experience, which are at the same time both 'complex enough, and subtle enough to defy our ordinary linguistic powers'.[27] The simple answer to the question of *what* it is about 'great music' that imparts a character-building experience is the following comment, which displays clearly the naively mystifying tendencies from which much analytical philosophical writing on music suffers: 'the beauty, the magnificence of the music'.[28] Two things are crucial here. First, the way in which this experience is described and, second, the fact that the accompanying moral effect is not lasting. The point made is that '*during* the experience of great absolute music, we are better people, with improved characters'.[29] Kivy also puts this in another way:

> [A]bsolute music *does* have the effect that it does, of character-uplifting, consciousness-expanding described above; and to that extent, it can, as well, be described as morally uplifting. There is no evidence that this ecstatic, character-uplifting experience has any lasting effect at all on moral behaviour or moral character in the long haul. Nor is it some mysterious Orphic or Pythagorean quality that music alone possesses .... But never mind all that. Music *does* possess it. And *while* you are experiencing its effect, *you* are the better for it, and so is the world.[30]

In the final chapter of the book this idea is used as further support for enhanced formalism and to defend what Kivy terms the 'empty pleasure to the ear'.[31] The paragraphs that end the book confirm that no further argument or explanation can be provided:

> Where is the *explanation* for the power absolute music, in its highest manifestations, has over its devotees? Alas, in the event, I have none to offer. I know what the explanation is *not*. It is not its narrative content, or its dramatic content, or any other literary content that it has been said from time to time to possess. For me, its power over us remains a divine mystery. Or, in other words, I haven't the foggiest.
>
> What I *do* know, by direct acquaintance, is the deep, powerful, ecstatic effect absolute music has on me, and by description, on others who have experienced

---

[27] Ibid., p. 231.
[28] Ibid. For a useful critique of these tendencies, see Aaron Ridley, *The Philosophy of Music: Themes and Variations* (Edinburgh: Edinburgh University Press, 2004), pp. 1–17.
[29] Kivy, *Antithetical Arts,* p. 230, emphasis added.
[30] Ibid., p. 232, emphasis in original.
[31] Ibid., p. 260.

and described it. It may not be, I am sure it is not, an enduring moral force in the world, or a revelation of a deeper reality. But it sure is great while it lasts.[32]

There is no doubt that music can have a profound effect as we experience it. But we do not have to succumb to ineffability and thereby settle for failure to explain what is *actually* going on in this experience or disregard the potential for effects to continue once we turn off the stereo or exit the concert hall. Nor (by implication) must we concede that this 'divine mystery' must remain a mystery, that we are forced to avoid more probing discussions of music. In fact, for ethical criticism, as we discuss below, *not* explaining it does justice neither to music nor to ourselves as listeners. Given Kivy's hermetic argument, it is not surprising that he has to conclude that we cannot explain further music's 'moral powers', but this is, to some extent, a cop-out. Instead of engaging with the actuality of musical experience, he surrenders to mystified universality. What makes Kivy's take on 'musical morality' so relevant for our account is that it shows some important methodological limits for an ethical criticism of music: to generalize about music in the way that he proposes is, in many ways, to reduce it to something it is not, namely an ahistorical and abstract entity. In his search for objective content like 'information', for specific albeit vague features such as 'harmoniousness' and concrete 'evidence', Kivy not only misses out, for example, on cultural contexts for meaning, and on levels of understanding and varieties of interpretation, but also ignores examples of where music does have particular effects and has inspired action. As Bowie succinctly puts it, Kivy 'gets the phenomenology of listening to and performing music wrong because he fails to discuss the differing kinds of contexts in which the question [about emotion] arises'.[33] We could add to this the point that the limited question about emotion itself gets music wrong in general. Kivy uncritically uses terms such as 'absolute' and 'canonical', but these are hugely problematic, as any musicologist knows. Even if we were to focus on 'great' composers of the Western art tradition, we would still have to place their music within particular cultural and stylistic traditions to account for their meanings, effects and expression. In the following, we take these points further in order to unravel more useful ways forward for our pursuit here. We argue that we do best justice to any ethical criticism of music if we explore in more depth the phenomenology of listening as well as engage in the discourse of explanation.

Breaking the hermetic seal: beyond logical necessities

Kivy's approach does not take us far enough for an ethical criticism of music because it fails to offer an explanation of music's power to engage our moral compass. We can return to his own example from *Schindler's List*, in order to

---

[32] Ibid., p. 261, emphasis in original.
[33] Bowie, *Music, Philosophy, and Modernity*, p. 25.

explore facets that could, and perhaps ought to, be included in the discussion, if we are to maximize our understanding of music's ethical potential.

As we saw above, Kivy makes reference to a scene from *Schindler's List* to support his argument that music cannot influence moral behaviour. About the scene in question, he notes:

> The point of the scene is all too clear …. Love of Bach does not engender love of humanity, or of the good. Or, put another way, the music of Bach is not a moral force in the world. A lover of Bach is no more likely to be a morally upright human being than a lover of chess or baseball.[34]

Even if we agree with this statement, there is much more to say, since the point of the scene goes much deeper than this, and mainly because of its music. Missing from our discussion of the ethical criticism of music so far is a consideration of how music can interact with, and influence, our imagination: by pointing to *film music*, Kivy has inadvertently chosen an example that would challenge his argument. As Elisabeth Schellekens has argued, there is a close relationship between aesthetic experience and moral engagement, since they both involve active imagination:

> If the element of actively imagining the implications, resonances and deeper structure of a work of art is germane to our aesthetic experience of it, then it seems plausible at least that it is this element that comes into play during our moral engagement with the world. In other words, it is the aesthetic, or lived and felt, aspect of our engagement with the real world – an engagement which is nurtured and perfected through our experience of art and nature – that keeps the genuinely moral aspect of our deliberations alive, preventing our moral life from collapsing into a set of ready-made propositions and decisions.[35]

Kivy is able to make his point about the scene *because* he knows something about the music of Bach, which allows him to observe that there is a striking juxtaposition between what we might consider great or high art, associated with noble sentiment, and the atrocity of the German slaughter of Jewish families.[36] (Indeed, for some viewers this juxtaposition will suggest the whole history of modern German *Kultur* and its terrible repercussions.) But the point does not end here. Another, more obvious, juxtaposition is simply that of a piece of music that is 'gay' or 'lively' in character being starkly opposed to images of brutal killing.

---

[34] Kivy, *Antithetical Arts*, p. 216.

[35] Elisabeth Schellekens, *Aesthetics and Morality* (London: Continuum International Publishing Group, 2007), p. 144.

[36] On one level, this can in itself can be considered a challenge to the formalism proposed through the argument that Kivy has not considered his own context and the cultural and educational baggage which allows him to make these points about Bach in the first place.

Here, we are no longer searching for logically necessary specific connections between inherent properties of the music and the perception of the listeners, but turn to evidence (although not evidence in Kivy's limited usage) drawn from our knowledge of the ways in which music, through conventions, creates associations and emotional responses. Furthermore, these conventions can offer insights into the ways in which music is able to shape the narrative of our lives, including those narratives that involve ethical or unethical action. To ignore associations provoked by music – be they related to musical, emotional, or social contexts – is, as Kathleen Higgins pertinently remarks, 'to sever from philosophical attention a basic way in which music can stimulate and guide reflection on the patterns of temporal and practical living'.[37]

Our claim to take conventions and associations seriously for an ethical criticism of music is part of our aim to take *listening* seriously. The phenomenology of listening is familiar in film music scholarship, and further explication of the scene under discussion will help to make clear why this is relevant to our approach to the ethical criticism of music. We work from the premise that music is never 'alone' (Kivy) but always 'in context': as soon as music (in any style) emerges in the composer's mind, even before it is shared with the world – notated or performed – it has already been contextualized. Based on well-known conventions of narrative film music, we can aim to understand the scene from *Schindler's List* in ways that may also be applicable to interactions with music in real life. This method is encouraged partly by philosophical suggestions that narratives can be edifying and deepen our moral understanding.[38] The following discussion will serve to support our point that critical engagement with listening is important for ethical criticism of music.

As film music scholarship has shown, music is a powerful tool by which to shape narratives, and also disrupt them, depending on the genre and style of the film.[39] Film music composition relies on a host of musical conventions, derived primarily, at least in the 'classic' Hollywood score, from nineteenth-century opera and symphonic music. These conventions, and listeners' expectations and responses, are historically and culturally embedded, and their effectiveness seems self-evident, although not supported by 'evidence' of a scientifically measurable kind. The conventions range from simple associations, such as lyrical

---

[37] Kathleen Higgins, *The Music of Our Lives* (Lanham, MD: Lexington Books, 2011), p. xvii.

[38] For more on narrative and ethics, see, for example, Noël Carroll, 'Art, Narrative, and Moral Understanding', in Levinson (ed.), *Aesthetics and Ethics*, pp. 126–61; and idem., 'Narrative and the Ethical Life' in Hagberg (ed.), *Art and Ethical Criticism*, pp. 35–63.

[39] The examples are countless, but standard sources here include: Claudia Gorbman, *Unheard Melodies: Narrative Film Music* (Bloomington: Indiana University Press, 1987); Michel Chion, *Film, A Sound Art*, trans. Claudia Gorbman (New York: Columbia University Press 2009); Mervyn Cooke, *A History of Film Music* (Cambridge: Cambridge University Press, 2008).

music in a medium tempo for love themes or slow music in the minor mode for 'sad' moments, to particular motifs or sounds to recall or forewarn of events. These methods extend to the employment of pre-existing music in films, such as the Bach Prelude, and additional associations may well arise in such cases. Listeners are often not aware of the sonic manipulation that occurs, however, and the most successful narrative film music is that which does not draw attention to itself (this is one of the 'unspoken' rules for composition). These musical conventions are undoubtedly effective in the context of film music because they not only correspond with familiar traditions of music, but also operate through associations, meanings and rituals in human life. And because the conventions are inextricably interwoven with lived lives, the causal relations are not clear-cut. It is, for example, entirely possible (if not inevitable) that associations first developed from knowledge of the standard Romantic repertoire have in turn – by the twenty-first century – been strengthened by our increasing familiarity with Hollywood films, and this, again in turn, has had an impact on our experience of that repertoire in the concert hall. We can perhaps consider it a self-perpetuating hermeneutic circle, in that these conventions are likely to continue to confirm themselves. We can therefore not only trace music's workings in film and other narrative genres employing music, but also to life experience as well. Although this functioning cannot be reduced to a universally constructed logical system, this does not diminish music's effectiveness for our emotional and moral responses. For the approach to ethical criticism of music that we are proposing it is important to take awareness and explanation of listening seriously.

Understanding possible responses to the scene from *Schindler's List* can be instructive. In film musicology parlance, the Bach Prelude is first heard *diegetically*, in that the source of the music is visibly observable in the film, being played on the piano. It is preceded by non-diegetic music, a subtle, melodious Jewish theme played by a clarinet, supported by a drone in the lower strings. Apart from providing a reference to the Jews, thereby steering us in the right direction as an audible 'point of view', this slow-tempo cue also helps establish a foreboding atmosphere for what is about to occur.

The Prelude functions on several levels and can lead to a variety of responses. Again drawing on terms from film music scholarship, the employment of the Prelude is an example of *anempathetic* music: music that is deliberately out of sync with the emotional quality of the images and narrative. The piece is quick and sparsely textured, and comes across as lively, joyous and carefree. It therefore serves as an obvious and stark contrast to the killing that takes place in this scene. Again, this tells us something about the strength of the musical convention and our knowledge of our affective responses, since this music draws attention to itself because it does not support our emotional reaction. Anempathetic music can confront us with moral issues, including our own responses.

In addition, for the less informed listener, it may well simply sound like any piece of classical music and thereby signify 'culture' and 'high art'. On this level, the Bach Prelude would inspire moral questions such as: 'Why and how could someone take pleasure in the activity of playing and listening to this piece while such killing is occurring?' One could take the view that a soldier who plays this kind of music in such a context must be desensitized and has lost his moral compass. The effect is disturbing, and it is the use of the music in particular that encourages the audience to question their own moral responses to the situation. Without the Bach, this level of reflection, or ethical criticism, would not occur. A similar response arises in Stanley Kubrick's version of *A Clockwork Orange*, in which Alex's love for Beethoven causes us to question our assumptions about core canonic repertory. We might also realize that our involvement with filmic effects leaves us vulnerable to being ourselves conditioned during our experience, similar to the way in which Alex is conditioned.[40]

For viewers with knowledge of the uses of the German musical canon by the Nazi regime, several further levels of morality may be apparent. Instead of simply assuming that Bach is 'great' music, we might be less convinced about the morally inspirational force of this music exactly *because* it is steeped in German national identity. Another response to the Bach Prelude would be to recognize the irony involved in the situation. Two German soldiers listening to the other's playing are not sure at first whether it is Bach or Mozart, but settle for Mozart. The irony here relates to the ownership of national identity, and the soldiers' ignorance in fact helps rescue the piece and Bach from the implication that this music can be associated with the soldiers' amoral mindset. If unfamiliarity of the piece may prevent some viewers from grasping this irony, it is ironic enough that there is a contrast between ignorance and sophistication, while suggesting that the music is somehow 'above' the soldiers, culturally and therefore, perhaps, also morally.

Finally, a listener may notice how the piece in some way does correspond to the violence that is depicted. It is performed in a mechanical manner – fast, percussive and without sensitivity – which may reflect either agitation or aggression, mirroring the brutality of the action. Also, this is supported by the effect of having the Prelude begin in synchrony with the firing of the first shots. The music is more than an example of anempathetic music, therefore, in that on a more subtle level it carries associations with violence, very much in opposition to the gentle and slow-moving material that introduced the scene. In other words, the anempathetic music has the capacity also to be empathetic by drawing on musical conventions, related here to tempo, 'attack' and nuance, which support (in this case) the impression of frenzy and barbarity. We are offered an opportunity to change our point of view and moral perception, and invited again to ask what kind of person we would be if we were to allow ourselves – steered by the music – to assume a particular perspective. If the agitation belongs to the Jews, the aggression belongs to the Germans, and we would hardly wish to partake in their emotional landscape. Towards the end of

---

[40] For a discussion of these issues, see Kate McQuiston, 'Value, Violence, and Music Recognized: A Clockwork Orange as Musicology'; in Gary D. Rhodes (ed.), *Stanley Kubrick: Essays on his Films and Legacy* (Jefferson, NC, and London: McFarland & Company, Inc., 2008).

the scene, the camera pans outside the house and on to piles of dead bodies and soldiers nearby, but we still hear the shots and the piano from afar. The distance to the houses in the background increases at the very end of the scene, and the Bach Prelude becomes entirely non-diegetic, part of the 'unreality' of the film, where it continues to play with our memory and imagination in powerful ways, tying our thoughts to the previous scene. The abrupt transition to the following scene is then itself violent, and the music is cut off.

This brief exploration should help us make the phenomenological point that once we begin entering the *explanations* of particular situations, we have an opportunity to do justice to what music is capable of 'doing'. This means engaging in the *discourse* of ethical criticism, rather than simply concluding that music's moral potential cannot be explained. One way of understanding the affective capacity of instrumental music is to put it in a context where – drawing from conventions – it is used to heighten emotional responses. This need not be proven scientifically: convention is based on longstanding cultural and artistic practices. Could this be the 'evidence' that Kivy is searching for, but cannot find, because his approach does not bridge the gap between subject and object, or allow for intersubjectivity? The kind of ethical criticism sketched here cannot be categorized as a purely speculative endeavour, since it is based on accepted knowledge about musical conventions. Of course, our example has clear limitations, in that it is relevant for an audience familiar with narrative film music, and possibly with the Western musical canon. To that extent, it is similar to Kivy's approach. We do not, however, purport to advance a theory that would have universal validity, but rather one that would be usefully applicable to a variety of situations. It is a call to take listening and affective response seriously in an ethical criticism of music, and to offer a commitment to explanation.

In real life we can understand our musical responses and their ethical implications in a wide variety of ways. Musical associations are, to some extent, tied to the fictional spaces of film and opera, but by no means entirely. As mentioned above, the link between art and life is easily made because we draw on situations and experiences from life (such as slow music at funerals) to shape our imagination. The point we are trying to make in this chapter is that it would be desirable for an ethical criticism of music to account for multiplicities of listening, in order to achieve a more thorough understanding of instances of moral engagement. Regardless of the context, humans possess a complex capacity for mental imagery and emotional evocation. Most people are able to recall not only themes and other musical details, but also specific associations (images, emotions, thoughts) that accompany the recollection of the music. Simply put, music has the capacity to shape the narrative of our lives. Narrative film music is one example that draws on this capacity, because otherwise it would not be so effective. One objection might be that film music is music working 'as an accompaniment' to a story, not as 'pure music' on its own. But the point here is that music is *always* to some extent working like this, shaping our experiences of a series of 'nows': even if we sit alone in a room listening to music, we still have the context of our imagination. Music can work in powerful ways to prompt memories and ideas, and therefore engage our emotional and intellectual faculties.[41]

So, to return to Kivy's question: can music 'influence moral behaviour'? Our answer would be: 'Yes it can.' As should be clear by now, limiting the parameters to a search for direct causal or logical relations is not very enlightening, since our experience of music is complex, and what is particularly interesting is the scope of possibilities of what *might* come about. As our brief exploration of the *Schindler's List* scene showed, as soon as we consider its role and how it engages us, music certainly has the potential to inspire further action in the form of reflection on ethical issues. We could argue that music can influence our moral behaviour both during our experience of it and afterwards: it can edify and help us reflect, become part of our imagination and influence further action just as many other moral experiences can. The edifying effects of music, and our awareness of these, has great potential for ethical criticism, because once we commit ourselves to explaining what these effects are, we gain an opportunity to account for our moral involvement and response. We now turn to exploring this commitment further as we expand on the concept of 'doing justice', which is inherent to ethical criticisms of music.

'Doing justice' (to an ethical criticism of music)

If Kivy's ethical criticism of music relies unhelpfully on the autonomy of the work-object, we can certainly find alternatives. Here we consider recent examples from musicology. We propose a focus on the idea of process rather than product, and would claim that ethical criticism must account for agency and responsibility. This is partly because aspects of agency and responsibility have increasingly informed critical approaches within musicology in recent decades; to ignore this would be to neglect this critical legacy. Needless to say, much has been written since Joseph Kerman's call for musicology to incorporate more criticism – that is, 'the study of the meaning and value of art works'.[42] An instructive example in terms of ethical criticism can be found in recent reviews of each other's work by Richard Taruskin and Susan McClary. These serve as meta-criticism, revealing much about the current position of musicology in regard to the topic of ethics.[43] The real significance of these reviews for our purposes here, however, is that they

---

[41] In this discussion, we are limiting ourselves to film music, but arguably a range of music, including serial music or minimalism, could offer the potential of similar responses, depending on context and situation (although some music may more easily be recalled).

[42] Joseph Kerman, *Contemplating Music: Challenges to Musicology* (Cambridge MA: Harvard University Press, 1985), p. 16.

[43] Susan McClary, 'The World According to Taruskin', *Music & Letters*, 87/3 (2006), pp. 408–15. Richard Taruskin, 'Material Gains: Assessing Susan McClary', *Music & Letters*, 90/3 (2009), pp. 453–67.

are not simply reviews of published work, but to a significant extent are reflections of the roles *and obligations* of musicologists as critics. Sometimes they touch on *ethical* obligations, relating to responsibilities in terms of shaping discourse about music. Rather than offering an assessment of whether either party is 'right' or 'wrong' in their criticisms, we concentrate on this critical role and its ethical dimensions.

In McClary's 2006 review of Taruskin's *The Oxford History of Western Music* entitled 'The World According to Taruskin', it is clear that she largely agrees with Taruskin's critical stance. She considers the *Oxford History* to stand 'as nothing less than the triumph of the New Musicology', thereby acknowledging that Taruskin's work participates in the same tradition as her own.[44] She praises his methodological adherence to what we, in this chapter, have presented as 'agency over object', exemplified by his claim that 'no historical event or change can be meaningfully asserted unless its agents can be specified; and *agents can only be people*'; he laments that, in many textbooks, the 'elimination of human agency is calculated to protect the autonomy of the work-object and actually prevent historical thinking'.[45] McClary's other main positive judgement relates to what she terms Taruskin's 'ethical position', namely his 'sociologically' informed approach, which pays attention to the particular contexts of musical creation and reception and grounds criticism in social history (without relinquishing detailed music analysis). It is clear that both McClary and Taruskin would hold that doing justice to musical discourse involves historical considerations.

Apart from noting that Taruskin is his usual polemical self and does not always manage to keep 'Taruskin the subjective critic' separate from 'Taruskin the objective historian', McClary makes only two major negative criticisms, and they both have ethical relevance. The first is that he all too often fails to quote the sources upon which he draws: he 'appropriates insights' from much North American New Musicology and only provides references when he wishes to make clear that an interpretation is going too far. In McClary's words, Taruskin 'incorporates 90 per cent of what such scholars have contributed, presents it as common knowledge, then all too often frames his source as part of a lunatic fringe'.[46] The reservation here is not a specifically musicological one; the necessity of acknowledging and respecting other scholars applies across the disciplinary spectrum. The second major criticism concerns an omission that McClary considers to be 'indefensible', namely Taruskin's exclusion of jazz, blues and hip-hop artists from his narrative. The ethical problem here is that he has missed an opportunity to write a different, more positive and more realistic ending to the narrative of Western music in his five volumes. While omitting

---

[44] McClary, 'The World According to Taruskin', p. 412.

[45] Ibid., p. 409 (pp. xxvi–xxvii in Taruskin, *The Oxford History of Western Music*, Volume 1: *Music from the Earliest Notations to the Sixteenth Century* (Oxford: Oxford University Press, 2005)), Taruskin's emphasis.

[46] Ibid., p. 412.

musics that are in many ways relevant to the recent history of Western music, and which because of their cultural impact and involvement with social needs and values would have fitted with his sociological aims, he misses out on potential insights into the development of music after the First World War. McClary seems to suggest that Taruskin has failed to live up to the obligation to represent history as fully as possible – to do justice to the task at hand.

Conversely, what lessons can we learn from Taruskin's review of McClary, in terms of doing justice to the history and criticism of music, and scholarly responsibilities in relation to explanation? His review, 'Material Gains: Assessing Susan McClary', is wide-ranging, covering much of McClary's work, although its particular reference is to two publications by Ashgate: a collection of various writings, and a *Festschrift* honouring her legacy.[47] The review begins with an interesting triple characterization in a passage in which Taruskin presents a bit of self-reflection while simultaneously accounting for the shared critical ground between himself and McClary. In addition, the passage provides an assessment of New Musicology's aims and achievements. Taruskin describes his outlook as follows:

> It is the vantage point or sensibility of one who just as fervently as McClary has yearned and striven to expand the horizons of musicology; to foster convergence between ethnomusicology and what in lieu of any better term I'll just call unprefixed musicology; to combat what I like to deride as the poietic fallacy, the assumption that the history of music is the history of composition; to rid the discipline of teleological narratives and a priori value judgements and metaphysical piffle; to seek explanations in the material world; to restore the political dimension to musicological writing; in fine (and in short) to dig out from under the dead weight of German Romanticism.[48]

On one level, the tension between ethics and aesthetics is already present in Taruskin's comment that McClary 'dares' to 'force on her readers a collision between aesthetic and ethical values'.[49] Here, he makes reference to some of her early publications from the years 1987–89, and makes the point that McClary's 'primary tactic' of 'finding the morally dubious or repugnant in the Adornian mother-lode of high humanistic culture challenges everyone's principles'.[50]

But an even more important ethical–aesthetic issue is inherent in Taruskin's main objection, namely his criticism of what he calls McClary's essentialism. He addresses a tension between hermeneutics and historical justification, and this

---

[47] Susan McClary, *Reading Music: Selected Essays* (Aldershot: Ashgate, 2007) and Steven Baur, Raymond Knapp and Jacqueline Warwick (eds), *Musicological Identities*: *Essays in Honor of Susan McClary* (Aldershot: Ashgate, 2008).
[48] Taruskin, 'Material Gains', p. 457.
[49] Ibid., p. 454.
[50] Ibid.

brings us into the (ethical) challenge of how best to approach *explanation* within musical discourse. Referring to McClary's article 'The Blasphemy of Talking Politics during Bach Year' (1987), in which she offered a reading of Bach in light of the social agendas of his own time, Taruskin expresses surprise at its inclusion in the Ashgate collection: '[is] she still standing behind these polemical fantasies?' This is just the beginning of a longer critique of what he calls a 'questionable hermeneutics', one that lacks historical evidence and thereby historical justification. He points out that McClary's reference to the internal evidence of the score is already an interpretation. Referring to her article 'Constructions of Subjectivity in Schubert's Music', Taruskin calls her arguments 'so blatantly essentialist as to amount to gay stereotyping',[51] and warns against readings that are not founded on 'observed social and historical realities'.[52]

The challenge of upholding a balance between hermeneutics and historical justification is not new for musicology, but what may be less familiar are the ethical dilemmas that Taruskin and McClary invite us to consider. As he calls directly for scholars to oppose the Bach piece, Taruskin – echoing Kant – becomes decidedly moralistic:

> There is more at stake here than a slippery slope. If scholarly constructions are justified by the political agendas they serve, then scholarship is no longer an end but only a means. And scholars, too, are turned into a mere means, which is to say into a subaltern class that cannot be allowed [to] speak on its own account unless conformingly.[53]

In other words, in order to avoid bias and manipulation both of material and of scholarly thought, we must maintain a balanced, critical standpoint. This ethical obligation of the scholar – to resist essentialism and do justice both to disciplinary standards and the role of the critic – is further elaborated in a broader claim in which Taruskin again turns self-reflective, and this time almost poetic:

> [I]f we are not first of all professional sceptics, then we are nothing. Being sceptics means regarding all stories as suspect, *especially* the ones that please us. For us, beauty can never be truth, or truth beauty. That is all we know on earth, though, sadly, not all we need to know. We'll never know all we need to know. But we must try not to believe all we need to believe.[54]

---

[51] Ibid., p. 462.
[52] Ibid., p. 465.
[53] Ibid., p. 460.
[54] Ibid., p. 461, emphasis in original. It is worth noting that McClary has put forward a point not dissimilar to Taruskin's in a 2002 article in which she discusses the ethical right to interpret music. As can be seen from the following quotation, her interpretive stance is thoroughly grounded in historical methodology: 'The past never stands still, for the interests of any given present spark new questions, many never before posed. That does not

Taruskin's point here is similar to our criticism of Kivy: while McClary (according to Taruskin) sometimes takes on too much power as an interpreter, Kivy grants the work 'itself' universal power. In both cases, explanation conforms to the parameters that have been set up in advance. To this extent, the following warning by Taruskin would apply equally to both approaches: the choice of semiotic codes 'needs historical justification. Otherwise one is merely displacing transhistorical validity – "timeless" values – from the musical object to the interpretative strategy'.[55] In other words, in order to avoid the pitfall of creating systems that predetermine any outcome in advance of engagement with the material, it is imperative to justify interpretative decisions through reference to empirical evidence ('to seek explanations in the material world'). Also, crucially, the factors of agency and responsibility would be recognized in the process, as the interpreter is aware of not only his/her personal and historical circumstances, but also the cultural and political contexts of the music under investigation. It is on these foundations that the 'right', justified explanation can be based.

In the musical discourse of the Taruskin–McClary reviews, scholarly values are circumscribed by 'oughts', 'shoulds', obligations and responsibilities. There are ways of doing (or not doing) justice to musical and historical material. The tension between hermeneutics and historical justification is one that cannot be eliminated, but it is important to take up the challenge, and to grant the problem sufficient attention, in order to espouse new ways forward for the ethical criticism of music within both musicology and philosophy. Based on our assessment of the shortcomings of Kivy's hermetic approach, and inspired by McClary's and Taruskin's assessment of each other's work, it appears that a potentially fruitful future for ethical criticism would be one in which discourse is framed by questions of agency and responsibility. The concluding part of this chapter draws on one recent argument from philosophy to suggest that the ethics at play in these debates can be adequately described as 'an ethics of commitment', and that music in particular invites us to take up the challenge. What follows is not intended to close the discussion, but rather to extend it to many possible philosophical avenues.

Towards an ethics of commitment

In this chapter we have argued that when music is treated as an isolated object, and its 'moral character' investigated through a focus on 'inherent properties' without

---

mean that anything goes: the historian must justify approaches and present viable evidence, even when broaching issues neither anticipated nor explicitly verbalized by the people under consideration. But the needs of our contemporary world – its attempts at configuring gender roles, at negotiating ethnic clashes, at dealing with the lethal legacy of imperialism – demand that the focus of research constantly shift along with the changes in social values' (*Dutch Journal of Music Theory*, 7/3 (2002), p. 183.

[55] Taruskin, 'Material Gains', pp. 459–60.

an account of how they may be perceived, the gap between subject and object remains wide open, neglecting any connection between music and the rest of the world. Underlying this formalist approach is arguably a wish to 'do justice' to the 'object music', which is put on a pedestal and removed from the material world. In the Taruskin–McClary debate we have seen other ways of trying to do justice within ethical criticism of music, involving offering interpretations that unravel music's meaning in a particular context, whether this relates to compositional or performance practice, or to social or political history. In this debate, music appears continually to *resist* both totalizing discourses and metaphysical readings that result in essentialism: we were warned that *that* is no way of doing justice. Finally, because entering into discourse about music involves, we might say, narration by 'professional sceptics', we can think of agency and responsibility in ethical criticism in terms of Jeanette Winterson's famous and ambiguous line: 'I'm telling you stories. Trust me.'[56] Stories are stories. They are not really trustworthy, because they are not stable objects but fluid entities. In Winterson's case, the entreaty for trust emerges because she, as the author, is the one in control. But whether she tells a truth or a lie, it will always be a story, and while we trust that it is indeed a story, we also trust in the power, agency and responsibility of a narrator. When writers on music narrate, readers trust that the story will do justice *to* something. But what exactly is being done justice to, and where does the (ethical) responsibility lie? Where are the 'oughts' and 'shoulds' inherent in the practice of musical storytelling? Who are the agents, where are the demands, and when are these demands ethical?

The preceding discussion has provided some possible answers, but in order to get closer to an understanding of the particular ethics involved in the examples of musical discourse covered here, and to support our claim that a focus on agency and responsibility is a fruitful way forward for ethical criticism, we turn for guidance to Simon Critchley's phenomenological theory of ethical experience and subjectivity as proposed in his book *Infinitely Demanding*.[57] Critchley believes that *the* fundamental question of ethics is: 'how does a self bind itself to whatever it determines as its good'?[58] To get to grips with this question, he offers a description and explanation of the subjective commitment to ethical action.[59] Ethical experience is necessarily active, not passive. 'Ethical experience is activity, the activity of the subject, even when that activity is the receptivity to the other's claim upon me – it is an active receptivity.'[60] Clearly, such a focus on activity tallies well with

---

[56] Repeated almost as a mantra in Jeanette Winterson's *The Passion* (London: Bloomsbury, 1987).

[57] Simon Critchley, *Infinitely Demanding: Ethics of Commitment, Politics of Resistance* (London, New York: Verso, 2007).

[58] Ibid., p. 8.

[59] For this theory, Critchley is particularly inspired by Alain Badiou, the Danish theologian Knud Ejler Løgstrup, Jacques Lacan and Emmanuel Levinas.

[60] Critchley, *Infinitely Demanding*, p. 14.

our argument to take listening and explanation seriously. Particularly relevant to ethical agency and responsibility is Critchley's account of approval and demand; in his theory, 'ethical experience begins with the experience of a demand to which I give my approval'.[61] Unlike a factual statement such as 'there are windows in this room', moral statements imply much *stronger* approval or disapproval, and Critchley's claim is that 'there can be no sense of the good ... without an act of approval, affirmation, or approbation'.[62] So, as he explains, if I were to say 'War is always wrong', then I am making a statement that demands approval. And it is approval of *something*. When I make this statement, I am committing myself to an experience of 'a demand that demands approval', and that can perhaps lead to action.[63] Other 'demands for approval' are the examples of 'the Good as the goal of desire for Aquinas' and 'the moral law in Kant'. Thus a wider picture emerges.[64] Critchley summarizes the point of demand and approval as follows:

> The essential feature of ethical experience is that the subject of the demand – the moral self – affirms that demand, assents to finding it good, binds itself to that good and shapes its subjectivity in relation to that good.[65]

The other cornerstone of this theory is the notion of the self. Critchley clarifies selfhood, or ethical subjectivity, by two theses. First, he asserts that the self 'is something that shapes itself through its relation to whatever it determines as its good'.[66] Whatever this good may be, it requires the approval of the self, for 'who else would be able to approve it?', Critchley asks. And so, he first defines an ethical subject as 'a self relating itself approvingly, bindingly, to the demand of its good'.[67] The second claim is that this demand of the good in fact *founds* the self, that the demand of the good is 'the fundamental principle of the subject's articulation'.[68] What we are particularly interested in emphasizing here is that this good can be anything, and that what matters is integrity to the choices made by the self – in other words, the *commitment* to the approved demands. Critchley sums up this point as follows:

> Such a claim ... does not presuppose any specific content to the good, let alone any moralistic prudishness. For example, my good could be perpetual peace or permanent revolution, merciful meekness or bloody vengeance, the Kantian moral law or the Sadean *droit de jouir*, where the Divine Marquis believed that

---

[61] Ibid., p. 14.
[62] Ibid., pp. 14–15.
[63] Ibid., p. 16.
[64] Ibid.
[65] Ibid., p. 17.
[66] Ibid., p. 20.
[67] Ibid.
[68] Ibid.

one's right to have an orgasm with whosoever one chose whenever one felt so inclined required the construction of specifically designated sex houses in the streets of Paris. The point here is that the ethical subject is constituted in relation to a demand that is determined as good, and that this can be felt most acutely when I fail to act in accordance with that demand or when I deliberately transgress it and betray myself. I can be as much a failing Sadist as a failing Kantian.[69]

Critchley takes these ideas down other avenues in his book, but, for the purposes of the current chapter, we can apply his approach to what we have tried to argue about agency and responsibility in musical discourse dealing with ethics. When we enter into ethical criticism and make statements about relationships between music and ethics, we can see this as committing ourselves to experiences of 'demands that demand approval'. And it would take understanding of our ethical subjectivities and experiences to *explain* why various ethical–musical demands would be so strongly felt. One keyword here is interaction and another is intersubjectivity: while moving beyond a specific 'content', Critchley closes the gap between philosophical abstraction and lived experience and crucially offers the space of intersubjectivity that Kivy ignored. Because this approach is predicated upon activity, engagement and a deep understanding of experience, it follows that neither ethics nor music should be placed in a sphere above and beyond of what it is to be human. In addition, by closing this gap, Critchley helps us understand the need for particularity in discussions about ethics. This corresponds with both Taruskin's and McClary's methodological endeavours. What is required, then, in accordance with Critchley's method, is to recognize demands that demand approval, bind our subjectivities to what we believe is good, and engage with ethical commitment in discourse. Crucially, as with any phenomenology that recognizes the continual interaction between subject and object in an intersubjective space, our subjectivities are in turn shaped by this commitment as it becomes a fundamental principle for our articulation in the world (these ideas will be further developed in Chapter 5, 'Voice', below).

The answers to the questions posed at the beginning of this concluding section – 'To *what* will be done justice?' and 'Who are the agents and where do the responsibilities lie?' – will depend on the particular circumstances of the music under discussion and the ethical questions that it raises. For now, some important perceptions and possibilities of some of the 'oughts', 'shoulds' and demands inherent in the ethical criticism of music should have emerged a little more clearly. Our Kivy discussion brought out the advantages for an ethical criticism that would take listeners' responses seriously, and pointed to the reasons why a commitment to explanation would result in a deeper understanding of music's ethical potential. Recalling the opening quotation to this chapter, if music can be world-disclosive, and change aspects of the world (or our perception of it), thereby offering new ways

---

[69] Ibid., pp. 21–22.

of understanding how we live, our response – in this case, our ethical discourse – needs to be adequate to the task. We have seen the strengths of considering music as historically and culturally embedded rather than as an object remote from the material world. Unravelling the McClary–Taruskin debate further clarified our argument for the importance of agency and responsibility for doing justice to music and explanations of how it engages (with) us, also ethically. Finally, by turning to Critchley, we found an avenue that offered further clarification of the ethics that may support future ethical criticism of music as we propose it. Comparing the Taruskin–McClary debate with Critchley's theory, we can see that Critchley's ideas about the ways in which individuals can take charge of their own ethical experience and agency are in fact echoed by recent musicological scholarship, in which a focus on agency and responsibility has been key for ethical criticism. And it is perhaps especially noticeable in Taruskin's comments that we can recognize the above idea of (necessary) circularity: this commitment and these ethical discourses in turn *found* who the critic is (as we saw when he warned about scholars being 'turned into a mere means'). If music is capable of interweaving with the narrative of our moral lives in complex ways, it appears that one way to maximize our understanding of its ethical potential and pave the path forward for the ethical criticism of music is to acknowledge not only its capacity to inspire interaction and engagement, but also its resistance to totalizing discourse that would invite essentialism (for example, by strictly separating categories such as subject and object). Judging from the examples covered in this chapter, it appears that music is able to work in this capacity by encouraging strong feelings of 'demands that demand approval', and that most justice is done when agents take responsibility and commit themselves to explanation, rather than letting music remain a distanced, mysterious and ineffable object.

In the next chapter we turn to a different kind of ethical discourse, namely that which occurs in improvised music. We explore ideas about response and respect between musicians as they seek interaction through music, while working towards and maintaining both individual and collective responsibility.

Chapter 3
Interaction

Marcel Cobussen

> The origins of music may be lost in obscurity but, from its earliest beginnings, it seems to have played an essential part in social interaction.
>
> Anthony Storr, *Music and the Mind*, p. 17.

> To learn step by step to cast off the supposed individual! To expose the errors of the ego! To see egoism as error! But not to mistake altruism for its opposite! That would only be love for other supposed individuals! No! To go beyond 'me' and 'you'!
>
> Friedrich Nietzsche, *Kritische Studienausgabe*, 9, 11 [7]

Non-listening

Il faut écouter. One must listen. Such was the concluding imperative of Chapter 1, 'Listening', in which we first searched for specific contributions that music can make to the discourse on ethics and ethical behaviour.[1] What music can teach us is, first of all, an attentive and perhaps unbiased listening attitude and, along with that, a way of being receptive towards an otherness that always already escapes the (discursive) domain of the Self. Music invites and entices us to listen; it compels us to listen to others and to otherness – to the unfamiliarity of certain sound worlds, to the unheard sounds of our environment, to non-discursive meaning or the sonorous elements within meaningful utterances and so on – and it thereby simultaneously evokes a feeling of responsibility, of duty. What can or should I do *to* music? I must listen. This categorical statement is, according to Peter Szendy, imposed on us as we encounter music.[2]

However, all too often it is precisely music and its producers who taunt and challenge such beguiling thoughts. Musical injunctions – for example, certain developments in improvised music – at least encourage some relativism. The duty to listen, the call to pay attention, although primarily directed at the audience, is

---

[1] Instead of locating and indicating certain formal characteristics in and of music as ethical, we are referring here to a *medium specific sensibility* – that is, a sensibility which is formed in and by a medium, in this case music. Neither an explicit or unique feature of a subject nor an intrinsic quality of an object, sensibility only comes into existence in, with and through the medium – as a working, not as a work.

[2] Peter Szendy, *Listen: A History of our Ears* (New York: Fordham University Press, 2008), p. 8.

certainly also meant for performing musicians. However, for a different view on this theme, consider former AMM guitarist Keith Rowe's description of his mindset during the recording of *Duos for Doris*, a CD he made with pianist John Tilbury:

> Being strangely aware of John's movements, but not necessarily listening to what he is playing; not reacting to his playing but being affected by it. The act of NOT listening is very important, preferring juxtaposition to confabulation, disturbing the congruity and avoiding Pavlovian laminates.
>
> Non Listening for me is about the intensification of the edge, or frame. This might be seen as an attempt to limit certain aspects of encroachment of the external environment, and it's almost always been part of my musical makeup. I'm very aware that it's almost heretical to praise not listening, but nevertheless I feel there is a place for it. I write these thoughts not needing or wanting to convince anyone of the correctness of these ideas, but only to explain how I approached playing these sessions.
>
> If I attempted not to actively listen to John's piano as my hand descended towards the guitar laid out before me, what might happen? Possibly I might avoid triggering memories of the piano, memories that by definition would take me away from the immediate context and towards some looping representations of past occasions. Clearly this is not an absolute state because I imagine that some memory is needed to comprehend the present. But given that my aim is to focus my attention on the situation in that room, that room will likely contain thousands of references which will in turn trigger memories. The question for me then is how I might relate to whatever is occurring in that room, certainly not with any loquacious clarity but rather with the obmutescence of an object on a shelf.
>
> So what I might mean by not listening is while I'm paying close attention to what I myself am doing, listening/hearing will be only a very small part of my comprehension of that complex room, or possibly listening might play no part at all. Listening will/may have become overwhelmed by the histories of painting/ music/the instrument/noise/the nature of success/the nature of failure/politics/ poverty/life/death/appropriation/who am I?, on and on.[3]

Non-listening as an alternative prerequisite for music-making; deliberately not paying attention to the performance of your fellow musician in order to arrive at an aesthetically satisfying result; consciously obstructing the possibility of letting yourself be influenced by the other's input and/or by (certain) memories: Rowe's playing seems permeated by an attitude of *de*-listening, an endeavour *not* to listen since the other might affect his actions negatively, an intentional secluding

---

[3] Keith Rowe, liner notes for *Duos for Doris* (Erstwhile Records, 2003).

oneself from the other in order to pay more attention to certain elements in one's own playing.

How can we understand this almost provocative position from the ethical perspective we developed in Chapter 1? What remains of Levinas's call that, before anything else, we are responsible for, and should respect, the face of the Other, when Rowe deliberately tries to ignore Tilbury's piano sounds? What remains of Derrida's explicit claim that ethics should, first of all, be regarded as an act of hospitality, when Rowe seems to keep the doors and windows of his musical house closed, even for the sonic contributions of a friend and kindred spirit? What remains of Elaine Scarry's direct link between an aesthetical and an ethical attitude, an increased sensibility for injustice aroused by an attentiveness to aesthetically valuable phenomena? And what remains of Garry Hagberg's statement that 'to allow episodic perception to occlude the memory-rooted view of the long form with its antecedents and its consequents is, in the forms of attention we give to both persons and players, simultaneously a moral and an aesthetic failing' when Rowe tries to marginalize memory?[4]

Is it sufficient to come to the conclusion that the concept of non-listening is a paradigmatic example of a more general evil that surfaces every now and then in our (contemporary and Western) society, namely the indifference towards the other, the almost exclusive orientation towards one's self, the tendency to prefer the sound of one's own voice over the receptive silence which is necessary to hear the other? In short, is Rowe's approach a case in point of unethical behaviour as Levinas, Derrida, Scarry and many others have 'defined' it – that is, as ignoring and obstructing an invitation towards, and respect for, the other?

These questions will guide this chapter. As in Chapter 1, the emphasis will be on the attitude of listening to explore a possible relationship between music and ethics, or better, to suggest a useful and perhaps even unique contribution that music can make to the discourse on ethics. Again, it will not be our aim to regard ethics as an adjective that can be added to music in order to disclose or emphasize some of its formal features. Nor do we intend to divide music into an ethical and unethical part.[5] If we speak of ethical music or musical ethics, we do not mean to say that there are some intrinsic characteristics which make (certain) music ethical, independent from a person's relation to (that) music, independent of an interpretation of and interaction with it: the ethical happens in a space between music and its listeners.

In this chapter we propose to regard the musical domain, and especially the field of improvised music, as a playground where, through (non-)listening,

---

[4] Garry Hagberg, *Art and Ethical Criticism* (Oxford: Blackwell Publishing, 2008), p. 267.

[5] It might be true that morality can reveal a work of art to be objectionable. However, in our opinion it is more interesting to investigate how art (music) can contribute to reflect on the moral point of view from which people judge a particular object or event as unwanted and reprehensible or, conversely, as valuable and desirable.

interactions between musicians take place that could be investigated in terms of their ethicality. In other words, in comparison to Chapter 1, both a wider and a narrower connection between listening and music will be addressed. On the one hand, listening will be treated as just one aspect of the more general concept of interaction. On the other hand, the focus will be only on performing improvisers, either during a concert or while recording in a studio, rather than on listeners in a more general sense.

Interaction and improvisation

With a wink at Peter Kivy we could call jazz and improvised music the fine art of interaction. Of course, all music-making is imbued with interaction between the participating musicians; one could even state for sound reasons that interaction is a prerequisite for real or true music-making. Playing together means paying attention to what the other musicians are doing and somehow attempting to attune to their contributions. But nowhere does this seem to be more in evidence than during the act of improvising.[6] Without the opportunity to fall back completely on a score or any other pre-established rules, structures or agreements, the performers of ostensibly free improvised music in particular must rely on their ability to cooperate musically as well as socially, in order to arrive at an acceptable musical result while playing.[7] At any given moment in a performance, the improviser makes musical choices in relation to what the others are doing – choices that might radically alter the orientation of the piece. The ability to respond in an appropriate manner to changing musical events is an attainment that any improviser has to learn. She/he constantly has to make decisions regarding what to play and when to play it, thereby also inevitably eliciting responses from the co-musicians. As

---

[6] Although we will restrict ourselves here to jazz and improvised music, we are very well aware that improvisation is an inextricable part of all *musicking*. To a greater or lesser degree, every performance is permeated by, and is only possible through, certain decisions made by the performers in the moment of playing. Even fully notated compositions can be regarded as solidified improvisations. However, from an ethico-political point of view, differences between primarily notated and mainly improvised music should not be neglected either. Ideal-typically, composed music starts from different power relations between the musicians involved, the composer included, than improvised music. Especially in so-called 'free' improvised music, every participating musician is, in principle, a composer, contributing to the total form and structure of the piece which is (often) not determined in advance. (The addition 'ideal-typically' is needed here to emphasize that the border between composed and improvised music is often hard to draw.)

[7] Just what is an 'acceptable musical result' is, of course, hard to determine satisfactorily, let alone universally. It differs between musicians mutually, as well as between musicians and audience and members of the audience mutually. Expectations, desires, knowledge, mood and so on – they all play a crucial role in this. Nevertheless, we like to maintain the idea, albeit in the most general, superficial and unscholarly sense.

Paul Berliner writes in *Thinking in Jazz*, 'anyone in the group can suddenly take the music in a direction that defies expectation, requiring the others to make instant decisions as to the development of their own parts'.[8] Musicians who miss opportunities to respond adequately to certain musical events are often said to be not listening to what is going on in the ensemble. To listen properly is essential to the process by which a specific musical idea is picked up on, developed or ignored.

> The ongoing process of decision making that takes place in the ensemble perhaps explains why musicians often say that the most important thing is to listen. They mean it in a very active sense: they must listen closely because they are continually called upon to respond to and participate in an ongoing flow of musical action that can change or surprise them at any moment.[9]

Explicitly connecting the musical and the social, musicologist Ingrid Monson states in *Saying Something* that musical roles in interaction are simultaneously human personalities in interaction, determining the success or failure of a musical event.[10] Thus, in the same moment, the social and the musical are fused. The point just made offers an opportunity to elaborate on the social side of improvisation, to investigate more closely the nature of that sociality.

An almost paradigmatic example of the importance and effect in jazz improvisation of interaction in general and listening in particular can be traced in an example taken from a recording by the second Miles Davis Quintet, with saxophonist Wayne Shorter, pianist Herbie Hancock, bass player Ron Carter and drummer Tony Williams. In the second version of 'Footprints' on the 1967 album *Winter in Europe* (the recording of a live concert at the Konserthuset in Stockholm), after the theme has been played on trumpet and sax, the solo by Davis almost immediately departs from the initial 6/8 time, into an ambiguous meter, until Carter picks up his 6/8 bass pattern again at a certain moment. Compared to other versions of the tune performed by the same quintet, it becomes clear that this rhythmic change, this dismantling of the groove, which occurs again in the subsequent sax solo, is not a result of predetermined and extensively rehearsed arrangements but emanates from subtle sonic and visual gestures – small yet significant bits of information which the players use to instruct and forewarn one another of impending shifts, and to comment almost immediately on musical events as they occur.

Somewhere near the end of his sax solo, Wayne Shorter – after having played three choruses in accordance with the harmonic scheme of 'Footprints' and having even quoted literally the last four bars of the theme – seems to indicate through his

---

[8] Paul Berliner, *Thinking in Jazz. The Infinite Art of Improvisation* (Chicago: University of Chicago Press, 1994), p. 349.

[9] Ingrid Monson, *Saying Something: Jazz Improvisation and Interaction* (Chicago: Chicago University Press, 1996), p. 43.

[10] Ibid., p. 7.

soloing that he is in for an abandonment of the rhythmic and harmonic structure of the tune. At first, the rhythm section allows him space to expose and develop his musical ideas by playing less dense figures under or next to Shorter's explorations. But soon, Tony Williams, in particular, begins to react to the quick notes, scales and phrases produced by Shorter in order to retort: instead of mainly using his cymbals as he did in the previous choruses, Williams now plays short and loud paradiddles on the floor toms, thereby acting more like an active conversation partner than a mere accompanist.

What is happening here is a sort of interaction quite different from common jazz practice: rather than maintaining the harmonic and rhythmic structure of the piece, the accompanists start to follow the lead of the soloist.[11] By the adoption of an extremely attentive listening attitude – both directed towards Shorter and the rest of the rhythm section – each group member attains a certain freedom in the development of the music outside the pre-given structure of the tune. An elastic form is created that can be stretched or reduced to accommodate the development of the improvisation.

It is primarily Ron Carter who, by playing the bass riff which also accompanies the main theme of 'Footprints', proposes (temporary) returns to the original form and rhythm. The roles of piano and drums are less defined; rather than providing a stable harmonic and rhythmic background against which the soloist can excel, they often throw in musical ideas which alter the direction the soloist had in mind. The accompaniment is replaced by challenges and provocations thereby increasing the level of interaction. However, rather less unusual are Hancock's and Williams's dialogues with each other rather than with the soloist, especially when Carter plays his ostinato figure. In this way, a complex network of actions, reactions and interactions is woven, one that is only made possible by extraordinary aural and visual attention and efforts to recognize and react creatively to cues and calls as they pass on the fly.[12]

How can we understand these forms of interaction in which musical risk, vulnerability and trust are so prominent? How can we relate to these interactions in which insecurity is often and consciously sought out, and almost constant provocations play such an important role? How can we appreciate those musical situations in which new ideas and prevailing emotions are tested for their

---

[11] Chris Smith, 'A Sense of the Possible: Miles Davis and the Semiotics of Improvisation', in Bruno Nettl (ed.), *In the Course of Performance: Studies in the World of Musical Improvisation* (Chicago: University of Chicago Press, 1998), p. 269.

The way in which the Miles Davis Quintet worked thus differs significantly from the more traditional model described by Kathleen Higgins, in which the solo instrument and the ensemble play against one another. We agree with Higgins's point that a jazz ensemble – described by her as a 'diversity in unity' – can be regarded as a model of ethical interaction, but we tend to think that the interactions taking place during a jazz performance are more complex and elaborate than she suggests.

[12] Ibid.

veracity, coherence and vitality? In our opinion, paying attention to the aesthetic contribution of the other players has transformed here, at least partly, into an ethics of paying respect; the musical response-ability has been converted into a shared and mutual ethical responsibility.[13] In other words, what the members of the second Miles Davis Quintet seem to share is a responsibility for their own actions as well as a consideration of how these actions might affect the others. Each performer acknowledges and accepts an individual responsibility for the decisions he makes and the way in which he engages with the others to produce a convincing and interesting piece of music. One proof of their ability to play is the way in which these musicians have learned to fit in with the broad gamut of sounds and the personalities encountered and available. In short, their playing is (in)formed by respect for the others and for the musical context – in other words, this respect has a musical as well as a social component. Whether to lead or to support, to complement or to contrast, to play or not to play; whether to play loudly or softly, quickly or slowly, inside or outside the pre-given harmonic and/ or rhythmic structure of the tune, and so on: all of these ongoing decisions involve close attention to the emerging piece in both an aesthetical and a socio-ethical way.

Musical interaction and the ethics of otherness

If we can agree on a close connection between genuine interaction and a careful attention for 'the other', it is not difficult to find philosophical arguments to support the claim that the performances of the Miles Davis Quintet carry traces of something that might be called ethical.

In a radical criticism of the Western metaphysical tradition, Emmanuel Levinas depicts ontology as the will to understand and grasp everything. It does not rest before the unknown has been identified completely and has been placed within the totality of what is and can be thought. Levinas deems this the reduction of an absolute otherness to the order of 'the Same' or 'the Self', a fundamentally unethical stance. Ethics is, for Levinas, precisely the location of a point of alterity or exteriority that cannot be reduced to 'the Same'.

His analysis focuses, however, not only and not even primarily on the object-oriented attention and appropriation of the philosophical conventions but primarily on the relation between human beings. The ethical relation is one in which I am related to 'the face of the other', 'the face' being defined as 'the way in which the other presents himself, which exceeds the idea of the other in me'.[14] The face is what resists me by its opposition; it opposes my power over it, my violence – that

---

[13] Garry Hagberg calls the capability to play what ought to be played and to hear that what is played is precisely what is needed in a given musical context a *moral sensitivity*. See *Art and Ethical Criticism*, pp. 275–76.

[14] Emmanuel Levinas, *Totality and Infinity*, trans. A. Lingis (Pittsburgh, PA: Duquesne University Press, 1969), p. 50.

is, it resists the assimilation of the other in the self. My behaviour can be called ethical when the face of the other – even or especially the stranger to whom I am indifferent, who does not affect me and whose well-being is not to my own advantage – nevertheless matters to me. It is exactly this otherness that concerns me. In the ethical relation, the other human being remains an other. And it is this otherness, an otherness which cannot be logically justified and which exceeds the differences that can be connected to salient features, that ethically connects her or him with me.[15]

The ethical can thus take place in my interaction with another human being, provided that I respect the absolute alterity of the other. In a conversation with François Poirié, Levinas argues that to respect the other is to be considerate of the other. It is courtesy which gives access to the face.

> To show respect is to bow down not before the law, but before a being who commands a work from me. But for this command to not involve humiliation – which would take me from the very possibility of showing respect – the command I receive must also be a command to command him who commands me. It consists in commanding a being to command me.[16]

What Levinas makes clear here is that this respect cannot be enforced by some ethical code or universal rule but should originate from a singular responsibility I have for the other. This thought especially is picked up by Zygmunt Bauman in his book *Postmodern Ethics*. Already in the first pages he downgrades the 'typically modern ways' of addressing ethical problems – that is, responding to ethical challenges with coercive normative regulation in political practice and the search for absolutes, universals and foundations in ethico-philosophical theories. Bauman advocates the substitution of learnable knowledge of ethical rules for an ethical self constituted by a truly personal and singular responsibility, a postmodern ethics which cannot fall back on prevailing norms and values, solidified in socio-political rules and laws which can be given universal form.[17] Following Levinas, he states:

> I take responsibility for the other. But I take that responsibility not in the way one signs a contract and takes upon himself the obligations that the contract stipulates ... My responsibility, which constitutes, simultaneously, the other as

---

[15] The face cannot be the possible object of a photographer. It cannot be reduced to the domain of the visual, to some pure and simple observation. The face cannot become something that thinking would be able to encompass. It exceeds thought; it is the incomprehensible and unobservable as only that can prevent the possibility of appropriation.

[16] Emmanuel Levinas, *Collected Philosophical Papers*, trans. A. Lingis (The Hague: Martinus Nijhoff, 1987), p. 43.

[17] Zygmunt Bauman, *Postmodern Ethics* (Oxford: Blackwell, 1993), p. 11.

the face and me as the moral self, is unconditional ... I am I in as far as I am for the other.[18]

Bauman's ethics is not about the duty correctly performed, but about the urge to act. An ethical person can never be entirely sure that she/he has acted in the right manner. Being more directly politically oriented than Levinas, Bauman sees the dismantling of the welfare state essentially as a process of putting ethical responsibility where it belongs – that is, among the private concerns of individuals.[19] Like his source of inspiration, Levinas, he sees no good in leaving ethics to an impersonal community; being ethical – that is, being *for* the other – precedes, or should precede, being *with* the other. We will come back to the distinction Bauman makes here.

Before investigating how productive and relevant Levinas's and Bauman's thoughts are for (improvised) music, one other issue needs to be raised. The problem of calling upon Levinas and Bauman in the context of a project on music and ethics is that both of them see no role reserved for art on the path towards a more ethical society and an improved moral relationship with other human beings. In *La réalité et son ombre* (*Reality and its Shadow*), Levinas judges severely what he sees as the exaggerated importance and values that are ascribed to art. 'Art, essentially disengaged, constitutes in a world of initiative and responsibility, a dimension of evasion' is his scathing assessment.[20] The aesthetical has a stupefying character; it contrasts with knowledge and keeps people from real problems. Therefore, one needs to exercise vigilance: 'Art is not the supreme value of civilization, and it is not forbidden to conceive a stage in which it will be reduced to a source of pleasure – having a place, but only a place, in man's happiness.'[21]

Levinas's main reproach is that the aesthetic disowns and refuses the face of the other because it confines itself to a play with forms. He notes that the receiving subject, the spectator or the listener, might be affected and carried away by artistic formalistic aspects, so that one cannot speak of consent, acceptance, initiative, or freedom. In other words, she/he recoils from the bewitchment and flush of art's intrinsic rhythms.

Decisive for Levinas is the idea that art gets its value from aesthetic pleasure instead of being able to establish truth or reality. By itself it knows no virtuousness; it is irresponsible. And the artist extricates himself from 'the real world' for the sake of that other world, the world of his art; with that, she/he is anything but available for the ethical demands of the 'real' world.

Granted, Levinas wrote this essay in 1948 in reaction, primarily, to the prevailing ideas of the art for art's sake movement. But Bauman still denies art any

---

[18] Ibid., pp. 74 and 78.
[19] Ibid., p. 244.
[20] Emmanuel Levinas, 'Reality and its Shadow', in Seán Hand, *The Levinas Reader* (Oxford: Blackwell Publishers, 1989), p. 141.
[21] Ibid., p. 142.

ethical expressiveness at the beginning of the 1990s. Dividing social space into three interwoven yet distinct processes – those of cognitive, moral and aesthetic 'spacings' – Bauman writes that 'neither the cognitively nor the aesthetically spaced worlds are hospitable to moral spacing. In both, moral urges are alien bodies and pathological growths.'[22] Like Levinas, Bauman understands the aesthetic space mainly as a site for amusement and enjoyment. To be sure, otherness and the other are tolerated in aesthetic spacing – Bauman even calls the aesthetic attitude *proteophilia*, love of strangers – but their only right to exist is that they offer pleasure; the other can appear solely as an object of enjoyment. Whatever sharing there seems to be is incidental and purely superficial; proximity depends on the volume of fun and entertainment the other is capable of purveying.[23] In other words, the aesthetic space is free of ethical constraints; the attention for the other lasts as long as the desire to be entertained is still present, whereas a real ethical stance entails keeping attention in place as long as the other may need it. This brings Bauman to the conclusion that 'amusement value is in principle an enemy of moral responsibility'.[24]

Encountering the other from a position of individual responsibility and respect; accepting fundamental uncertainties because particular decisions regarding the contact with others cannot be grounded in established rules; not attempting to reduce the other's input to the structures (conventions, laws) of the self: those thoughts or concrete recommendations traverse and/or determine the ethics of Levinas and Bauman. However, they also seem to be a rather adequate description of the interactions taking place during the performances of the Miles Davis Quintet. To play 'beyond themselves', to do something different from that which they normally do, using their imagination to be more creative and more innovative – that is what Davis demanded from his fellow musicians. Wayne Shorter recalled, in an interview, the magic and excitement of working together: 'We all knew that we were going into some territory, some virgin territory or some points unknown.'[25] To anticipate the possible directions of the other musicians requires a developed and empathetic sense of listening as well as a more social and ethical sensitivity towards those others. In our opinion, Levinas's and Bauman's rather rigorous rejection of the arts and the aesthetic realm as domains that exclude ethical responsibility requires some reconsideration and modification. In a space where people collaborate on a joint artistic process and product, as in musical improvisation, the ethical and the aesthetical often overlap and reinforce one another.

Although hardly included in the index of books on the subject of improvisation, respect, responsibility and successful improvisations are almost always bracketed

---

[22] Bauman, *Postmodern Ethics*, p. 180.
[23] Ibid., pp. 178–79.
[24] Ibid., p. 180.
[25] Jeremy Yudkin, *Miles Davis, Miles Smiles and the Invention of Post Bop* (Bloomington: Indiana University Press, 2008), p. 5.

together by both scholars and musicians.[26] In sketching the outlines of a major research programme on improvisation, community and social practice (ICASP) in Canada, Ajay Heble states that 'improvisation demands shared responsibility for participation ... an ability to negotiate differences, and a willingness to accept challenges of risk and contingency'.[27] In *Sync or Swarm*, David Borgo remarks that 'in the moment of performance and through the act of listening, our personal, social, and cultural understandings – and interpersonal and intercultural sensibilities – can also be powerfully changed in the rapture and rupture of improvisation'.[28] In *No Sound is Innocent*, drummer Edwin 'Eddie' Prévost writes:

> ... if intra-personal relations are uncooperative, unless there is some element of interchange, even if it's only sparring, then the possibility of productive new music transcending individual sensibilities is slim ... Speaking and acting in response to another human being is the very essence of human existence.[29]

And, further on in the same book, he notes that the success of a performance depends on knowing the appropriate action:

> The guide for this is essentially *moral*: will it lead to beneficial effects upon me, upon fellow musicians, upon the performance, upon the audience?[30]

The improvising musician has a musical, social and ethical responsibility to deal with all the direct and indirect stimuli that somehow determine the musical outcomes.

The ethics of musical conversation

Although not always explicitly expressed, most texts on improvisation are pervaded with ethical considerations made operational through such concepts as

---

[26] Cf. Derek Bailey, *Improvisation: Its Nature and Practice in Music* (New York: Da Capo Press, 1992); Bruce Ellis Benson, *The Improvisation of Musical Dialogue: A Phenomenology of Music* (Cambridge: Cambridge University Press, 2003); Paul Berliner, *Thinking in Jazz*; Ingrid Monson, *Saying Something*; Daniel Fischlin and Ajay Heble, *The Other Side of Nowhere: Jazz, Improvisation, and Communities in Dialogue* (Middletown, CT: Wesleyan University Press, 2004); and Gary Peters, *The Philosophy of Improvisation* (Chicago: University of Chicago Press, 2009).

[27] Ajay Heble, 'About ICASP', *Improvisation, Community, and Social Practice*, at: http://www.improvcommunity.ca/about.

[28] David Borgo, *Sync or Swarm: Improvising Music in a Complex Age* (New York: Continuum, 2005), p. 30.

[29] Edwin Prévost, *No Sound is Innocent* (Harlow: Copula, 1995), pp. 72 and 80.

[30] Ibid., pp. 126–27, emphasis added.

respect, openness, responsibility, hospitality, attentive listening and receptivity as well as cognate terms such as vulnerability, risk, courage, hesitation, insecurity and so on; these terms become relevant because, almost by definition, improvisation leaves space for invention, discovery, experimentation, trials and various musical options.

Within a musical framework, this sincere interest in the roles of the other participants during a performance or a recording should not necessarily lead to an agreement on the formal continuation of a piece, its musical language, or the use of certain (sonic) materials.[31] It is perhaps here, with this observation, that we can trace an explicit musical contribution to the ethical discourse, a more media-specific ethics made manifest in and through improvisation – a musical ethics which oscillates between assimilation and indifference, between the efforts to incorporate the other's input into one's own idiom and the total negation of the other's involvement in the musical process and product, between a colonizing reduction of otherness to sameness and an absolute unwillingness to relate to the other. The game piece *Cobra* by American composer, saxophonist and producer John Zorn can function as a sonic realization of this in-between-ness. *Cobra* is a conducted or controlled collective improvisation for one prompter and an unlimited number of musicians with any kinds of instrument. In front of the prompter are several colour-coded cue cards, each referring to a specific operation. A yellow 'S' stands for 'Substitute', meaning that those musicians who are playing must stop and those not playing must come in. When the blue 'MΔ' card is held up, the same group of players should radically change the music they are playing at that moment.[32] Raising the white 'D' card (Duos), the prompter indicates that one of the players can (or should) choose someone to play with. Through these cards, more than 20 musical signs or directions can be communicated.

The last example also indicates that it is not necessarily the prompter who sets the course of the piece. Although she/he can certainly take some initiatives, she/he is mainly an intermediary, transferring cues from the musicians to the rest of the ensemble. In other words, holding up the red card with a '1' on it – write down what you are playing and reproduce it when called – is an instruction which might come from a request by one of the group members. This request can be submitted by first catching the attention of the prompter, followed by a specific gesture, in this case touching one's head and raising one finger.[33] As more than one instruction can be operative simultaneously, what arises with a performance

---

[31] We are not referring here to the famous 'sax battles' that sometimes mark the end of a jazz or blues festival as these 'fights' are waged on the basis of a common musical ground, either literally, when the harmonic framework is determined, or ideologically, when all sax players share more or less the same musical background and conventions.

[32] To be more precise, during the upholding of the cards, the ensemble can see and prepare; only at the downbeat does the instruction become operative.

[33] When a musician wants the yellow 'S' card, she/he has to touch her/his mouth and then raise three fingers; touching the ear and raising one finger means that the prompter

of *Cobra* is a kind of musical theatre, starring a prompter, often holding up more than one card, and several performers, playing, listening, paying attention to each other and to the prompter, waving, touching body parts and raising fingers, and all this within a matter of seconds. Although the recognition of the next call is subject to the discretion of the prompter, her/his influence on the sounding result of a particular *Cobra* performance is, of course, quite limited: she/he is unable to affect the exact choice of tones the individual performers wish to produce when, for example, playing a duo. And this equally applies to the musicians: choosing one of the other performers with whom to play a duo primarily means choosing an instrument; the manner in which that instrument will be played, the volume, the number of notes, the speed and so on all has to be left to the discretion of the chosen one. Put differently, an invitation to participate extended by one player to one or more others can simply never be grounded on the stipulation to comply with the musical ideas of the 'host' but can still be aesthetically, as well as socially (and ethically), acceptable.

The point we want to make here is that although many musicians and scholars (Monson, Berliner, Hagberg) regard improvisation as a kind of conversation there seems to be a fundamental difference between the preconditions for a verbal and a musical 'conversation'. A meaningful and exciting musical conversation does not necessarily have to be built on a consensus about its form and content. It is not only that the propriety to let someone have his say does not have to be observed in music-making; nor do the attention and respect for the other's input have to be articulated in a mutual agreement on the output. Whereas a verbal dialogue or group discussion can only be satisfying when people react to each other's contributions using more or less the same formal standards and discursive language, this is no absolute prior condition for an interesting and meaningful musical improvisation.[34] Rather, in the latter, otherness is accepted as a given, a sonic challenge, an opportunity perhaps to transgress one's own restrictions, to be creatively stimulated. Pieces like *Cobra* derive their aesthetical and (thereby) also their ethical attraction precisely from the tensions at work in the impossibilities of total assimilation and complete indifference, both musically and interpersonally.

However, in order to investigate a possible contribution of musical improvisation to the ethical discourse, we leave this track for another, in order to consider more fundamental objections against the emphasis in both Levinas and Bauman on individual responsibility.

---

should pick up the blue 'MΔ' card; playing a duo (the white 'D' card) becomes possible after touching the nose and putting up one finger.

[34] Therefore we tend to disagree with Garry Hagberg, who states that, in a dialogical conversation, the simple attitude of mutual respect is a precondition for success and precisely this is true in dialogical improvisation, too (*Art and Ethical Criticism*, p. 273). In our opinion, musical conversations open the possibility of rethinking and extending the linguistic mores of mutual respect. Musical aesthetics and ethics allow for disregard, cacophony and completely unexpected turns.

From the individual to the collective

Through music, the question might be asked to what extent we can be held fully responsible at all times. To what extent can musicians individually assume liability for their actions and the final sonic outcomes? Musical improvisation might become a means not to abandon individual responsibility for some kind of aesthetic irresponsibility as Levinas and Bauman seem to intimate, but to reconsider the strict individual character of ethical behaviour. Without intending to be exhaustive, we see three musical realities that could implicitly query the dominant conditions of an ethics as proposed by Levinas and Bauman – an ethics which requires a subject somehow being able to weigh up situations, conscious of ethical feelings and able to accept the consequences ensuing from certain actions. In other words, although ethical behaviour cannot be based on rational arguments, according to Levinas and Bauman, what nevertheless seems to be postulated is a rational and sentient being, knowable for himself, and always responsible for her/his actions and thoughts. It seems clear that improvising musicians cannot at all times fulfil these stipulations.

First station

Drawn Inward is a CD by a septet led by the British saxophonist Evan Parker, creating a mix of free improvisation, live electronics and real-time sound processing. Five of seven musicians operate a computer, two of them in addition to the more traditional instruments of percussion and violin. Only Parker himself and bass player Barry Guy do not have any electronic equipment at their disposal. The electronics are not used simply to thicken the texture; rather, they are employed to process sounds in real time and to improvise with and from them. These sounds can be taken from any or all of the other performers and may also include sounds already transformed. They can then be processed or manipulated further either singly or in combination.

The input of a particular player can thus be transformed continuously. Indeed, the performance as a whole can be sampled and used as raw material for further transformations and development, the results then being fed back into the collective pool of sounds. The electronic sound manipulations thus veil to a large extent the 'original' sounds of the more traditional instruments. Cut off from their source from the very beginning, the processed sounds wander around in an uncanny sonic territory.[35]

The simple question we would like to pose here (and leave as yet unanswered) is how we can think responsibility in musical improvisation once the sounds are processed by electronic equipment and are (therefore) hardly recognizable and no longer controllable by the individual musicians? Put differently, how does personal responsibility relate to a kind of techno-aesthetical manipulation? If the

---

[35] For a more detailed description of *Drawn Inward* in relation to the ethics of Alain Badiou, see Marcel Cobussen, 'Noise and Ethics: On Evan Parker and Alain Badiou', *Culture, Theory and Critique*, 46/1 (April 2005), pp. 29–42.

consequences of one's playing are unable to be anticipated in any way, how can one be accountable for one's (re)actions?

Second station

Sigmund Freud has already undermined the notion that we are always in control of our ethical choices.[36] An individual's instinctual and unconscious desires obstruct a total domination and therefore subvert the ability to be completely responsible for one's behaviour. The (ethical) choices a human makes are not always 'his', but are somehow influenced by the instinctive psychic structures at work in the unconsciousness. If we are almost uninformed about at least some sources or causes of our behaviour, how can we ever be fully responsible for our ethical lives?

Freud's perspective is primarily psychological, not philosophical or moral. He is less interested in what we should do than what we in fact do. In his psychology the idea of an autonomous 'self' becomes a fiction. This is evident also in music-making (and perhaps especially in improvised music). The level of intensity that John Coltrane and, in his wake, Pharaoh Sanders reach at *The Olatunji Concert* takes them beyond themselves – that is, beyond the safe and familiar place where musicians still have control over what they are doing. Their states of mind may be described as ecstatic: literally 'out of place', a displacement of a self. The example of Coltrane is all the more interesting because this ecstasy is not only (or not primarily) achieved through some direct manipulation of the mind, but perhaps first of all through the activities of the body. Coltrane's body takes over, doing things not previously directed by his conscious mind. This is what the French phenomenologist Maurice Merleau-Ponty calls *praktognosia*: a (tacit) knowledge that is not only expressed in action, but, in addition, results from the acting itself, without resting on mental knowledge. The extreme corporeality of his later music does not turn Coltrane into a ruler and commander. He does not possess 'his' music; he is not mastering it, leading it with full consciousness in a desired direction. Rather, he is the obedient servant and the listener.[37] Can he be held fully and truly responsible for "his" improvisations? Freud's psychoanalytical insights and Coltrane's ecstatic music-making seem to question the supposition of a self in complete control of her/his musical achievements and related social and ethical actions. Another otherness, always already present within the self, can block the conscious initiative to take responsibility for the other.

Third station

What the modest analyses of socio-musical interactions of the Miles Davis Quintet, the musicians performing Cobra and Evan Parker's electro-acoustic ensemble made clear was that collective music-making, especially when improvisation is

---

[36] See also Chapter 1.
[37] For more on Coltrane, embodiment and the transgression of control, see Marcel Cobussen, *Thresholds: Rethinking Spirituality Through Music* (Aldershot: Ashgate, 2008), pp. 89–106.

a part of it, is primarily a group process. This could lead to the conclusion that the individual responsibility of any of the participants is thereby exceeded and transcended during a performance. The third station takes us to the field of collective responsibility. Even Keith Rowe's non-listening, a deliberate attempt to be released from conventional systems of interaction, the input of real-time processing that exceeds the individual musicians' ability to control, as in Evan Parker's band, and Coltrane's ecstatic playing, a combination of conscious, subconscious and embodied actions, do not exclude any responsibility: being a group, the musicians are collectively responsible, at least to a certain extent, for the musical outcomes. And this aesthetical orientation directly implies a socio-ethical one.

To think this collective responsibility takes us from the continental philosophers to a mainly American movement that arose in the mid-1990s: communitarianism. Although a diffuse movement incorporating quite divergent theories – from Alasdair MacIntyre to Charles Taylor, and from Amitai Etzioni to Philip Selznick and even back in time to John Dewey – some general and shared principles might be traced that can provide further insight into the ethics at work in the interactive process of group improvisations.

The most basic idea that communitarians argue against is what Canadian philosopher Charles Taylor in *The Malaise of Modernity* calls 'social atomism', the inclination to seek the ideal of self-realization within the individual human being, whereby affiliations become purely instrumental, used only to achieve that ideal.[38] Taylor calls this 'the ethics of authenticity'. He considers this ethics, crystallized in fragmentation, narcissism and relativism, as the biggest danger of our contemporary society. It represents the inability to form common purposes and enter into joint projects and allegiances.[39] His arguments are not so much directed against any form of self-fulfilment but are meant to make us aware of the fact that we always need relationships to develop ourselves. If authenticity means being faithful to ourselves, this will only be possible if we recognize a stronger, more inner sense of linkages.[40]

In much the same way, political philosopher Michael Sandel reacts against 'the unencumbered self', the present-day individual who seeks to determine his life in complete freedom: 'What is denied to the unencumbered self is the possibility of membership in any community bound by moral ties *antecedent to choice*; he cannot belong to any community where the self itself could be at stake.'[41]

American sociologist and legal scholar Philip Selznick states that 'the label communitarian can be applied to any doctrine that prizes collective goods or

---

[38] Charles Taylor, *The Malaise of Modernity* (Concord: House of Anansi Press, 1991), p. 58.
[39] Ibid., p. 112.
[40] Ibid., p. 91.
[41] Michael J. Sandel, 'The Procedural Republic and the Unencumbered Self', *Political Theory*, 12/1 (1984), p. 87, emphasis added.

ideals and limits claims to individual independence and self-realization'.[42] Of importance is a commitment to the group, which shows itself in communication and confidence. The latter is the cement of communities; it is the condition for attaining collaboration. Bonds of community arise from interdependence, from the virtues of cooperation and from an awareness of shared identity, although Selznick hastens to point out that communities can be made up of relatively loosely coordinated activities and persons.[43]

In some way analogous to Zygmunt Bauman, Selznick argues in favour of an ethic of responsibility which calls for reflection and understanding instead of mechanical or bare conformity.[44] Rather than through control and command, Selznick defends an ethos of open-ended obligation. Striving after the good is always tentative, incomplete and responsive with respect to external developments; more than Bauman, however, he emphasizes that doing one's duty presumes commitment not only to an ideal, but first of all to a community. The open-ended obligation fosters trust, the indispensable binder of group life. The good is decided on by 'collective intelligence' and social learning.[45] Selznick still recognizes a certain individual autonomy since responsibility requires judgement, but besides this personal integrity he also propounds a responsibility for the practical needs of a community;[46] it is always pertinent to ask how the pursuit of individual goals affects communal values and interests. Conversely, a community 'shows collective responsibility when it provides the resources and opportunities people need for personal responsibility'.[47]

Communitarian responsibility thus emerges from the experience of connectedness and the imperatives of interdependence. To a greater or lesser degree all communitarians start from the idea that members of a community gear their actions towards the realization of the common good. According to the British philosopher Alasdair MacIntyre, morality only displays inner consistency when it is defined in reference to a collective goal.

This seemingly measured balance between interdependence and autonomy, between singular duties and more institutionalized obligations, between diversity

---

[42] Philip Selznick, *The Communitarian Persuasion* (Washington, DC: Woodrow Wilson Center Press, 2002), p. 4.

[43] Ibid., p. 18. Selznick casts doubt on forms of multiculturalism that support separation instead of unity and confrontation instead of reconciliation. Diversity in itself can never be self-justifying; threshold standards of shared morality are necessary (ibid., pp. 47–50).

[44] Ibid., p. 29.

[45] Communitarianism advocates open, responsive communities with a human moral which can be disputed and adjusted by its members if particular circumstances require this. Nevertheless, certain bonds of commitment and culture have to be shared in order to establish a community; to participate in a community is to be aware of, and responsive to, a complex set of communal interests and values.

[46] Selznick, *The Communitarian Persuasion*, p. 37.

[47] Ibid., p. 119.

and unity, and especially the mutual influence of collective and individual responsibility, applies very well to various social interactions that take place during a group improvisation. The idea that the context determines what can be valuable, without this being fixed for ever, can be the result of a reflection on socio-political aspects of improvisations, but it is a keynote in (liberal) communitarian thought, too.[48] Trust and commitment are the hobbyhorses of communitarianism as well as important features in making successful musical improvisations possible; they provide self-regulation and a positive feeling of self-control, without deteriorating into dogmatism (solidarity should never degenerate into subordination). The idea of a collective safety net or framework within which personal responsibility (and perhaps even irresponsibility) is operative but also controlled, seems appropriate for the improvised music discussed above. The responsibilities of the individual musicians in John Zorn's *Cobra*, as well as their abilities to respond, cannot be understood in full depth through an exclusive concentration on *ethical atomism*. The musician's interrelated aesthetical and ethical behaviour depends on a complex and extensive network of interactions with cultural traditions, musical pasts, the environment, the possibilities and impossibilities of the musical instrument and, presumably first of all, with fellow musicians. The best proof for the unmistakable existence of human interdependency in *Cobra* might be the possibility offered to the musicians to become a so-called 'guerrilla'. This allows players to become a renegade, to subvert the entire proceedings and to disregard the input of the others. This seems to be a rare opportunity to exchange a primarily collective responsibility for a primarily individual (ir)responsibility.

As in Zorn's conducted improvisation games, the attention for the other and otherness in the Miles Davis Quintet appears to be coordinated and kept together by some shared principles which make risky explorations of new musical interactions possible. These principles are not made explicit or laid down in contracts; rather, these are tacit agreements emanating from concrete experiences which result in certain ideas, often less clearly describable, about making music together and about improvising.

Undeniably, commitment and interdependence were two of the driving forces behind the successful explorative expeditions in the jazz idiom by the Miles Davis Quintet. But even in the (non-)collaboration between Keith Rowe and John Tilbury, the example with which we began this chapter, only the virtues of loyalty and commitment and a shared background make it possible to come to successful musical results through the concept of non-listening, if only because Rowe is dependent here on the susceptibility of Tilbury.[49] A small community indeed, this duo, but enough to show that Rowe cannot exist as a self-determining,

---

[48] 'The context tells us what kinds of liberty, creativity, or discipline are appropriate.' This sentence doesn't originate from a biography of some famous jazz musician but can be found in Selznick's *The Communitarian Persuasion*, p. 75.

[49] 'In the interest of liberty people should endure some disorder, perhaps even some danger and abuse,' Selznick writes (*The Communitarian Persuasion*, p. 59).

self-sufficient individual whose desired freedom can simply ignore the other. What can(not) be done – musically, but also socially and ethically – is decided by the participating musicians, either before or during the performance.

Criticizing collective ethics through improvisation

What communitarianism shows us is that personal responsibility arises most often from collective responsibility, from a framework of rules and premises accepted in advance. Considering, for example, the state of ecstasy that certain improvisers reach during performances as well as the sonic transformations via real-time processing of laptop musicians, both of which hamper the possibility of taking full responsibility on an individual level, the musico-ethical interactions that take place during an improvisation can best be understood from a communitarian point of view.

However, somehow the shoe doesn't quite fit. We agree that communal musical life is held together by traditions and by those dispositions or virtues that groups encourage in individual members. But improvising musicians cannot hide themselves behind a collective body or institution. An improvising ensemble is irreducible to a community regarded as a fusion of beings, a unified organic whole, a transparent socio-musical organization based on the specular recognition of the self in the other. By studying musical improvisation and the social interactions taking place between improvisers, communitarianism can also be criticized. For example, communitarian theories do not make clear to what extent a community is allowed to impose rules on individuals in order to create or maintain a well-defined and closed social identity or own-ness. Ultimately, communitarianism seems to aspire to a surveyable whole in which divergences of views are solved at the risk of producing forms of oppression and disintegration; and all this under the pretext of social coherence, desired reconciliation and the necessity of accepted rules.[50] A potential disappointment for communitarianism finds its origin in the possibility that individuals will not do exactly that which the so-called whole demands from them.[51] Although we have tried to argue that the ethicality of improvisers cannot be traced back completely to the responsibilities of each individual separately, the inescapable subordination of the individual to the collective in communitarian theories

---

[50] Ibid., p. 61. Perhaps Nietzsche can anachronistically be called the greatest critic of communitarian thinking. At the end of the nineteenth century he already warned against forms of friendship marked by a need for constant closeness, thereby paralysing the stranger's hostility.

[51] In a certain way, communitarianism seeks after the same as Plato's political-religious treatise, Book 10 of the *Nomoi*. In it, rebellious individuals have to be convinced that it is a mistake to think that there exists a natural multitude of more or less equal individualities that have every right to look after themselves in their own way.

seems to do injustice to the musical and social dynamics taking place during an improvised performance.

All communitarians to a greater or lesser degree begin from the notion that members of a community gear their actions to the realization of the common good. As stated above, MacIntyre emphasizes the importance of moral goods defined in respect to a community and a collective goal, supported by tradition. However, in such a predilection for unity – albeit Selznick's liberal, organic unity that tries to preserve the integrity of all the parts – the individual only counts insofar as she/he contributes to the case, the project, the whole. The community is presented as an immanent entity, oriented towards the fulfilment of a pre-established destiny.[52] However, through improvised music it can be shown that the irreducible multitude of self-willed individuals and neighbouring, analogously motivated lives and actions thus seem to be neglected. In its own way, communitarianism blocks the outlook for independent spaces of being together; it has to deny heterogeneity. Its legitimate plea for the fairness of coordinating interests of the commonwealth can rapidly change into resentment towards the obstinacy of the declared smaller units (the individuals). And this freedom for the individuals that together form a collective is of essential importance in improvised music.

One thing that interacting improvisers can oppose against the communitarian idea(l) is a more dynamic way of thinking and working: at least partially, the rules that govern the collective interplays of the Evan Parker ensemble, the Rowe–Tilbury duo, the quintets of Miles Davis and John Coltrane, and the *Cobra* musicians are only invented and established during performances. Perhaps with the exception of making (good) music together, the musical goals – if predefined at all – are almost constantly debatable and changeable. The ethical question (these) improvising musicians implicitly pose is how a community can remain a place for commonality while at the same time being an open, interrupted community that is both respectful of difference and resists closure. Through musical improvisation it becomes obvious that communitarianism obscures and obstructs dynamic and sometimes disharmonious interactions within (social) groups. Furthermore, the nature of musical collaborations and their outcomes might criticize more trenchantly the idea that identity is, first of all, an auto-constitutive whole which only at a later stage begins to relate to something or someone else. This last

---

[52] MacIntyre's thoughts echo those of the German sociologist Ferdinand Tönnies who, in the first decades of the twentieth century, made a distinction between *Gemeinschaft* (community) and *Gesellschaft* (society). Whereas the former stands for family, solidarity and friendship, the latter represents individualism, contractual relationships, segregation and alienation. MacIntyre's ethics and morality seem to be grounded on the idea that in the course of history a decline has taken place – that is, a transferral from *Gemeinschaft* to *Gesellschaft*. His moral proposals, like that of many communitarians, are based on the possibility of returning to a supposed original situation, the *Gemeinschaft*. In the rest of this chapter, we emphasize and elaborate the notion that this retrograde is foreign to (most) interactions taking place during musical improvisations.

remark is not so much a final surrender to communitarian thought, but offers an alternative to Theodor Adorno's analysis and criticism of 1930s jazz in order to arrive at an ethics that rejects neither individual nor collective responsibility and, simultaneously, refutes both.[53]

In the essay 'Über Jazz' ('On Jazz'), Adorno's rejection of (most) jazz music proceeds along four lines: the application of vibrato, the use of syncopation, the structural form of jazz pieces, and the contribution of improvisation. According to Adorno's analysis, the use of vibrato ascribes to sound subjective emotions, but without this being allowed to interrupt the fixedness of the basic sound-pattern; the vibrato cannot change the fundamental.[54] In much the same way, the syncope always remains connected and subordinated to the founding and ongoing beat. The syncope does not lead to new rhythmic developments but, in the end, conforms to a predetermined meter. In other words, the opposition against the compelling beat is temporary and weak.[55] Regarding the overall form of jazz pieces, Adorno notes that these are most often simple and symmetrical. The structure is usually dominated by the function instead of emanating from an autonomous formal development: in particular, the improvised parts are merely ornamental and never determine or affect the basic construction of the pieces.[56] And if improvisation can be regarded as a moment of musical freedom for a soloist, one cannot deny that in jazz this freedom is immediately and severely restricted by the pre-established and inflexible harmonic scheme to which the soloist has to conform. In that sense, jazz maintains an inexorably rigid stereotypology; its individual elements are merely illusionary.[57]

All these objections can be traced back to Adorno's fundamental problem with jazz music – that is, the subordination of the individual to the collective.

> The sacrificial meaning of the jazz subject is now clearly mitigated under the pressure of dream censorship. It falls out of the collective just as syncopation does from the regular beat; it does not want to be engulfed in the prescribed majority, which existed before the subject and is independent of it, whether out of protest or ineptitude or both at once, – until it finally is received into, or, better, subordinated to the collective as it was predestined to be; until the music

---

[53] Of course, it has to be kept in mind that Adorno's definition of jazz in the mid-1930s will, most probably, not correspond to prevailing definitions. For Adorno, the term 'jazz' also included the worst manifestations of (German) popular dance music. Nevertheless, the thought behind his criticism of, for example, improvisation is, within the context of this chapter, still relevant.

[54] Theodor W. Adorno, 'On Jazz', in *Essays on Music*, ed. Richard Leppert (Berkeley: University of California Press, 2002), p. 471.

[55] Ibid., p. 490.

[56] Ibid., p. 477.

[57] Ibid., p. 472.

indicates, in a subsequently ironic manner as the measures grow rounder, that it was a part of it from the very beginning.[58]

The improvising individual relates to the collective as the verse does to the refrain, as the syncope does to the meter, and as the vibrato does to the fundamental: she/he seems to claim freedom and the right to be different, but in fact she/he is just obeying the pre-given laws. That is why Adorno defines the improvisator as the sacrifice or victim of the collective. Not only is the alleged opposition of the soloist against the collective without prospect because she/he is isolated; her or his individual efforts are still determined by the stereotypes which she/he seems to oppose. 'This subject is not a free, lyrical subject which is then elevated into the collective, but rather one which is not originally free – a victim of the collective.'[59] Adorno concludes that jazz represents nothing but pseudo-individuality and pseudo-freedom – an almost deadly sin in his philosophical ideology which is based on every individual's right to compose a meaningful existence, free from dogmatic restrictions imposed by others.

Whereas the communitarian aspiration for unity inclines towards too much amalgamation and unification, Adorno could be accused of being too wary of the collective. If ethical behaviour has something to do with being responsible for the other, the former movement introduces the possibility for an individual to hide behind a collective and thereby anonymous responsibility, whereas for the latter the attention for the other is a purely individual affair, only true and sincere if the subject is free of restraints. The question is whether through music, through musical improvisation, through an emphasis on the interactive process taking place among musicians while improvising, another position is possible: namely another outlook on ethics, somewhere between individuality and collectivity. In order to think this in-between-ness we enlist the help of the French philosopher Jean-Luc Nancy and the German philosopher Peter Sloterdijk, although it should be firmly stated from the outset that their writings have not been aimed at the construction or the analysis of ethics.

Improvisation and ethics: between individuality and collectivity

What the musical examples above have shown is that playing is always playing *with* – playing with others. This is obviously the case for ensembles, but it is equally true for solo performances: soloists, too, are constantly connected to other human beings, other musicians, other entities, either diachronically, by pursuing a certain tradition, or synchronically, by playing the same instrument, in the same style or in the same venues. John Zorn's solo saxophone concerts, for example, connect him to the illustrious reedist Anthony Braxton, who in 1968 released the first solo

---

[58] Ibid., p. 489.
[59] Ibid., p. 488.

saxophone record, *For Alto*. Simultaneously, Zorn's way of experimenting with various musical parameters relates him to many more musicians from the 'free jazz' movement, from saxophonist Ornette Coleman to guitarist Derek Bailey and from keyboard player and band leader Sun Ra to trombonist George Lewis or pianist Thelonious Monk. However, his playing bears the traces of many more musics, from twentieth-century classical music to surf, film and cartoon music, and from klezmer to punk and noise. Zorn draws his inspiration from the complete history of music; nothing or nobody is excluded *a priori*. Spatial and temporal connections, musical and social relations, ethnic and cultural–political associations, technical innovations and discoveries and so on – the multitude of potential influences that forms, informs and transforms his work is inevitable. Even though Zorn appears to be alone on stage, he is continuously communicating and playing with many others. Following Peter Sloterdijk, we could call these synchronic and diachronic relations (being-together and being-together-after-one-another) *resonance communities*.[60]

This rudimentary example should make it sufficiently clear that improvising musicians – and, for that matter, all (human) beings – are always situated in a certain world, always in relation to this world and to others, always being-in-common even before it is a matter of common-being. According to Jean-Luc Nancy, in *La communauté désoeuvrée* (*The Inoperative Community*), being has no meaning other than being together with other beings.[61] In other words, being does not precede the possibility of being-with-others: our ontological condition is fundamentally social. Existence is always already coexistence:[62] people assemble, encounter one another, share experiences and separate again. This constitutes our being-in-common. However, with this statement, Nancy does not ally with the communitarians. He contends that community can never be the idealized fantasy of common-being or a unity of experience or perspective. A community is not a project of fusion, Nancy observes.[63] The reason for this is entrenched in the 'with': 'with' gestures to the possibility of connection but simultaneously exposes distance, difference and space. Similarly, the 'co' in coexistence marks deferral and difference as well as relation and bond (somewhat analogously to

---

[60] Peter Sloterdijk, *Sferen. Schuim*, trans. Hans Driessen (Amsterdam: Boom, 2009), p. 208.

[61] Jean-Luc Nancy, *The Inoperative Community*, trans. P. Connor *et al.* (Minneapolis: University of Minnesota Press, 1991), p. 3. It is obvious that Nancy's thoughts take their inspiration from Martin Heidegger's reflections on *Mitsein*. Social fragmentation, alienation and individuality only arise as secondary issues out of the primordial togetherness of *Dasein*.

[62] Similar thoughts can also be found in the philosophy of Hannah Arendt. She argues that the conditions of cohabitation are prior to contract, voluntary assent and decision. Arendt conducts a critique of the liberal contract theory. Her ethics starts from the idea that the ones who live here with us are the ones whose lives we are obligated to protect by the sheer fact of our coexistence.

[63] Nancy, *The Inoperative Community*, p. 15.

the structure of Derrida's concept of *différance*). 'There is proximity, but only to the extent that extreme closeness emphasizes the distancing it opens up.'[64] In most definitions, community becomes a single thing (body, mind, fatherland) and loses the paradoxical working of the 'with' or the 'together' that defines it. Instead of a fusion, Nancy suggests a double bind in which sharing and dividing occur concurrently: *partition*. 'With' is both a mark of union and a mark of division, leaving each one to its isolation and its being-with-others. It is a mark drawn out over a void, which crosses over it and underlines it at the same time, thereby constituting the drawing apart and drawing together of the void. A community thus exists in a space between integration and disintegration. Opposed to an idea(l) in which the voice of each member aligns with all others, literally being in tune with the other voices, Nancy's thoughts give space to a plurality of singularities or a multitude of voices. Partition refers to both multiplicity and communality at the same time.

This ontology of existence is in itself not only social, but also ethical. The 'I' is no Self who is unmediated present to itself. One appears to oneself insofar as one is already an other for oneself. Self-consciousness means that the self knows itself principally as other than itself. The individual is thus an intersection of singularities and always already exposed to a heteronomy, a partition, even before there is a matter of 'self', even before a deliberate choice for pluralism can be established. Following from this thought, Nancy claims that 'to exist' means to be-outside-oneself, to connect to the world, to be exposed; it means to be in relation, to be open to the other or otherness, not to coincide with oneself and to exceed the self. It is our ontological condition to be exposed. To share a world means to relate to each other and to be consigned to others. Therefore, being-in-common means taking responsibility.

> Such is our responsibility, which is not added to us like a task, but which makes up our being. We exist as this responsibility; that is, in Heidegger's words we *ek-sist*, we are exposed to one another and together to the world – the world which is nothing but this very exposure. Existence is responsibility for existence.[65]

This existential responsibility does not give guidelines how to act; we have to justify ourselves constantly with regard to this existence, to the world, to others. And because we *are* always already an opened existence, we cannot escape from this responsibility. Respecting or disdaining the other can only arise because there is, on an ontological level, already a relation between me and the other.

Implicitly, Nancy reacts to some of Levinas's and Adorno's thoughts. In Levinas's philosophy, the capitalized Other can never belong to my community.

---

[64] Jean-Luc Nancy, *Being Singular Plural*, trans. R.D. Richardson and A.E. O'Byrne (Stanford, CA: Stanford University Press, 2000), p. 5.

[65] Jean-Luc Nancy, 'Responding for Existence', *Studies in Practical Philosophy*, 1/1 (1999), p. 8.

Conversely, for Nancy each community implies by definition a fundamental otherness (lower-case) that cannot be reduced to the order of the same. Levinas's claim that the ontology has to yield to ethics is replaced by Nancy's ontological condition in which we are connected to an infinite number of others from the outset. Coexistence puts me in an irreducible openness not, as in Levinas, to an infinite Otherness, an instance transcending the world, but to an alterity or alteration *of* the world.[66]

Contrary to Adorno, Nancy states that freedom only takes place in community; it thereby presupposes relationality. Freedom is not the free space preceding existence; it happens in-common. Freedom as independence only reveals the impossibility to relate, to connect, to bond. Each form of freedom as independence already appeals to the dependence of others to practise this independence. However, once more, Nancy's rejection of freedom as an autonomous, individual affair is not replaced by the non-subjective freedom of a communitarian collective. Freedom always presupposes relationality, and this relationality is not fixed in advance but is contingent.

Peter Sloterdijk does not take the ontological course; his bulky trilogy, *Spheres*, is a cultural analysis of how people live and act together. But, like Nancy, he recoils from embracing communitarian holism or liberal individualism. Supporting the basic idea that humans coexist before they exist – in his terms, the 'we-immunity' exceeds the 'I-immunity' – Sloterdijk attempts to present an alternative outlook on associations and the natural aim towards closeness and mutual commitment. Instead of the ontological unity of the individual organism, he proposes a poly-perspective unity of a simultaneously experienced but differently symbolized common situation by a number of intelligent beings.[67] Therefore he links up with one of the German founders of sociology, Georg Simmel, who developed a non-totalitarian analysis of social units: each element of a group is not only a part of society, but also something else. However, Sloterdijk does not understand this being-something-else-than-society as the intimate last being-for-itself of an atomic individual. Rather, he coins the concept of *co-isolated associations*: societies are multitudes of more or less autonomous spaces, in which people participate thanks to their always already present 'psychotopical differences'.[68] To put it differently, a society is an aggregate of micro-spheres that border on one another without really being accessible to one another or effectively separable from one another.[69] Sloterdijk refers to Pierre Lévy, who in his book *L'Intelligence collective* (*Collective Intelligence*) writes that 'in the knowledge space active exhalations work together, not to bring about some hypothetical fusion of individual

---

[66] Nancy, *Being Singular Plural*, p. 11. See also Ignaas Devisch, *Wij. Nancy en het vraagstuk van de gemeenschap in de hedendaagse wijsbegeerte* (Leuven: Peeters, 2003), p. 170.
[67] Sloterdijk, *Sferen. Schuim*, p. 202.
[68] Ibid., p. 211.
[69] Ibid., p. 39.

beings, but to collectively inflate the same bubble, thousands of rainbow-tinged bubbles, provisional universes, shared worlds of signification'.[70] Like Nancy, Sloterdijk seems to be pursuing a space between a segregating individualism and a coordinating collectivism – a space where making an undertaking and being separated from one another can be considered as two sides of the same coin.

It is not our aim to contend that interactions in improvised music link up perfectly with Nancy's or Sloterdijk's philosophy; nor is it our intention to present musical improvisation as an exemplar of their work. Rather, their meditations put us on a track to rethink the interactions within improvised music from ethical principles. As we have demonstrated above, the responsibilities for interactions among improvising musicians cannot always be thought of as stemming from an individual or a self: certain agents (technology, ecstasy, intensive collaboration) obstruct the idea that ethical contact with others can be retraced to a personal responsibility. Nor can an ethics at work in musical improvisation merely be regarded as a set of predetermined, predefined rules, principles and duties that function as some kind of common ground on the basis of which musicians start collaborating. What Jacques Attali in 1977 formulated as an ideal, namely 'to play for the other and by the other, to exchange the noise of bodies, to hear the noise of other's in exchange for one's own, to create, in common, the code within which communication will take place',[71] was at that time already one of the unstable pillars of free improvised music: perhaps the musicians worked towards a common goal, but this goal was not established, formulated or known in detail in advance.[72] Out of many possibilities, a common route was chosen – a route that could constantly be negotiated, challenged and adapted. This is not to say that this free improvised music (movement) offered the kind of 'absolute' freedom Nancy is arguing against. Conventions and traditions, both intra- and extramusical, transect this form of musicking as they do any other. Physical (im)possibilities of musicians, instruments, technology and acoustics furthermore determine the music's upper and lower limits. And operating within a collective is not only the opening up of unforeseen possibilities; it carries with it certain inevitable restrictions as well. However, the fundamental openness, the acceptance and even the (conscious) suspension of too much security, as well as an aesthetics which allows for disruption and dissolution, are almost diametrically opposed to the communitarian consensus ideal of agreed and pre-established social and ethical rules. Musical improvisation knows no law or ultimate value but the one that makes the relation towards a law or value possible: the decision.

---

[70] Pierre Lévy, *Collective Intelligence. Mankind's Emerging World in Cyberspace*, trans. R. Bononno (Cambridge: Perseus Books, 1997), p. 169.

[71] Jacques Attali, *Noise: The Political Economy of Music*, trans. B. Massumi (Minneapolis: University of Minnesota Press), p. 143.

[72] Of course, the main goal of making music, of improvising, can indeed be having fun, but what we mean here is that the musical results of free improvised music are usually not predetermined or predictable.

Playing with others

Nancy's conceptualization of the 'with' and Sloterdijk's cultural analysis of isolated coexistence provide us with an opportunity to situate the interactions that take place during a performance of improvised music in a space between individual and collective responsibility – a space that can be entered neither through Levinas's and Bauman's emphasis on an ethics based on the responsibility of a human being sufficient to itself nor through Selznick's and MacIntyre's advocacy of collective responsibility preceding individual self-realization. If we can agree on the idea that, within each musical improvisation, interactions are present that at least contain traces of what can be called ethics, this music and these interactions allow us to encounter a different ethics or a different view on ethics. This ethics can be understood through a reflection on the meaning of the word 'with', based on the consideration that musicking is always a playing-with, a playing-with-others. Miles Davis plays with Herbie Hancock, Evan Parker plays with Paul Lytton, John Coltrane plays with Pharoah Sanders, the musicians performing *Cobra* play with each other and so on. And, likewise, Keith Rowe plays with John Tilbury. Musicking is always already and unavoidably *Mitsein*, being-with, and it therefore encompasses, by definition, ethical aspects as well. At first sight, this being-with seems to oscillate indefinitely between two meanings without ever coming to a point of equilibrium: it is either the 'together' of gathering *totum intra totum*, a unified totality where the part is determined by, and dependent on, collective arrangements, or the 'together' of juxtaposition *partes extra partes*, isolated parts that aspire to complete self-fulfilment, relatively independent from the collective interests. However, the 'playing-with' of improvising musicians can be situated precisely on the point of equilibrium between the two meanings: 'together' is neither extra nor intra.[73] Playing-with constitutes the mark of unity and disunity, the traction and tension, the repulsion and attraction of the 'between', of the always already existing interval between performing musicians.

Returning to the Miles Davis Quintet once more, we could perhaps argue that this is a community without unity, working on and through communication without communing. Each of the musicians is permanently exposed not only to the other, the other as human being, as musician, but also to the other as intervening musical input, the other as a de- and recontextualization; it is precisely through their interplay that the musicians can experience another otherness – an otherness between themselves and their respective instruments as well as an otherness inside themselves. Davis put together a group of musicians who he could lead but from whom he could learn at the same time. This eagerness to learn – an attitude that characterized all five members – is nothing else than opening oneself to the other and to otherness. And opening oneself can be understood as making space for, admitting, inviting and deliberately calling on the other of/in oneself. During performances of this quintet, this learning process was almost guaranteed

---

[73] Nancy, *Being Singular Plural*, p. 60.

because the musical material and the musical frame were not pre-established but formed in and during the interactive play in which arrangements ranked mostly as guidelines and not as compulsory instructions. This becomes especially clear at the indecisive, scrappy ending of 'Footprints' as it appears on the album *Miles Smiles*. Three times Davis signals an ending and, in all three cases, members of the rhythm section carry on regardless until bass and drums finally slow down and find a stopping place.[74] What this masterly example of (failed) interplay makes heard is that performing regarded as a playing-with always implies being exposed to an otherness that can never be reduced to the order of the same but simultaneously co-constitutes the self.

Sloterdijk would perhaps speak of the Quintet as a 'phonotopic cell' – a cell with sonically based interwoven isolations that are neither united nor really separated – or, what comes down to the same, isolations that are both connected and separated – closely entwined, yet divided, units. It is the ethical responsibility of the musicians not to obstruct the learning process, not to hamper the possibility to be open to the other, not to impede the exposure to insecurity and vulnerability. But before this ethical imperative operative within the Quintet, an ethics of being-in-common, of playing together, is already postulated. This playing together happens in a collective frame that makes space for individual freedom. In other words, the 'phonotopic cell' provides its individual members with possibilities to discover unknown sonic–ethical and socio-ethical places, the result being that the cell itself evolves, reorientates and rediscovers itself. In the case of the ending of 'Footprints' on *Miles Smiles*, the awkward result is that trumpet and sax are playing the 6/4 theme over a 4/4 accompaniment.

'One is not "with" in some general sort of way, but each time according to determined modes that are themselves multiple and simultaneous.'[75] Put simply, the playing-with of the Miles Davis Quintet differs from the playing-with of the other musicians discussed in this chapter, such as the Rowe–Tilbury duo. The initial question whether Rowe's concept of non-listening is a convincing example of unethical musical behaviour can now be recaptured. Let us recall once more Rowe's words:

> Being strangely aware of John's movements, but not necessarily listening to what he is playing; not reacting to his playing but being affected by it. The act of NOT listening is very important, preferring juxtaposition to confabulation … If I attempted not to actively listen to John's piano as my hand descended towards the guitar laid out before me, what might happen? Possibly I might avoid triggering memories of the piano, memories that by definition would take me away from the immediate context and towards some looping representations of past occasions.[76]

---

[74] Yudkin, *Miles Davis*, pp. 93–94.
[75] Nancy, *Being Singular Plural*, p. 65.
[76] Rowe, liner notes for *Duos for Doris*.

Rowe's non-listening is not meant to prevent any form of interaction. It is meant to avoid relapsing into a musical performance which is built on previous explorations and discoveries; it is meant to avoid too many conventions, too many tricks that have already proven their success; it is meant to stay open to another otherness.[77] Rowe opens an ethical space of creativity and change through resistance. His attitude makes space for musical interactions that demand a response-ability that is not already prescribed, a praxis of risk for which there can be no rules, no codes, no principles and no guarantees.[78] 'Playing-with' is a formula in which the 'with' implies exposition. Rowe's attitude is the constitutive fact of an exposition to the outside. He is thus able to be affected by the other's alterity, to experience alterity in the other together with the alteration that in him sets his singularity outside him and infinitely delimits it. What is exposed is the following, and Nancy insists that we must learn to read it in all possible combinations: '"you (are/and/is) (entirely other than) I". Or again, more simply: you shares me.'[79] Non-listening as a form of playing-with, as a possibility of becoming exposed to alterities in and of the (musical) world; non-listening as a research into the possibilities of interaction on another level than the conscious, accepted, articulated, crystallized ones; non-listening as a concern not for the other improviser but a care for the work itself: perhaps that is the difference between reacting and being affected to which Rowe refers. Or, as Gary Peters summarizes, 'collective, yes, communal, no'.[80]

'Community cannot arise from the domain of work because one does not produce it, one experiences or one is constituted by it,' Nancy writes in *The Inoperative Community*.[81] Without purposely producing it, without consciously working on it, Rowe and Tilbury form a community. 'Community necessarily takes place in what Blanchot has called "unworking," referring to that which, before or beyond the work, withdraws from the work, and which, no longer having to do either with production or with completion, encounters interruption, fragmentation, suspension.'[82] Rowe and Tilbury experience community as they are first of all exposed to each other, and exposed to the exposure of the other. It is not possible for Rowe not to play with the other. Because playing is always playing-with, Rowe cannot not take responsibility; as a being-in-common he is always already responsible.

---

[77] Though writing about a different musical context, Garry Hagberg also warns musicians not to become too close to the other players as that diminishes their individuality and turns an autonomous ethical gesture into bland agreement. The right thing to do is to provide a fellow musician with 'something to play against'. Hagberg thus encounters a paradox: working with becomes working against (*Art and Ethical Criticism*, pp. 277–78).

[78] Geraldine Finn, *Why Althusser Killed His Wife: Essays on Discourse and Violence* (Atlantic Highlands, NJ: Humanities Press, 1996), p. 176.

[79] Nancy, *The Inoperative Community*, p. 29.

[80] Peters, *The Philosophy of Improvisation*, p. 58.

[81] Ibid., p. 31.

[82] Ibid.

Rowe's attitude does not seek to eradicate hospitality but rather to subject it to transvaluation.[83] His is an agonistic mode of hospitality. Quite analogous to Nietzsche's scattered remarks on ethics and morality, he *desires* resistances instead of evading or trying to subvert them. This requires a strong nature and, at least according to Nietzsche, will lead to personal growth, freedom and a continual self-overcoming. But the community will also benefit as such an attitude ensures that one's actions are measured and judged against one another and tested again and again. Only through contest can existing values be questioned, tested and, when necessary, reformed or created anew. This way, Nietzsche's anti-religious agonistic ethics seems to resonate and find fertile soil in the Rowe–Tilbury community. Instead of a sensitivity 'where virtually every mark interferes with or intrudes into the marked space of the other',[84] Rowe's non-listening attitude shows that resistance and the freedom to actualize this resistance aesthetically, as well as ethically, can be an integral part of improvisation.[85]

From 'the good' to 'the best'

Bass player Ron Carter recalls his experiences as a member of the second Miles Davis Quintet: 'Collectively, we were a mind of one.'[86] It might be productive to interpret this reflective remark in the light of our preceding quest for a musical ethics. Following Nancy and Sloterdijk (but also many psychoanalysts), it is first expedient, and perhaps even justifiable, to add that 'a mind of one' most often encompasses many different ways of thinking and experiencing; besides rationality and combinatorial powers it knows many antinomies and inconsistencies; besides causality and linearity it often takes many side-roads and is constantly haunted by feelings of insecurity and indeterminacy. Granted, the Quintet made a good team, which is a prerequisite for their ways of experimenting. But musical as well as social analyses of their improvising practice make clear that their collectivity cannot be reduced to 'feeding in the same place, as it does when applied to cattle'.[87] The collaborations within the Quintet cannot be equated with bodily

---

[83] This paragraph is inspired by Rainer J. Hanshe's 'Agonistic Ethics: On the Hospitality of Warriors', a paper presented at the East–West Passage Conference in Pécs, Hungary, 3–6 November 2010.

[84] Peters, *The Philosophy of Improvisation*, p. 54.

[85] Similar thoughts can be found in Peters, *The Philosophy of Improvisation*, pp. 53–55. Peters states that a profound concern and care for the other might create improvisations in which attentiveness, responsiveness and support can produce works of great sensitivity and delicacy. However, too much mutual respect for the improvisatory space of the other can also be suffocating and lead to a loss of creative possibilities, thereby harming the work.

[86] Quoted in Yudkin, *Miles Davis*, p. 5.

[87] Aristotle, *The Nicomachean Ethics*, trans. H. Rackham (Ware: Wordsworth Editions, 1996), p. 249.

organs that make an altruistic contribution to the healthy eudemonia of the whole. The virtuosic interactions never lead to a complete unification, but provide a space where each individual member can explore unknown musical sites without being restricted by collective rules. Davis, Shorter, Hancock, Carter and Williams play in a space between total subordination to the interest of the group as a whole and complete individual self-realization where none of these poles is ever touched. Better yet, this supposed opposition between the collective and the individual is deconstructed in the praxis of the Quintet's improvisations.

'Collectively, we were a mind of one.' Perhaps this could be understood as a kind of *collective intelligence* as described by the French anthropologist and sociologist Pierre Lévy in his book of the same name. Lévy describes the transition of self knowledge into forms of group knowledge, collective thought and sophisticated systems of networked intelligence. The simple premise is that no one knows everything; everyone knows something. Through enhanced interaction people share their knowledge, and this transpersonal knowledge exceeds the sum of individual intelligences. What is important for music is that, throughout the book, Lévy emphasizes that his definition of collective intelligence cannot and should not be restricted to the exchange of rational knowledge only: there are body-thoughts, affect-thoughts, percept-thoughts, sign-thoughts, concept-thoughts, gestural-thoughts, machine-thoughts, world-thoughts.[88] Sharing memories and experiences thus also belongs to the 'cooperative brain' which Lévy has in mind.

Collective intelligence is the result of continuous discoveries, developments, fluctuating uses and evaluations and it will (therefore) constantly develop in many unforeseen directions; it is in a perpetual state of becoming. That is why Lévy calls it the 'utopia of the unstable and multiple'. Being volatile and open, it responds to an ethics of the best rather than a morality of the good.

> Static, definitive, decontextualized, the good is imposed a priori, on top of any existing situation, whereas the best (the best possible) is situated, relative, dynamic, and provisional. The good doesn't change; the best is different wherever it is found. Good opposed to evil; it's exclusionary. The best, however, includes evil since logically equivalent to the lesser evil, it is satisfied with minimizing it ... Members of intelligent communities promote the growth of the best; they create a best that is always new and always different. The best is continuously displaced not only because objective situations evolve, but because our understanding of situations develops or becomes confused (which also constitutes a changed situation), because the criteria of choice change as a function of the transformation of the environment and the evolution of our plans.[89]

It is our claim that the interactions taking place during musical improvisations such as the ones described above can be regarded as a good example of a 'displaced

---

[88] Lévy, *Collective Intelligence*, p. 139.
[89] Ibid., pp. 250–51.

ethics of the best'. Since any of the members of the Miles Davis Quintet, the Evan Parker group and the John Coltrane Quintet, as well as the *Cobra* performers and the Rowe–Tilbury duo, can, in principle, shift the direction of the music, there is an ongoing process of decision-making taking place among all musicians during an improvisation. Each one has constantly to reconsider and remodel her/his own part as a result of certain decisions taken by others that change the development of the music to a lesser or greater extent.[90] Improvisation can thus be(come) a suitable medium for problem analysis, group discussion, the development of an awareness of complex processes, collective decision-making and evaluation.[91] Musical improvisation can provide a site where aesthetical, social and ethical relations are enacted, negotiated and established simultaneously over and over again. Naturally, these relations can never be fixed forever or in advance; that would frustrate the basic premise of improvisation. An improvisational ethics of the best will always resist foundation, codification, formalization and universalization. It is an ethics that will always stay singular, though not merely individual.

The contribution of improvised music to the ethical discourse could consist of the understanding that ethics takes place in a space between personal and collective responsibility. However, this positive contribution cannot disguise the fact that music is frequently used in ways and for reasons which seem diametrically opposed to the ethics we have been tracing here. In the space between the personal and the collective, music often contributes to strategies of exclusion, disciplining and control, thereby obstructing a real and open quest for an ethics of the best. The initial rationale behind the next chapter, 'Affect', is to show 'the dark side of the tune' – the relation between music and amorality.

---

[90] 'More important for morality than a willingness to judge others is the courage to critically examine one's own actions or responses and motivations,' philosopher Craig Taylor rightfully remarks ('Art and Moralism', *Philosophy*, 84/3 (2009), p. 343).

[91] Lévy, *Collective Intelligence*, p. 59.

Chapter 4
Affect

Marcel Cobussen

> Every disease is a musical problem; every cure is a musical solution.
> Novalis, *Schriften: Die Werke Friedrich von Hardenbergs*

The auralization of an ethnic conflict

The location is an elegant and noisy restaurant in Istanbul, at the turn of the millennium. Five people of different nationalities – a Greek, a Serb, a Macedonian, a Turk and a Bulgarian woman – sit at one of the tables. Their animated conversation is accompanied by live music, and at a certain moment the band strikes up a familiar folk tune. A rather peculiar dispute breaks out, each of the diners claiming that the tune is a well-known national song that belongs to his or her country.

This is the beginning of *Whose is this Song?*, a documentary by Adela Peeva (the Bulgarian member of the group of diners). What follows is a fascinating 'road movie' through South-east Europe, as a quest for the roots of the tune takes Peeva from Turkey to Greece, Albania, Bosnia, Macedonia, Serbia and Bulgaria respectively. In most of these countries, the tune is a love song with varying domestic lyrics, but in others, such as Turkey and Bosnia, it has also been used as a war song. In each country, however, the reactions to the study are the same: people display shock, anger or disbelief when Peeva suggests that the same tune is also claimed by their neighbours. 'The Serbs can never do a song like this; they have no traditions,' a young Albanian man says curtly. 'It might be that the Turks took it from us,' the conductor of a local Albanian orchestra replies to Peeva's remark that the Turks regard it as their song. In other words, for him it is beyond dispute that the song originates from Albania. For Sarajevo Sevdah singer Emina Zecaj, meanwhile, the song is 'Bosnian only'. This is confirmed by a Bosnian choir director, although he admits to Peeva that it is not (only) a sweet love song as Zecaj claims, but a religious (Muslim) song as well, used as a call to arms, brought by the Turks and forbidden during the communist rule in former Yugoslavia. Confronted with this second, belligerent Bosnian version during a festivity in Vranje, a town in southern Serbia, Peeva's hosts tell her that this is theft and a pure provocation: it is a Serbian love song. Suddenly, the festive atmosphere changes and a scuffle seems almost inevitable. Returning to her home country, Bulgaria, Peeva finds out that the song is sung there as well, particularly during an annual commemoration near southern Strandja, where the Bulgarians fought against the Ottoman Empire a century earlier. Cautiously intimating to the nationalist participants that the song might be Turkish, Peeva is met with a furious response: 'You risk being stoned if you say that it was a Turkish song,' replies a man sipping his local brandy; 'I'll hang the one who says that song was Turkish on that oak tree' is the reaction of one skinny accordion player.

The documentary is open-ended in its findings. Suggestions that the song might have Jewish or Central Asian origins are conditional, requiring further investigation, although this will probably not serve to soothe tempers.

Music and identity

In an interview, Peeva states that music is one of the fundamental aspects of our identities. Nevertheless, she asks with genuine bewilderment, 'How can one song cause so much hatred?' And, indeed, research indicates that 'while there is a demonstrated causal link between music and arousal, including the arousal of aggressive and violent inclinations, this does not necessarily ... lead to violent social conduct'.[1] And we could further add, to Peeva's astonishment, the fact that the predominantly amiable lyrics would not seem especially likely to have been a factor in the obvious animosities.

So, after several explorations in tracing how music as music – that is, as a sonic art form, rather than as another manifestation or intermediary of discursive meaning – might contribute to ethical discourse and concrete ethical behaviour, we strike here a very different note, to reveal 'the dark side of the tune', as Bruce Johnson and Martin Cloonan have it. It is time to twist things around and confront the question of whether music can be unethical, whether it can incite people to do evil, provoke them into doing harm – an almost rhetorical question judging from Peeva's documentary.

Music is no source of harmless entertainment or diversion, Plato has already warned. It has significant potential to move and stir the emotions, a power that can be used for good but certainly also for ill. It can nurture temperance and moderation, but it can also undermine self-control and disrupt the harmonious balance of the virtuous soul. That is why Plato worried about music's seductive pleasure: it appeals less to the reasoned than to the passionate parts of the soul. The persuasiveness of music must be controlled at any cost and used in service of proper moral ends, as hedonic pleasure is a lesser value than rational or moral behaviour. Because music's affective and emotional character is able to introduce distortions that corrupt understanding and responsible action, it should be treated with great care and only by those who are educated and good, a section of the population from which musicians themselves, in Plato's ideal society, were usually excluded.[2]

---

[1] Bruce Johnson and Martin Cloonan, *Dark Side of the Tune: Popular Music and Violence* (Aldershot: Ashgate, 2008), p. 138.

[2] Plato, *The Republic*, Book III, trans. Benjamin Jowett (Charleston, SC: BiblioBazaar, 2007).

There is the question of whether Plato's objections against music's power to work on, to affect and to infect human emotions can be averted by something like George Steiner's belief that music cannot lie: 'Is there a lie, anywhere, in Mozart?' he asks provocatively.[3] The crucial aspect of this remark is that Steiner is not referring here to the librettos or other textualities that accompany and surround music; his attention is focused explicitly on the musical sounds. Indeed, it may be difficult to find falsehoods in musical parameters such as melody, harmony, or rhythm. Nevertheless, Steiner has to admit in the same paragraph that music can indeed 'release springs of cruelty'. If it doesn't lie, but can do much harm otherwise, music, of course, cannot claim to be on the safe side of morality. Besides, Theodor Adorno had already stated by the end of the 1940s that music actually can be untrue.[4] If music somehow fails to express the state of affairs of a contemporary society, and if a composer does not avail himself of the current (semi-autonomous) development of the musical material, the result will be a music that can be called false.

The conclusion from the examples above is obvious and well documented elsewhere (see also Chapter 1, 'Listening'): music cannot withdraw from socio-political or ethical concerns, and it cannot retreat to the ivory tower of pure aesthetic pleasure, pretending or hoping to be completely unaffected by so-called 'extramusical' events or experiences, nor, therefore, should it be approached only through formal analyses. What is referred to by the term 'contextualization' – as if 'the outside' can be kept at a safe distance or simply regarded as an avoidable supplement – always already affects the production and determination of a certain musical event. Social, political, economic, religious, cultural, ethnical, ethical, juridical and psychological matters operate on, and resonate with, the production, distribution, reception and actual sounding of music. And, conversely, music exercises influence on these 'contextual' matters: social, political, economic, religious, cultural, ethnical, ethical, juridical and psychological matters are transformed or even only come into existence through music. As Tia DeNora writes in *Music in Everyday Life*, music is a 'medium for making, sustaining, and changing social worlds and social activities'[5] (a point confirmed in Peeva's documentary). Disclosing possible connections between music and ethics – the main subject of this book – inevitably means dealing with and trying to understand musical affect more than analysing the structure of musical works; the emphasis should be on how particular aspects of music come to be (ethically) significant

---

[3] George Steiner, *In Bluebeard's Castle: Some Notes Towards the Redefinition of Culture* (New Haven, CT: Yale University Press, 1971), p. 122.

[4] Theodor Adorno, *Philosophy of New Music* (Minneapolis: University of Minnesota Press, 2006). See especially his accusations directed at Stravinsky's neo-classical music. This music was untrue as it fell back on music and values from previous centuries. Instead, true music is critical music, showing the disharmonies of contemporary society.

[5] Tia DeNora, *Music in Everyday Life* (Cambridge: Cambridge University Press, 2000), p. x.

in relation to particular recipients at particular moments and under particular circumstances.[6] Consistent with DeNora's ideas, Edward Said states that music cannot be separated from political and social processes. Music is a social force influencing how people conduct themselves, how they feel about themselves, about others, and about situations.[7]

Whereas DeNora emphasizes the constant interplay between music and its recipients, Simon Frith propounds the idea that music not so much reflects or represents (social) groups as produces and constructs them. Music is a key to identity because it offers a sense of both self and others. Frith reverses the idea that a social group has beliefs which it then articulates in its music; instead, he claims that music articulates in itself an understanding of group relations, on the basis of which ethical codes and social ideologies can be understood.

> What I want to suggest, in other words, is not that social groups agree on values which are then expressed in their cultural activities (the assumption of the homology model) but that they only get to know themselves *as groups* (as a particular organization of individual and social interests, of sameness and difference) *through* cultural activity, through aesthetic judgment.[8]

Music thus stands for, symbolizes and offers an experience of collective social and cultural identity. Music constructs senses of identity through experiences which enable people to place themselves in imaginative cultural narratives.[9]

In short, music has a dynamic relation with social life, helping to invoke, stabilize or change parameters of individual as well as collective feeling, perception, cognition, consciousness, identity, energy and comportment.[10] Music does not represent identity; it intervenes to rearrange things and bodies into identities. There is not music on one side, and social reality on the other. Music is part of reality. Music makes identity out of individual bodies, not through meaning but through force; no mediation or representation, but sonic interventions.

Seemingly less astonished than Peeva about music's effects and affects, Croatian writer Dubravka Ugresic in *The Culture of Lies*, the author's often personal observations and analyses of former Yugoslavian society and politics before, during and after the wars of the 1990s, dedicates a whole chapter to the various roles music

---

[6] Ibid., p. 23.

[7] See, for example, Daniel Barenboim and Edward Said, *Parallels and Paradoxes* (New York: Vintage Books, 2002).

[8] Simon Frith, 'Music and Identity', in Stuart Hall and Paul du Gay (eds), *Questions of Cultural Identity* (London: Sage, 1996), p. 111, emphasis in original.

[9] Ibid., p. 124. In much the same way, Alan Merriam argues that music provides a rallying point around which the members of society gather in order to engage in activities which require the cooperation and coordination of the group. See Alan Merriam, *The Anthropology of Music* (Evanston, IL: Northwestern University Press, 1964), p. 227.

[10] DeNora, *Music in Everyday Life*, p. 20.

played in the creation and destruction of (new) national identities in the Balkans.[11] 'Balkan Blues' – the chapter's apt title – describes music's power to evoke hidden memories, to create identity, to preserve emotions and to maintain feelings of solidarity and alliance beyond rational foundations.[12] Ugresic argues that music's (symbolic) power to (de)construct ethnic, national, and/or religious identities, and its potential to contribute to the politics of (social) in- and exclusion, takes place on many different levels and in different types of music, from supposedly innocent children's songs, the prominence of the minor key in expressing the melancholy of Balkan people, and music lessons in primary school,[13] to commercial *turbo folk* with its often explicitly political lyrics, and the use of specific musical instruments to convey political ideologies. As an example of the latter, Ugresic refers to a documentary by Paul Pawlikowski about Radovan Karadzic, the leader of the Bosnian Serbs from 1992 to 1996. Gazing sorrowfully over half-ruined Sarajevo, then besieged by Karadzic's army, the movie includes a scene of Karadzic murmuring a few folk songs, in alternation with readings of his own poems. He holds a *gusle*, a single-stringed musical instrument of the Balkans with a round wooden back, a skin belly and one horsehair string secured at the top of the neck by a rear tuning peg. *Gusle* players or *guslari* are among the few performers who maintain the oral tradition of epic Balkan poetry, and their instrument and music could be said to symbolize the history and the soul of the people living in that part of Europe. It is clear that Karadzic could not have chosen a more accurate instrument, Ugresic claims. Through the *gusle*, Bosnian and Serbian war criminals are connected to the national heroes of times long past; Karadzic presents himself as their true heir. Ugresic coins his appropriation '*Gusle* laundering'.[14]

Peeva, Frith and Ugresic all point to the fact that music is often deployed to establish, maintain or deconstruct group identities, where 'identity' can be understood as the condition that a group is itself and not something else, as the ability to hold on to a coherent image of 'who one knows one is'. Group identity

---

[11] Dubravka Ugresic, *The Culture of Lies*, trans. Celia Hawkesworth (London: Phoenix, 1996).

[12] Most interesting in this respect is Ugresic's mentioning of the so-called *rere*, a wordless, heterophonic intoning usually performed by men from the Croatian and Herzegovinian countryside. With their arms on each other's shoulders, they let out throaty, usually clashing, dissonant sounds. Solidarity, identity and emotions are bunched in sound and rhythm instead of, outside of, or before discursive meaning.

[13] 'And we all knew everything: the sound of the "bajs" from Zagorje, the tune of the ballads from Medjimurje, the songs of Dalmatian groups, the words of Slavonian jigs and Bosnian "sevdalinke", the beat of Albanian drums, the sound of the Serbian trumpet and the rhythm of the Slovene polka' (Ugresic, *The Culture of Lies*, p. 132).

[14] Ibid., p. 139. In *Dark Side of the Tune*, Bruce Johnson and Martin Cloonan make mention of three main uses of music in the Yugoslavian conflict: encouragement to participants; provoking and humiliating the enemy; and calls for the involvement of those not directly involved (p. 149). All three seem applicable to Karadzic's *gusle* performance.

presupposes the sameness of the group at all times and in all circumstances. 'To be is to be one,' Mark C. Taylor summarizes in a few words.[15] The group has to appear as a simple or undivided being-for-itself; it is identical to itself. This can only be done by defining and positioning itself in and through opposition to other isolated groups. In other words, creating identity always takes place through what Derrida calls a 'logic of exclusion'. Creating a group identity implies isolating that group and presenting it as opposed to everything that is not that group: 'the outside is out and the inside in'.[16]

Creating or maintaining an identity is a struggle for mastery in which the group often asserts itself by negating the other, which it regards in thoroughly negative terms. The group's elaborate strategies of self-assertion are actually various efforts to secure its identity as a group by excluding difference and otherness.[17] Although the creating of group identities is a feature of all times, Peter Sloterdijk writes in *Spheres* that, just as the nineteenth century knew its social questions, so the twentieth and twenty-first centuries know the question of exclusion. It is the postmodern figure of the unhappy consciousness.[18]

The 'logic' of identity implies an economy of ownership in which one seeks security by struggling against dispossession, impropriety and expropriation. The group can seek to possess itself by possessing other groups. Such possession then takes the form of oppression, in which the oppressed group also confirms the autonomy and identity of the dominant group.

---

[15] Mark C. Taylor, *Erring: A Postmodern A/Theology* (Chicago: University of Chicago Press, 1987), p. 130.

[16] Jacques Derrida, *Dissemination*, trans. B. Johnson (Chicago: University of Chicago Press, 1981), p. 128. According to Judith Butler, to claim self-identity is an act of irresponsibility, an effort to close off one's fundamental vulnerability to the other. This claim prevents the self from entering into an ethical relation of responsibility. See her chapter 'Ethical Ambivalence', in Marjorie Garber, Beatrice Hanssen, and Rebecca Walkowitz (eds), *The Turn to Ethics* (New York: Routledge, 2000), pp. 15–28, esp. p. 25.

[17] Taylor, *Erring*, p. 140.

[18] Peter Sloterdijk, *Sferen. Schuim*, trans. Hans Driessen (Amsterdam: Boom, 2009), p. 614 (our translation). It is remarkable that Sloterdijk recognizes the logic of exclusion through sound already in pre-historical groups. In *Im selben Boot. Versuch über die Hyperpolitik*, Sloterdijk describes the way in which sounds created and demarcated spaces at the dawn of human history. Rhythm, music and language united the members of prehistorical communities so that they formed close groups. For these nomadic hordes, belonging-together meant approximately the same thing as being able to hear each other. To a certain extent, psycho-acoustic umbilical cords tied each individual to the 'sonospheric continuum' of the group. In woods and grasslands, a primary and invisible boundary was drawn between 'the self' and 'the other', by the differentiation between group sounds and sounds of the world around that group. With its own specific talking, mumbling, singing, drumming and clapping, the small group secured its acoustic continuum and ascertained that this horde was a horde. See Peter Sloterdijk, *Im selben Boot. Versuch über die Hyperpolitik* (Frankfurt am Main: Suhrkamp, 1995), p. 25 (our translation).

As Nancy Fraser makes clear, a collective identity puts moral pressure on individual members to conform to the group culture:

> The result is often to impose a single, drastically simplified group identity, which denies the complexity of people's lives, the multiplicity of their identifications, and the cross-pulls of their various affiliations. Likewise, the model entrenches a reified conception of culture. Ignoring transcultural flows, it treats cultures as sharply bounded, neatly separated, and noninteracting, as if it were obvious where one stops and another starts. As a result, it tends to promote separatism and group enclaving in lieu of transgroup interaction. Denying internal heterogeneity, moreover, the identity model assumes that a 'culture' contains a single coherent set of ethical values whose meaning is clear and uncontested.[19]

What we have suggested so far is that music may function as a tool to establish and essentialize identity, to maintain integrity, to oppress or discriminate other identities, and to protect propriety as well as property. Music plays a role in collective ordering such that 'disparate individuals and their actions may appear to be intersubjective, mutually oriented, coordinated, entrained, and aligned'.[20] But when music has the power to contribute to the existence of group identities – that is, when it is able to operate within the logic of exclusion – there is, inevitably, already a certain relation between music and violence. Of course, the nature and scale of this violence, and music's part in this, varies. The fact remains, however, that music often plays an important role in the realization and preservation of a self–other opposition and, therefore, in violent acts of separation.

I live a stone's throw from the biggest football stadium in Rotterdam, and I regularly visit it to support the local team, Feyenoord. And as Les Back rightly claims, 'experiencing football as a fan is always as much about the sounds of the stadium as the visual exhibition of the game itself'.[21] It is primarily through the culture of sound, including the songs that are sung, that identity and identification are animated and felt. This is especially true when competing teams from other parts of the city or from the capital are visiting. The regular singing to support the home team is alternated with very specific songs that are usually meant to insult the visiting team and its supporters, thereby offering extreme contrasts between self and other, between inside and outside, between here and there. In particular, the mass singing of the club anthem generates shared feelings, an atmosphere of sociability and the expression of a collective presence, thereby stifling the

---

[19] Nancy Fraser, 'Recognition without Ethics?', in Marjorie Garber, Beatrice Hanssen and Rebecca Walkowitz (eds), *The Turn to Ethics* (New York: Routledge, 2000), p. 100.

[20] DeNora, *Music in Everyday Life*, p. 109.

[21] Les Back, 'Sounds in the Crowd', in Michael Bull and Les Back (eds), *The Auditory Culture Reader* (Oxford: Berg, 2003), p. 311.

opposition.[22] These club anthems, however, confirm one of the results from the Johnson and Cloonan study that sonic violence is not reducible to, or exclusively situated in, the lyrics. Indeed, lyrics are almost never the originary cause leading to uncontained social violence.

Hand in hand, kameraden	Hand in hand, mates
Hand in hand voor Feyenoord 1	Hand in hand, for Feyenoord 1
Geen woorden maar daden	Actions speak louder than words
Leve Feyenoord 1	Long live Feyenoord 1

Although the lyrics of this club anthem seem far enough removed from direct attempts to harm the supporters of the opposing team sonically, they often act like a red rag to a bull. The 'answer' from the fans of the team from the capital in this 'antiphonal singing' is already less friendly. Based on the first lines of Max Bygraves's song 'Tulips from Amsterdam' – 'When it's spring again, I'll bring again / Tulips from Amsterdam' – their usual reply is 'Als de lente komt dan gooien wij bommen op Rotterdam' ('When it's spring again, we throw again, bombs on Rotterdam'), referring to the destruction of Rotterdam by Nazi Germany in May 1940. The Feyenoord supporters often have a ready answer: 'Hamas, Hamas, joden aan het gas' ('Hamas, Hamas, Jews to the gas'), followed by a hissing noise. By calling the supporters from Amsterdam 'Jews', they make reference to the traditionally large Jewish community in the Dutch capital – the fans from Amsterdam almost always carry with them Israeli flags. This way, images of self and other are invented, created and sustained, although these are inconsistent images: 'the other' is alternately identified as a Nazi or a Jew. Nevertheless, through the interconnection of memory, ritual and the symbolic use of city names

---

[22] This observation seemed to be falsified by the *sonic strokes* (the term has been coined by Vincent Meelberg) of the vuvuzelas during the 2010 FIFA World Cup in South Africa (which often thwarted a quick materialization of this chapter): the sound of these tooters appeared to unite fans of competing teams and more or less independent spectators instead of marking the differences between each of them. Nevertheless, the vuvuzela is also an instrument of both inclusion and exclusion. Instead of sonically indicating different groups of supporters, it marks the distinction between those who are attracted to this soccer feast and those who are not. It is inextricably bound to football: blowing the vuvuzela means 'I am watching (world cup) football'; the vuvuzela is the sonic representation of this mondial event.

But, besides this, the vuvuzela represents something else, another mark of inclusion and exclusion, another identity mark. More uncomfortably perhaps, this simple instrument defines the border between self and other in the realm of semantics, affecting cultural, geographical and ethnic differences. Whereas some national broadcasting organizations chose to convey as much as possible the stadium's sonic atmosphere, TV watchers complained that it was quite difficult to hear the commentators. The non-semantic and non-Western other became a serious and annoying threat for the Western spectators oriented towards linguistic meaning as an important means of communication.

(most supporters of both teams live outside Amsterdam and Rotterdam), senses of identity, belonging, inclusion and exclusion can be musically produced. Not only does music play an important role in fostering feelings of animosity, the mere melody of a tune might suffice to arouse a sense of belonging or aversion.[23]

Visiting a football match in a stadium means entering a place determined by a certain sonic architecture in which self and other are also sonically constituted. Individuals and groups intervene, obstruct, resist and enter into the soundscape created around a match; conversely, the soundscape intervenes, obstructs, enters and offers resistance to the being of individuals and groups. Self, other and their (social) relations are constituted through music and sound and vice versa. The creation of place through sound is thus relevant to notions of identity and belonging. Activating a sense of belonging, however, also means that personal boundaries dissolve; it problematizes the neat separation of an individual self and non-self, patterning an entire field with intensities, passing through and within bodies, without respect for traditional epidermal – and indeed epistemological – boundaries.[24] Especially when participating in the singing, supporters are immersed in a sonic environment, becoming a singular-multiplicity (the one-who-is-many and the many-who-are-one). They are enveloped by sound, drawn or plunged into it as the produced sounds not only enter their ears, but also pass through their whole bodies, which might give rise to an illusion of continuity with the surrounding world. Flows of this kind open up an entire world for affective connections. The sound of the supporters' singing is a vehicle for imagining and reimagining the self in relations to other selves and the spaces in which those selves interact, as it at the same time constitutes those spaces and other selves. On a more general level, one could conclude that the insides and outsides of a community are constituted through music in the very acts of people engaging with that music.[25]

---

[23] This can also be illustrated by the tunes that are played when the home team scores a goal. Feyenoord, for example, uses the slightly adapted instrumental interlude of Gloria Gaynor's monster hit 'I Will Survive' to incite their supporters. Whether the supporters associate this interlude with the song title is doubtful.

[24] Julian Henriques, 'The Vibrations of Affect and their Propagation on a Night Out on Kingston's Dancehall Scene', *Body & Society*, 16/1 (March 2010), p. 75. In agreement with these thoughts, Judith Butler ('Ethical Ambivalence') argues that the loss of discreteness is an inevitable part of sociality. We have to loosen the self's boundaries to recognize that we are fundamentally sustained by others. The ethical implications of this idea will be further developed throughout this chapter.

[25] Michelle Duffy, 'Inhabiting Soundscapes', *ASCA Conference Sonic Interventions: Pushing the Boundaries of Cultural Analysis*, Reader for Panel 4: *Soundscapes: Sound, Space, and the Body* (2005), p. 52. Peter Sloterdijk aims to rethink human history as a history of space – a history of the creation of space and of organizing space. In this thought, the conviction finds its expression that the acts of taking and giving space are the first ethical exploits. See Sloterdijk, *Sferen. Schuim*, p. 615.

Music and the body

In *La revolution du langage poétique* (*Revolution in Poetic Language*) Julia Kristeva writes that the constitution of the self through music is not situated on the level of the symbolic order, a regulating system mainly functioning through (discursive) signification and (rational) meaning. Like modern poetry, music primarily works on the level of what Kristeva calls 'the semiotic', a non-verbal, pre-signifying and heterogeneous energy. Constructions of self and other through music thus rely on signification through the drives of affects, sensations and gestures. That is, one may, will, or even must respond to music prior to ordering those responses through language, through the symbolic order. It is here that we will try to situate the (un)ethical aspects of music, of music as sound. (Musical) sounds act on and penetrate the autonomy of the body, the individual *ethos*; they induce affects in the subject's body – a body which appears to be vulnerable as it can hardly, if at all, protect itself against external sonic influences. This impact is ethical in nature, exactly because it is a penetration, positively or negatively, of the subject's body.[26] We join in here with an idea of Alasdair MacIntyre who, in *Dependent Rational Animals*, proposes to treat the vulnerable and afflicted human body as central to the human condition. To disregard this idea means a refusal to acknowledge adequately the bodily dimensions of our existence; human identity is primarily, even if not only, bodily.[27] According to MacIntyre, this insight should have an impact on our ethical thoughts and behaviours. In short, he addresses the ethicality of unreflective and pre-reflective bodily experiences.[28] Continuing along this line of thought, one could state that every event that acts on the autonomy of the body has at least an ethical component. And as music and sound operate on the subject's body, there is an ethical dimension in their encounter. What needs to be investigated are the ethical implications of these sonic encounters.[29] Following Kristeva and MacIntyre, the main question here should not be what a specific sound or a piece of music could possibly mean but how they are able to influence subjects on a primarily physical level.[30]

---

[26] See also Vincent Meelberg, 'Sonic Strokes and Musical Gestures', in Jukka Louhivuori *et al.* (eds), *Proceedings of the 7th Triennial Conference of the European Society for the Cognitive Sciences* (Jyväskylä, University of Jyväskylä, 2009), p. 327. Vulnerability could be considered a precondition for openness towards others.

[27] Alasdair MacIntyre, *Dependent Rational Animals. Why Human Beings Need Virtues* (Chicago: Open Court, 1999), p. 8.

[28] 'I now judge that I was in error in supposing an ethics independent of biology to be possible' (ibid., p. x).

[29] Similar thoughts can be found in Vincent Meelberg's *Kernthema's in het muziekonderzoek* (Den Haag: Boom Lemma, 2010), p. 126.

[30] 'The "meaning" of the musical message is expressed … in its operationality' (Jacques Attali, *Noise: The Political Economy of Music*, trans. B. Massumi (Minneapolis: University of Minnesota Press, 1985), p. 25).

Put differently, we propose to shift attention from *bios* to *zoë*, from culture to nature, from the political body to biological life, from the qualified life of a citizen to bare life as such[31] – shift attention, that is, to the relation between music and what Foucault terms biopolitics and biopower, concepts that should indicate a transition in the development of the exercise of power, a transition that results in managing, regulating and controlling (human) beings on the level of life itself. 'The control of society over individuals is not conducted only through consciousness or ideology, but also in the body and with the body. For capitalist society biopolitics is what is most important, the biological, the somatic, the corporeal.'[32] The effect of biopolitics is that biological existence passes into knowledge's field of control and power's sphere of intervention. Power, conceived by Foucault in terms of the 'multiplicity of force relations' immanent to the plane in which they operate, gets access to man's physical or material existence. According to Foucault, biopower, being the result of a number of shifts, mutations or redeployments of power during the seventeenth, eighteenth and nineteenth centuries, can be understood as regulating, normalizing and disciplining the biological life of man. Biopower is literally having power over other bodies, 'an explosion of numerous and diverse techniques for achieving the subjugations of bodies and the control of population'.[33]

In *Homo Sacer* Giorgio Agamben follows Foucault's track, although he tries to situate the beginning of biopower in the ancient world, more specifically in the work of Aristotle. According to Agamben, it is the entry of *zoë* into the sphere of the polis – the politicization of bare life as such – that signals a radical transformation of more classical political–philosophical categories: 'much would not have been possible, from this perspective, without the disciplinary control achieved by the new biopower, which, through a series of appropriate technologies, so to speak created the "docile bodies" that it needed'.[34] Like Foucault, Agamben analyses, in his work, the concrete ways in which power penetrates subjects' very bodies and forms of life, but whereas Foucault concentrates on medical, educational, scientific and punitive institutions, Agamben mainly focuses on concentration camps and fringe figures.

Neither Foucault nor Agamben mentions music as a possible accomplice in the execution of biopower. Nevertheless, the principal idea of this chapter is that music plays a significant role in the increasing inclusion of man's natural life in the mechanisms and calculations of power, and therefore connects to something that

---

[31] See, for example, Giorgio Agamben's *Homo Sacer: Sovereign Power and Bare Life,* trans. D. Heller-Roazen (Stanford, CA: Stanford University Press, 1998); Michel Foucault's *The History of Sexuality, Vol. I*, trans. Robert Hurley (New York: Vintage Books, 1990); and Walter Benjamin's 'Critique of Violence', in *Walter Benjamin: Selected Writings, Volume 1: 1913–1926*, ed. M. Bullock and M.W. Jennings (Cambridge, MA: Belknap/Harvard University Press, 1999).

[32] Michel Foucault, 'La naissance de la médecine sociale', in *Dits et écrits*, vol. 2 (Paris: Gallimard, 1994), p. 210 (our translation).

[33] Foucault, *The History of Sexuality, Vol. I*, p. 140.

[34] Agamben, *Homo Sacer*, p. 5.

could be called (un)ethical. Music can be considered a form of organization that is very well suited to the task of assuring the care, control and use of bare life. Thus, as a tool to regulate and exercise power, music can be connected, both implicitly and explicitly, to ethics and morality.

People as different as Plato, the nineteenth-century Romantics, music therapists and the Afghan Taliban in the late twentieth century all discerned correctly the fact that music has the potential to deeply affect human beings. The nature of this affect, however, has often been assumed to be situated on a transcendental level. Alternatively, the influence of music on human behaviour has been reduced to its textual components: specific lyrics and/or supplementary commentaries seemed to give music its ethic-political meaning.[35] Rarely has music's power been located on a primarily biological and physical plane: sounds penetrating the body, cutting across the duality of physical and emotional processes. Nevertheless, when Fran Tonkiss writes in her essay 'Aural Postcards. Sound, Memory and the City' about the connection between sound and urban atmospheres, she is (also) referring to the sensuous relation we have to the city through listening: sounds influence the ways in which we relate to and experience a city, both mentally and physically.[36] We can read Gernot Böhme's essay 'Die Atmosphäre einer Stadt' ('The Atmosphere of a City') in much the same way. Setting up oppositions between theories that attempt to describe music's so-called emotional effect, Böhme defines music as a modification of space as it is experienced by the body. Music forms and informs *das Sichbefinden*, the listener's sense of self in a space; it reaches directly into her or his corporeal economy.[37] A less innocent example can be found in the American High-frequency Active Auroral Research Program (HAARP), a scientific and technological project aimed at future warfare in the ionosphere. Part of the program investigates the effects of ELF (extreme low frequency) waves, or infrasonic sound waves, on living organisms, especially on parts of the human brain that operate on low-frequencies. This 'ecological' warfare is aimed at damaging the (living) environment or the aural preconditions of life, and makes it clear that a corporeal being-in-the-world always also has a sonic component.[38]

---

[35] One could think here of sexist lyrics in a lot of rap and hip-hop music, or the subversive texts used by punk and metal bands. Also, the American Parents Music Resource Center (PMRC) has been founded just to warn parents about the coarsening of language in popular music.

[36] Fran Tonkiss, 'Aural Postcards: Sound, Memory and the City', in Bull and Back, *The Auditory Culture Reader*, p. 304.

[37] David Toop, *Haunted Weather: Music, Silence and Memory* (London: Serpent's Tail, 2004), p. 63.

[38] Sloterdijk, *Sferen. Schuim*, pp. 93–106.

Discipline and control

A first step towards a more systematic consideration of the triangle music–body–ethics might be to reread Jacques Attali's analysis of the functioning of music throughout human civilization. Early in his book *Bruits* (*Noise*), he states that music – which he defines as an organization of sounds or as giving form to noise – was an attribute of religious and political power signifying order – for example, by channelling violence and, more specifically, by repressing bodily activities.[39] The ordering and controlling side of music becomes evident in 'the monopolization of the broadcast of messages, the control of noise, and the institutionalization of the silence of others … Musical distribution techniques are today contributing to the establishment of a system of eavesdropping and social surveillance.'[40] Demonstrating the effectiveness of its participation in social regulation and showing how its production has the maintenance of order as its function, Attali distinguishes between three strategic uses of music by power. First, music is used and produced in (politico-religious) rituals in an attempt to make people forget a general violence, an uncontrollable chaos, an existential disorder. Second, it is employed to make people believe in the harmony of the world. And, third, the current omnipresence of music serves to silence and censor other human sounds.[41]

Attali concretizes the effect on the body through his focus on the training of musicians: the advent of the conservatories in the eighteenth century was an effective and institutionalized way of disciplining musicians' bodies. Attali's findings on this topic are supported, extended and specified by Katherine Bergeron in her prologue to the book *Disciplining Music*. For a performer, practising scales, for example, is a measure of both instrumental and bodily discipline: both instrument and body become submitted to certain rules, conventions and, more concretely, positions. The performing and composing body is further ordered through tuning or playing in tune, which is simultaneously a disciplining of the ear. 'The tuned scale, or canon, is a locus of discipline, a collection of discrete values produced out of a system that orders, segments, divides.'[42] Social control is exerted through the presence of the canon of big names, the Great Men – Bach, Mozart, Beethoven, Schubert: 'To uphold the canon is ultimately to interiorize those values that would maintain, so to speak, social "harmony."'[43] Bergeron comes close to Foucault's ideas about the disciplining of bodies expounded in *Surveiller et punir* (*Discipline and Punish*) when writing about the role of the conductor in an orchestra, whom she describes as 'the master of acoustic surveillance'. Analogous

---

[39] Attali, *Noise*, pp. 4–5.

[40] Ibid., p. 8.

[41] Ibid., p. 19.

[42] Katherine Bergeron, 'Prologue: Disciplining Music', in Katherine Bergeron and Philip V. Bohlman, *Disciplining Music. Musicology and its Canons* (Chicago: Chicago University Press, 1992), p. 2.

[43] Ibid., p. 3.

to the captives in Bentham's Panopticon who are unable to tell whether they are being watched, the orchestral musician cannot escape her/his own audibility: she/he never knows the precise moment when the conductor may be listening to her/him. Paraphrasing Foucault, one could state that she/he who is subjected to a field of audibility, and knows it, assumes responsibility for the constraints of power.[44] In other words, subordinated to a potential disciplining and punishment taking place within the orchestra – by both fellow musicians and the conductor – musicians start to take responsibility for their own musical actions, thereby learning to conduct themselves according to the standards of the performance they share.[45]

What is reflected in music here, or, better, what is executed by and through music is what Michael Hardt and Antonio Negri in *Empire* describe as the passage from a disciplinary society to a society of control.[46] The former works through a diffuse network of *dispositifs* or apparatuses that produce and regulate customs, habits and productive practices, whereas the mechanisms of command in the latter are distributed throughout brains and bodies – that is, interiorized within the subjects themselves. Slightly different from Hardt and Negri's linear analysis, discipline, imposed from the outside by the conductor, and control, imposed from the inside by the musicians themselves, converge and operate simultaneously in the institution called 'orchestra'. Music's power is thus expressed as a control mechanism that extends throughout the depths of both (sub)consciousness and the body. In many ways, the classical orchestra produces corporeal normalization – normalization being regarded here as a subtler version of morality under the politics of power/knowledge. Supported by extensive education and training in specialized spaces, it directly brings bodies under the expanded grid of control not by physical punishment, but rather by tactics that value certain types of bodily behaviour as normal – behaviour that individual musicians diligently and voluntarily work towards. In addition, orchestral control is internalized by the obedient musicians, the docile bodies, as an invisible ear tirelessly listens for signs of deviance.[47]

---

[44] Foucault, *The History of Sexuality, Vol. I*, p. 202.

[45] Bergeron, 'Prologue', p. 4. Besides demonstrating the disciplinary workings of music, Bergeron also examines the ways in which music itself is disciplined: for example, by classifying it under different disciplines (musicology, music theory, ethnomusicology), by submitting scales to ratio – that is, to mathematical subdivisions – and by developing various measuring devices such as notation, biographies and the so-called 'standards' in jazz. See ibid., pp. 1–5.

[46] Michael Hardt and Antonio Negri, *Empire* (Cambridge, MA: Harvard University Press, 2000), pp. 22–23.

[47] Music's capacity to normalize can also be traced in Oliver Sacks's bestseller *Musicophilia* in which he describes many examples of patients with different diseases or disabilities who, when playing or listening to music, are able to function (more or less) 'normally' (again). See Oliver Sacks, *Musicophilia: Tales of Music and the Brain* (New York: Vintage Books, 2007).

Of course, this short and incomplete description of the functioning of an orchestra is not meant to discredit orchestral music or the enormous achievements of orchestral musicians. Here, our principal aim is to show how music subtly contributes to the disciplining and controlling of bodily activities and corporeal actions. The musician's body is mastered by training, performance conventions and the supervising role of the conductor, and this contrasts sharply with an ethics as a practice of the sort that might entail what Foucault describes as 'the care of the self', the care of the body, of bare life.

What is often denied in discourses on ethics is the subject's lack of power, its vulnerability and dependence, particularly when it concerns the influence of sonic interventions on the body – that is, when sound or music manipulates a human being beyond or before her logos of sense and signification, beyond or before her intellectual, cognitive and conscious abilities. To these unsignified and unsignifiable sonic events – events that cannot always be turned into objects of cognition – the subject cannot *not* respond; she cannot *not* participate – that is, assume a relationship. For before or beyond being the indication of a concept, category, value or desire, the sound of music grips the body, enters the body, solicits the body's participation, the corporeal consent, the e-motion. Sound has the capacity to modulate the physical, affective and libidinal dynamics of the body. Beyond or before the activation of semantic or cognitive listening, the sonic is a force of contact that has the seductive power to affect the body, the skin, the brain.[48]

The sound of music is infectious: not the grammatical part, not its organization, its system, structure or sense, but the acoustical part – frequency, timbre and rhythm. The acoustical part gives the grammatical (signifying, structural, semantic) part effectiveness, agency and force, by giving it direct access to the body. And this force of corporeal inf(l)ection always exceeds the cognitive structures of signification.[49] Sonic events are felt and processed as modes of feeling beyond or before they are cognized and categorized in schemas of knowledge.[50] Rhythms, frequencies and intensities affect bodies before they are transduced by regimes of signification and before they are picked up by human emotions and cognition.

Derrida, in his phrase 'ce qui reste à force de musique', also recognizes music's power beyond or before signification, against a linguistic imperialism that subordinates the sonic to merely communicative meaning. The sense of music always exceeds whatever is or can be expressed by its means, and it is here that we can trace a specific musical or sonic ethics. How music or sound (directly) affects

---

[48] Steve Goodman, *Sonic Warfare: Sound, Affect, and the Ecology of Fear* (Cambridge, MA: MIT Press, 2009), p. 10.

[49] Geraldine Finn, 'Giving Place – Making Space – For Truth – In Music' (unpublished paper, 2002). According to Nietzsche, we listen to music with our muscles, be that by tapping our feet, singing along or 'conducting' the music.

[50] Goodman, *Sonic Warfare*, p. 96.

the body has (also) ethical implications. This bio-ethical influence of music on human behaviour is often neglected in favour of its meaning, content, narrativity or capacity to represent exterior ethical–political realities. Likewise, it has escaped the attention of philosophers dealing with ethics.

Sonic weapons

The first stage of reflection on the relationship music-body-ethics concentrated on the disciplining and controlling of musicians. But in the first two sections of this chapter we have already indicated how music also affects the recipient's behaviour – for example, in times of social or ethnic conflicts. Given this, we were less interested in the effects that textual parts of and around music (for example, programme notes) have on people; rather, it was the influence of music as a primarily sonic phenomenon that we were emphasizing and investigating.[51] Whether in armed conflicts between nation-states, in clashes between a state and its citizens, or in problems among citizens within a state, music can be used as a sonic weapon so that sound becomes a potential instrument of both power and violence. Sonic violence can be brought into action to exercise power over other people and the soundscape. As such, music can be both the site and agent of violence.

Basically, the relation music–violence can work in two overlapping ways. The first is chiefly psychological: music used as a tool for disorientation (for example, through the repetitive exposure to noise music for sustained periods outside the recipient's control), humiliation (for example, through forced singing of the enemy's national anthem or through forced playing of (mainly) soothing classical music by Jews in the Nazi concentration camps), and insult of one's identity as a human being (for example, the playing of (extremely loud) Western pop music to Iraqi detainees by US soldiers as a symbolic claim to supremacy and global sovereignty).[52]

The second and connected step is primarily biological: music used as a sonic force – for example, when it is played at high volume, at particular registers, or in other ways that physically hurt or cause organic damage.[53] Of course, volume has a major somatic impact on human behaviour and can even be lethal. But there

---

[51] Concluding their study on music and violence, Johnson and Cloonan explicitly state that it is a profound misunderstanding to think that musical violence is generated primarily by what words mean. Instead they place sonority in the centre: sound itself proves to be an instrument of enormous (social) power. The failure to recognize this is, according to them, a residue of the scopic model of knowledge that still seems to be prevailing in the Western world. See *Dark Side of the Tune*, p. 193.

[52] Ibid., pp. 150–58. These examples show how the line between mind and body becomes blurred.

[53] Ibid., p. 147.

are many more and subtler ways in which people can be sonically manipulated.[54] In order to illustrate this, we have to leave the realm of music for a little while in order to concentrate on sound only. In November 2005, international newspapers reported the use of 'sound bombs' in the Gaza Strip by the Israeli army. These high-volume, deep-frequency effects of low-flying jets caused ear pain, nosebleeds, anxiety attacks, sleeplessness, hypertension and an effect of 'shaking inside'. The objective was to create a climate of fear through a non-lethal threat, a fear induced by sound.[55] In the same year, the Israeli launched another sonic weapon, the 'Scream', with which public demonstrations from both Palestinians and Jewish settlers could be controlled. The 'Scream' sends out bursts of audible, though not loud, sounds. As the device targets a specific frequency towards the inner ear, it produces dizziness and nausea.[56]

By its ability to penetrate and damage parts of not only the body but also the living environment of adversaries, sound enters the domains of human rights, ecological politics, and morality and ethics. This does not have to imply noise pollution in terms of decibels; so-called infrasounds and ultrasounds escape man's auditory organ and work as vibrations directly on the inside of the body. Together with new sophisticated technologies, they make a drift towards corporeal or subliminal effects possible. It has been noted that certain infrasonic frequencies plug straight into the algorithms of the brain and nervous system. Frequencies of 7 hertz, for example, coincide with theta rhythms, thought to induce moods of fear and anger.[57] Other vibrations can disorder the working of the vestibular system as well as the organ of balance, thereby influencing someone's movements, sensations and mood. As Steve Goodman states in his book *Sonic Warfare*:

> It is hardly controversial to suggest that, as more has been learned about the neuroeffects of very high and very low frequency sound, and bionic audition develops, then the perceptual battlefields of sonic warfare have broadened ... Working on microscopic scales, often pathogenic, many electromagnetic fields

---

[54] Traditionally, noise pollution has been mapped and combated through (the reduction of) decibels. However, it is becoming increasingly clear that non-acoustical variables, such as perceived control, personality traits like noise sensitivity, and attitudes towards the sound and its source, play very important roles in the experience of noise pollution. It has been found that the more control a person perceives to have over the noise, the smaller the negative impact. In other words, power relations rather than physical or aesthetical discomfort primarily determine people's reactions towards noise pollution. This also implies that any sound or any music can cause annoyance. To impose music on people in a way that is beyond their control will take them closer to irritation.
[55] Goodman, *Sonic Warfare*, pp. xiii–xiv.
[56] Ibid., pp. 21–22.
[57] Ibid., p. 18.

interfere with the cellular structure of the body. Paranoia accompanies dealing with such hertzian machines.[58]

Sonic branding

The sound of music is complicit in relations of power. Demarcating or rearranging a territory through (musical) sounds simultaneously entails invading, marginalizing, appropriating or obliterating the other, be it an individual or a group. This becomes clearer in what seems to be a less destructive and therefore more innocent sonic device, the 'Mosquito'. An ultrasonic sound device in a small metal box emits a very high tone ranging from 17 to 18 kHz which can only be heard by young people of less than 25 years of age and is experienced by them as extremely annoying. In several cities in the USA, the UK and the Netherlands, the 'Mosquito' is used to chase away 'inconveniencing youth' from public spaces such as playgrounds, shopping malls, parks and school grounds. Some schools have even installed it in busy hallways to reduce congestion and encourage the flow of traffic to and from classes. Although the device cannot solve the general 'problem' of youth loitering, it does help in certain locations.

The 'Mosquito' is just another example that fits into a way of thinking that recognizes the potential of sound to have a hold on public space, to have control of social human behaviour, to regulate and discipline people outside their private lives.

In an even more normalized and accepted way, Muzak or background music serves the same purpose, albeit in a less striking and equivocal way. Jonathan Sterne describes the use of Muzak in indoor shopping centres as a form of sonic architecture created for specific aesthetic and social purposes. Being an essential part of the mall's total(izing) infrastructure, the role and working of Muzak is based on two assumptions. The first assumption is that people who are shopping like it, that they feel welcome and safe. The flip side is, of course, that unwanted persons will be deterred as they find this kind of sonic wallpaper offensive and hostile. Welcoming the spenders simultaneously means driving out those who do not fit in the ideology of citizens as paying consumers. The second assumption is that these unwanted persons can all be lumped together: teens, drug-dealers, the homeless, sex workers, skateboarders and low-income populations are all included in the same category and ordered by Muzak to avoid the temples of consumerism.[59]

True and successful or not, Muzak is

> ... built on the belief that people – especially upper-middle class people – should not have to encounter people of lower social classes in their daily or leisure

---

[58] Ibid., pp. 184 and 188.
[59] Jonathan Sterne, 'Urban Media and the Politics of Sound Space', in *OPEN 9 Sound: Sound in Art and Culture* (Rotterdam: NAi Publishers, 2005), no page numbers.

travels ... Programmed music used outdoors is an attempt to code space, and specifically to code it in terms of social class, race, and age.[60]

Turning mixed-use spaces into single-use spaces, Muzak marks a particular moment in the history of urban design: behind this 'nonaggressive music deterrent' is a real aggressiveness towards the poor, the young and all other 'nonconsumers'. It is about excluding these people from the 'front' spaces of consumerism.[61]

According to Sterne, Muzak has thus become a weapon in a form of social warfare by trying to limit social interactions between different social strata. Besides aesthetical aspects, *acoustic design* therefore clearly has both political and ethical dimensions. It is meant to regulate mood and behaviour of people in specific situations, to turn them into more biddable citizens. And it is a small step from producing those who are biddable, to expelling those who are not.[62] Muzak provides a background, atmospheric control that no longer needs to correct individual actions directly. As such, it may function as another element in what Hardt and Negri, following Deleuze, label control society.[63] As a form of environmental conditioning, Muzak, often on an unconscious and subliminal level, aids in the general mood of its listeners.

The use and role of Muzak raises crucial moral and ethical questions about social responsibilities, human rights, cultural formations and diversity. 'Music preferences become sites of conflict within and between communities, between state and citizenry, between hegemonic and subordinate blocs.'[64] The psychological and biological converge in Muzak's working on muscular energy, personal desire and economics.[65]

---

[60] Ibid.
[61] Ibid.
[62] Johnson and Cloonan, *Dark Side of the Tune*, p. 182.
[63] Hardt and Negri, *Empire*, pp. 22–26.
[64] Johnson and Cloonan, *Dark Side of the Tune,* p. 186.
[65] What is sketched here is how Muzak might function ideally or in theory. In practice, its working will probably be less unambiguous as the assumption is simply that it will work well enough for most people most of the time. In other words, Muzak plays against a law of averages. The potential consumers Adorno labels as 'experts' or 'good listeners' might be offended just as much as the alleged non-consumers. Conversely, the non-consumers most probably cannot be equated just like that with Muzak-haters. Several years ago, German and Dutch railways experimented with playing classical music at some stations in order to deter drug addicts and prostitutes. In a cynical reaction in a Dutch daily, a columnist asked the following questions: 'Does the railways management truly believe that among non-junkies nobody will be irritated by classical music? Does the management disdain music so much that it is found suitable as a spray against vermin?' Humorously the columnist continues: 'One addict I know thinks it is a cool plan. He loves classical music and now wants to spend even more time on train stations. However, he takes the view that orchestra and conductor should be carefully chosen. For example, Mahler only conducted by Bernard

The legacy of Muzak has activated more contemporary approaches toward scripting the auditory environment. Sonic branding and sonification are currently active design strategies to catalyse the motivation to consume. From advertising jingles and sound logos to ringtones and sounds for gaming devices, sonic branding entails an intervention into the affective sensorium's mnemonic system. However,

> ... a catchy tune is no longer sufficient; it merely provides the DNA for a whole viral assemblage. Instead of an outmoded associative psychology, most branding theory has already moved on to invest in the modulation of emotion by nonverbal means, signalling a mutation of capital logic into a more subtle colonization of memory through the preemptive sonic modulation of affective tonality.[66]

Muzak and sonic branding are concrete, everyday examples of the power to audio seduction, music's power to allure human beings. Consciously or unconsciously, intentionally or unintentionally, music guides human behaviour by being able to enter a personal sound sphere. *Sonic effects* are operative in the space between the physical sound environment, the sound milieu of a socio-cultural community and the 'internal soundscape' of every individual.[67] It is these potential effects that give music its moral or ethical dimension and, with that, a certain responsibility. This implies a shift from a concern with what music means to a concern with what it does and how it works.

Music has an important role as an ordering device; it can serve as a constitutive property of bodily being. If it can be regarded to have effects upon bodies, hearts and minds – effects that lie for the most part outside a person's control and in which she/he is caught up – then music works not only on an aesthetic plane, but certainly also on (micro)political and ethical planes.

Haitink and played by the Royal Concertgebouw Orchestra. And not continually interrupted by timetable announcements.'

Brandon LaBelle suggests that Muzak could just as well contribute to opposite effects: deterritorializing experiences, non-totalizing structures and distracted listening: 'The script of the mall is also prone to slippages, generating boring tedium as well as certain flirtations, both of which supplement the directness of spending' (Brandon LaBelle, *Acoustic Territories: Sound Culture and Everyday Life* (New York: Continuum, 2010), p. 180). Instead of a univocal meaning resulting in a desired behaviour, Muzak also gives rise to possible mishearing and to a fragmentary richness of relating.

[66] Goodman, *Sonic Warfare*, p. 148. In *Musicophilia*, Oliver Sacks calls this catchy or sticky music 'earworms' or 'brainworms' (p. 45). Sacks is interested in the characteristics that make such a tune 'dangerous' or 'infectious': 'Is it some oddity of sound, of timbre or rhythm or melody? Is it repetition? Or is it arousal of special emotional resonances or associations?' (ibid., p. 47).

[67] Jean-François Augoyard and Henry Torgue, *Sonic Experience: A Guide to Everyday Sounds* (Montreal: McGill-Queen's University Press, 2005), p. 9.

From affect to ethics

As stated in this chapter, music as a manipulative or violent intervention thoroughly pervades contemporary life, ranging from its availability during times of war and its uses in processes of social or ethnic exclusion to the regulation and 'normalization' of public order. National anthems, the 'Mosquito', football songs, Muzak, folk tunes, conducted music, ringtones, jingles, middle-of-the-road pop songs – the sound of music is potentially an instrument of power and violence and is thereby connected to moral and ethical issues. What these examples demonstrate is: first, there are no intrinsic characteristics of music that make it more or less violent, more or less powerful, more or less suitable for causing noise pollution; second, it is not the music 'itself' that disciplines, controls or causes violence but how it is being used; third, the music–violence–power nexus should not be traced back to lyrics and discursive meaning for the affective responses are defined by music's sonority, by the sound of music, by its direct impact on the body.

But perhaps the most important idea that the examples reveal is that these 'dark sides of the tune' refer to music's 'amoral' and 'unethical' potentialities, to its overt and covert connections to disciplining and controlling powers, to its various contributions to actions of inclusion and exclusion, and to its co-maintenance of social, economic, political, racial, ethnic and cultural inequality. And music simply cannot withdraw from that.

However, would it be possible, by unfolding the amoral and unethical role, position and function of music, to open another, more positive perspective on the relation between music and ethics? Would it be possible to envisage another ethic, beyond or through the presented unethicality of music? Is there some light on the other side of the putative darkness?

The opening we are cautiously referring to here has already, perchance unnoted, been created in the section on the singing of football supporters. There, the sense of where the self ends and the non-self begins precisely problematizes the formation of individuality and identity. Personal boundaries are blurred and transgressed through a sense of belonging evoked by singing loudly. Here, we will elaborate on the potential ethical implications of this intrusion on the autonomy of the body. In order to do so, we need to rethink the relation between music and affect once more.

Affect, according to Gilles Deleuze and Brian Massumi, is a pre-personal intensity and pre-individuated surface corresponding to the passage from one experiential state of the body to another.[68] It is an autonomous reaction of the body

---

[68] Affects should thus be distinguished from feelings and emotions. A feeling is *personal and biographical*; it is a sensation that has been labelled and checked against previous experiences. An emotion is *social*; it is the projection or display of a feeling. Furthermore, an emotion is a very partial expression of affect. It only draws on a limited selection of memories and only activates certain reflexes or tendencies. No one emotional state can encompass all the depth and breadth of our experiences. See, for example, Brian

when confronted with another entity, a reaction always prior to and outside of consciousness. The body has a grammar of its own that cannot be fully captured in awareness.

If the body can be defined through its capacity to affect and be affected by other bodies, affect, then, connects man to others, to other entities, events, bodies. It plays an important role in determining the relationship between bodies, environment and others. Affect moves; it is a wave of energy, a flow of vibrations. Put differently, intensities or affects can be propagated and embodied through vibrations. But these are not unidirectional vibrations; they go from one body to another and back again. Affects resonate and include feedback.

The transmission of affect means that human beings are not self-contained in terms of energies. There is no secure distinction between self and other or between self and environment. A body resonates with the intensity of the contexts it enfolds. In that sense, the idea of affect undermines the separateness and self-consistency of the autonomous individual in favour of the birth of the human being consisting of resonating frequencies.

This Deleuzian idea somehow resonates in Jean-Luc Nancy's *À l'écoute* (*Listening*) in which he rethinks the human subject, the self, on the basis of its ability to listen:

> A *self* is nothing other than a form or function of referral: a *self* is made of a relationship *to* self, or of a presence *to* self, which is nothing other than the mutual referral between a perceptible individuation and an intelligible identity ... – this referral itself would have to be infinite, and the point or occurrence of a *subject* in the substantial sense would have never taken place except in the referral, thus in spacing and resonance, at the very most as the dimensionless point of the re- of this resonance: the repetition where the sound is amplified and spreads, as well as the turning back [*rebroussement*] where the echo is made by making itself heard. A subject *feels*: that is his characteristic and his definition. This means that he hears (himself), sees (himself), touches (himself), tastes (himself), and so on, and that he thinks himself or represents himself, approaches himself and strays for himself, and thus always feels himself feeling a 'self' that escapes [*s'échappe*] or hides [*se retranche*] as long as it resounds elsewhere as it does in itself, in a world and in the other.[69]

According to Nancy, the self is not an entity towards which one can return; it cannot be objectified and it is not present in and of itself. A subject feels – that is, he is able to affect and be affected. Nancy presents the self as resonance, as a coming and going, from the sensory perceptions of a self to a self as a theoretical

---

Massumi, *Parables for the Virtual: Movement, Affect, Sensation* (Durham, NC: Duke University Press, 2002).

[69] Jean-Luc Nancy, *Listening*, trans. C. Mandell (New York: Fordham University Press, 2007), pp. 8–9, emphasis in original.

construct and back again, in an endless movement, never arriving at a stable position or origin. This self has not been the subject of the Western philosophical tradition; perhaps, Nancy contemplates, it is no subject at all, except as a place of resonance.[70]

Nancy arrives at this rethinking of self and subject through a meditation on the sound of music – a meditation on music as sound. He observes a correspondence between subject and sound. Like a self, the sonorous is never a simple being-there; it appears always in a return (*renvoi*) 'from one element to the other, whether it be between the emitter and the receptor or in one or the other, or, finally, and especially, between the sound and itself'.[71] Sound turns out to be intrinsically and unmistakably relational: it leaves a body and enters others; it sends the body moving, the air oscillating, the space reverberating. Sound is also relational because it is always referring back to itself, because it is vibration: 'To sound is to vibrate in itself or by itself: it is not only, for the sonorous body, to emit a sound, but it is also to stretch out, to carry itself and be resolved into vibrations that both return it to itself and place it outside itself.'[72] By force of resonance, sound doubles itself infinitely. Without this internal resonance there would be nothing to listen to – even a single sine wave produces its own resonance.

> All sonorous presence is made of a complex of returns. Thus, sound does not consist in a being-present-there, in a stable, fixed being. Yet, it is not elsewhere or absent either. The place of sound is a taking-place, a vibrant place; the one does not precede the other.[73]

Through this ontological reflection on sound and subject, Nancy concludes that both can be 'defined' through vibration, movement and the ability to affect.

Music, regarded as a sonic phenomenon – that is, as consisting of sound waves that vibrate and resonate – affects the listener's body; it induces intensities in the listener.[74] But the listener also affects the music: 'Resonance is at once that of

---

[70] Ibid., p. 22.
[71] Ibid., p. 15.
[72] Ibid., p. 10.
[73] Ibid., p. 16.
[74] See also Meelberg, 'Sonic Strokes', p. 325. Neurologist Oliver Sacks gives a fine example of music affecting a human body. Sacks recalls a climbing accident he had, tearing off the quadriceps tendon of his left leg. After a 14-day period in which he was not allowed to use the leg, he found out that he had 'forgotten' how to walk. The proprioception, the unconscious perception of movement and spatial orientation arising from stimuli within the body itself, was blocked. Imagining music, however, his body started to remember how to walk and, along with this, the feeling of his leg as part of his body (Sacks, *Musicophilia*, pp. 254–26) Music thus acted as an activator, a de-inhibitor. What will alone could not do, musical affect could. Music as a sonic phenomenon can act on the autonomy of the body. It has *physical effects* which differ from its potential *meanings*. In many cases, the working

a body that is sonorous for itself and resonance of sonority in a listening body that, itself, resounds as it listens.'[75] The body is no longer a property of the self but a locus of impulses, the locus of their confrontation. Since it is a product of these impulses, the body becomes fortuitous.[76] The stable subject of modern Western philosophy, knowable to itself, has turned into a vibrating subject, always already in relation before being petrified by metaphysical conceptualizations and categorizations. The self is not something fixed but a cohesion formed out of the various impulses and affects of our fortuitous bodies.

Conclusion

What does this short reflection on music and affect, on sound, subject and self, yield for the relation between music and ethics? How can it influence our thinking on the specific role music can play with regard to ethical and moral discourses? At the beginning of this chapter we referred to Alasdair MacIntyre who promoted an ethics that takes the autonomous body as a point of departure. Perhaps it is now possible to provide his 'proposal' with some additions, coming from the previous meditations on how music affects humans. This chapter made clear that investigating potential connections between music and ethics cannot skip the direct influence music has on the human body – an influence that lies before or beyond consciousness, signification and will. However, both the ideas on affect and music presented here seem to undermine the separateness and self-consistency of an autonomous individual. Just as affect can be recognized relationally, sound waves pattern relationships; they exhibit remarkable powers of diffusion against an individual's conventionally fixed boundaries:[77]

> The vibrations of affect offer an escape from the cage of the autonomous, self-consistent, rational subject – liberating the *relational* subject. The practice of listening, in the broadest sense and senses, allows us to sink under and sync up with the dynamics of the vibrating world of intensities.[78]

Music shatters the illusion of separate individual wholeness because sound enters the body.

---

of music has less to do with the communication of meaning and far more with the way in which it is able to 'move' people.

[75] Nancy, *Listening*, p. 40.

[76] Pierre Klossowski, *Nietzsche and the Vicious Circle*, trans. Daniel W. Smith (London: Continuum, 2005), p. 26. See also Rainer J. Hanshe, 'Agonistic Ethics: On the Hospitality of Warriors', paper presented at the East–West Passage Conference in Pécs, Hungary, 3–6 November 2010.

[77] Henriques, 'The Vibrations of Affect', pp. 58 and 75.

[78] Ibid., p. 79.

Through the disciplining and controlling influence of music we thus gain insight in 'an ethic' which is permeated by, and even grounded in, a *relationality* that ontologically precedes bodily autonomy and individuality. If bodies can be characterized by their intercorporeality and trans-subjectivity, then it is possible and perhaps even necessary to decouple such experiences from a singular, bounded and distinctly human body. What previously might have been thought of as separate entities which then interact should be rethought of as vibrating and resonating sites of co-enactment, co-emergence and co-evolution, thereby assuming that we are dealing with thoroughly entangled processes.

Nancy's reflections on the self as well as Massumi's and Deleuze's reflections on affect shift the focus from distinctly bounded bodies, from subjects as unitary, autonomous, self-sufficient entities to an exploration of bodies as dynamic knots which are more aligned to forces that take form by means of pre-individual and pre-conscious tendencies as well as by the relational connections which are immanent to such taking-form. 'In the beginning is relation,' Martin Buber writes.[79] Shifting the focus to a body as a site or intersection for affective resonance requires us to rethink some of our inherited basic principles from which we commonly start thinking about ethics and morality.

Although coming from very different musics and theories in comparison to the previous chapter, our present line of thought seems to lead to the same conclusion: the working and function of music implicitly criticizes the premises of most ethical and moral discourses in the Western world, namely corporeal autonomy and conscious responsibility. To discipline and control the human body through music also reveals, as Steven Connor puts it, that 'the self defined in terms of hearing rather than sight is a self imaged not as a point, but as a membrane; not as a picture, but as a channel through which voices, noises, and musics travel'.[80] Such a model not only confronts us with 'the dark sides of tunes', with music's amoral and unethical roles; it also vitally introduces a relation of self to otherness that is based on a literal 'inter-esse' of human beings, a being amidst things and events (see Chapter 1) instead of a world-view in which man dominates his environment and posits himself as separate from, and even opposed to, the surrounding world. Perhaps music can thus teach us some restraint, some modesty and a bit less overestimation of our 'selves' – affects that already have profound ethical connotations.

However, the emphasis on the permeable borders of subjects and selves, the primacy of relationality, does not relieve us from the possibility and/or necessity

---

[79] Martin Buber, *I and Thou*, trans. W. Kaufmann (London: Continuum, 2004), p. 22. The difference with the line of thinking presented here is that Buber still thinks this relationality in a *meta*physical way, whereas we emphasize, through sound, mainly corporeal connections.

[80] Steven Connor, 'The Modern Auditory I', in Roy Porter (ed.), *Rewriting the Self: Histories From the Renaissance to the Present* (London and New York: Routledge, 1996), p. 211.

to investigate how ethics can be rethought by paying attention to one of our most individual 'properties', our voice. On the contrary, it is also with and through our voices that we are able to give shape to a fundamental intersubjectivity which makes ethics possible. The way in which human and musical voices interact, supplement and contradict one another, and the implications that these interactions have for a rethinking of ethics through music, is the main topic of the next chapter.

Chapter 5
Voice

Nanette Nielsen

> Ethics requires a voice, but a voice which ultimately does not say anything, being by virtue of that all the louder, an absolute convocation which one cannot escape, a silence that cannot be silenced. The voice appears as the non-signifying, meaningless foundation of ethics. But what kind of foundation?
>
> <div align="right">Mladen Dolar, <i>A Voice and Nothing More</i>, p. 98.</div>

Towards a vocal ethics

The voice is ubiquitous. Even before we are born, we hear the sound of our mother's voice. As we draw our first breath, our cry becomes our first autonomous expression in the world. Throughout our lives, we are surrounded by voices: familiar, foreign, whispering, shouting, electronically manipulated, singing. The voice is one of the most fundamental human attributes; it is a means of rational communication and emotional expression, and is imbued with subjectivity. With this in mind, there are some relatively obvious links between voice and ethics. While voice has been theorized extensively by philosophy, psychoanalysis, critical theory and musicology, there has been little indication of how the *musical* voice might link with ethics. Through the multifaceted concept of voice, music, as a key player in the construction of subjectivity, can offer insights into expressions of selfhood. In this chapter we think musical ethics as a vocal ethics. We will explore how voice – understood in a variety of senses – relates to ethics through music, and how music can be regarded ethical or unethical through a theoretical framework focusing on voice. By summarizing some of the useful ways in which voice has been theorized, and by applying some of these ideas to a case study, Berg's *Wozzeck*, which concentrates on subjectivity, humanity and meaning, we propose a foundation for musical interpretations that may wish to follow a similar path.

We begin with a fundamental question, one of considerable breadth: what layers of 'voice' are potentially involved in music? The concept 'voice' occupies both physical and metaphysical spheres. Clearly, there is the existence of voice as an aesthetic object in itself: the voice-object, the voice of the singer, which attracts attention to itself *as* voice. For Mladen Dolar, attending to the voice as an aesthetic entity turns it into a fetish object, most often at the expense of linguistic meaning and concrete communication. By bringing voice to the forefront as something with which we can engage aesthetically, and which can offer emblematic meaning, singing lets 'the voice be the bearer of what cannot be expressed by words'.[1] So, in what appears to be the most immediate and perhaps superficial (physical) layer of voice in music, there is already potential for further (metaphysical) depth. Dolar's thoughts on the voice-object have important implications for the ethical potential of music and have fed into our discussion in this chapter, particularly into our exploration of perceived tensions between music and language.

Within musicology, Carolyn Abbate has argued along lines similar to Dolar, and a brief sketch of some pertinent points emerging from her groundbreaking book, *Unsung Voices*, will offer preliminary insight into the layers of voice involved in music as well as their ethical import. The idea of narrative is central to Abbate's account of musical voices. She avoids a conventional concept of narrative, and seeks to move beyond the tendency in both nineteenth- and twentieth-century opera criticism to equate the drama with the music – that is, to create an analogy between the plot and (linear) musical development. Activity and agency are crucial aspects of her narrative theory. Richard Taruskin's summary is helpful: for Abbate,

> ... a narrative is not simply a tale but a telling, requiring a teller (as well as a hearer). Who- or whatsoever is marked as a teller – be it animate or inanimate, be it actual or virtual (sung or 'unsung'), be it singer, player, character, instrument, composer, or any of these in combination – is a 'voice'. And this voice, transcending text and action and plot, is the ultimate musical doer, the Lord High Illocutioner.[2]

Agency in Abbate's framework extends to include the role of the listener (who decides what is 'marked as a teller'). For her, the narrating voice is defined simultaneously by being both enacted and perceived: her comment that 'certain gestures experienced in music constitute a narrating voice' appears paradoxical, because it implies that the existence of the voice is dependent on its construction via the listening audience.[3] Also, she does not consider music to *be* a narrative, and refuses to read music and plot as linearly combined.[4] Her framework encourages us to listen for moments that *disrupt* narrative flow, for it is in such moments that powerful, meaningful gestures occur. She writes:

> I propose that we understand musical narration not as an omnipresent phenomenon, not as sonorous encoding of human events or psychological states,

---

[1] Mladen Dolar, *A Voice and Nothing More* (Cambridge, MA: MIT Press, 2006), p. 30.

[2] Richard Taruskin, 'She do the Ring in different voices' (review), *Cambridge Opera Journal*, 4/2 (1992), pp. 187–97, at p. 188.

[3] Carolyn Abbate, *Unsung Voices: Opera and Musical Narrative in the Nineteenth Century* (Princeton, NJ: Princeton University Press, 1991), p. 19.

[4] Ibid., p. 28.

but rather as a rare and peculiar act, a unique moment of performing narration within a surrounding music.[5]

So what initially appears to be a paradox is, at second glance, founded on a particular way of proposing what is involved in being a recipient: Abbate's listener is an active listener. This is a phenomenological argument, based on the view that music occupies a real space in the world, and the consequence is that the musical voices will only emerge via the listener's active interpretation and understanding. It is with this (intended) heuristic move that Abbate reaches the final claim of her introduction, that voice needs 'not remain unheard, despite the fact that it is unsung'.[6] On one level, this simply means that voice is not just that of the singer: it can equally be carried by the orchestra. But the meaning of 'unsung' extends beyond this; as Taruskin explains, making a connection to phenomenology via Roman Ingarden's concept of the 'nonsounding', and reiterating the point about active listening: 'unsung' covers

> ... everything from expression to form to rhythmic or harmonic structure – everything which, while indisputably a part of the experience of the music as music rather than noise, nevertheless is not given in the sounds but has to be constructed by a competent listener.[7]

In her departure from structuralist narratology and conventional explanations of musical narrative, Abbate's critical strategy encourages resistance to simplistic comparisons of language and music. In particular, she argues that important insights into voice are not achieved by drawing analogies between music and language, and that by focusing on voice we can clarify the ways in which music is in fact *not* like language. Like Dolar, Abbate would argue that it is important to understand that music's voices, although devoid of linguistic meaning, add hermeneutic depth and offer other dimensions of meaning. Finally, the way in which Abbate's voices are interpreted as 'disruptive' is not unlike practices familiar from film. Such techniques as jump cuts, flashbacks and manipulation of visual and aural perspectives create a narrative distance ('discursive disjunctions'), and are accepted and understood in this way by audiences accustomed to interpreting them.[8]

In this chapter we take from Abbate the fundamental idea that music's voices participate in an active interplay between phenomenology and hermeneutics. On the phenomenological level, we work from the basis that music's voices emerge when they are actively perceived by the listener. In a sense, therefore, we as authors are also listening out for 'disruptions' and 'discursive disjunctions', for

---

[5] Ibid., p. 19.
[6] Ibid., p. 29.
[7] Taruskin, 'She Do the Ring', p. 189.
[8] Abbate, *Unsung Voices*, p. 26.

voices that open up new possibilities for understanding. These ruptures, when explored phenomenologically as musical experience, generate meaning, and this is not meaning that is 'discovered' as if it were already present in the musical fabric, but meaning that is instead created by the attentive listener. In Taruskin's words, '[n]ew meaning is created when old works are asked new questions, questions that arise out of new intellectual climates and concerns'.[9] We are, of course, concerned here with ethical questions. On the hermeneutical side, then, we aim to take advantage of the interpretative potential involved in exploring voice and ethics, and would argue that only by fully appreciating the potential meanings in music's voices can we also realize their ethical relevance.

From the above, it should be clear that the elements within music we can refer to by means of the term 'voice' are manifold. In a broad sense, the voice can be understood as a 'musical doer' or 'teller', ranging from the composer through a singer to an instrument to any detail in the musical texture. The crucial point is that only when the telling is perceived actively is it possible to deduce this musical voice. In this relatively brief chapter, a case study on *Wozzeck* focuses on only a few avenues by which we might explore voice and ethics, particularly in relation to the possible ethical and aural experience of the (ordinary) listener. Before coming to that example, we need to explore further how the musical voice, by offering something which language cannot, sets itself apart from the other narrative arts, such as literature, theatre and the cinema. Furthermore, once we have drawn out some of the tensions between language and music, it will be appropriate to consider an example from the genre of opera, which obviously involves a powerful and often ethically revelatory interplay between language and music. In the following section it will also emerge what more precisely we mean by 'ethics' within this chapter.

Phenomenology, hermeneutics and the musical voice

In engaging with the concept of voice, we move at the same time both closer towards and further away from philosophical tensions related to language. As Andrew Bowie has shown, current philosophical and musical debates can be linked to arguments made during the second half of the eighteenth century concerning the development of language, in which it was recognized that the nature of neither language nor music was clear.[10] According to Rousseau and Condillac, for example, music played a role in establishing the very origin of language, because it was not language, yet comprehensible. Rousseau singled out 'voice' as a crucial aspect of music, linking music and the origin of language (the human cry is one of his examples). In Bowie's gloss, for Rousseau '[l]anguage is not generated by

---

[9] Taruskin, 'She do the Ring', p. 193.
[10] Andrew Bowie, *Music, Philosophy, and Modernity* (Cambridge: Cambridge University Press, 2007), p. 48.

natural needs, but by human emotions. Needs give rise to 'gestures', passions to 'voices', and it is the voice that is essential for music.'[11]

Conceptual tensions intrinsic to music and language, which were carried forward to philosophical discussions in the twentieth century and our own time, are related in particular to questions of representation and expression. While mapping the historical and philosophical developments, Bowie asks: 'Is language a means of representing things in the world or of communicating information, a means of expressing emotions, a form of social action, a manifestation of *Geist*?'[12] An important point here is that the same questions could arguably be asked of music. Drawing on the work of Richard Rorty (who does not actually discuss music), Bowie offers an alternative to the focus on representation by encouraging recognition of music's and language's active engagement in the shaping of human action, as inherently human practices.[13]

Some discussion of music's relationship to human action is useful for understanding and revealing the ethical potential of the musical voice. Rather than attempting to show how or what voice may *represent*, we can uncover how or what it may *articulate*. Unlike language, music does not offer propositions, but it can nevertheless make the world comprehensible in new ways. And we would argue that music – and voice – is crucial to the ways in which we articulate our being-in-the-world. Relevant to this discussion is, of course, the work of Martin Heidegger (1889–1976), especially his thoughts on emotions as 'world-disclosive' entities and silence as meaningful articulation. In order to explore the close relationship between the musical voice and Heideggerian Being, we can turn to the complementary combination of phenomenology and hermeneutics in philosophical scholarship emerging in the early twentieth century.[14]

Central to Heidegger's insights into the world-disclosive nature of emotion is *Stimmung*, a concept by no means exhausted by the English translation as 'mood' or 'affectedness'. *Dasein*, the form or state of our 'being-in-the-world' as we exist alongside others,[15] can be affected by *Stimmung* in a number of ways. As Hubert Dreyfus has summarized:

---

[11] Ibid., p. 57.

[12] Ibid., p. 49.

[13] Ibid., p. 59.

[14] Following Edmund Husserl (1859–1938), the aim of Heidegger's phenomenological investigation is a hermeneutic and existential philosophy. As Don Ihde aptly summarizes, 'The phenomenology of essence, structure, and presence in Husserl leads to the phenomenology of existence, history, and the hermeneutical in Heidegger' (Don Ihde, *Listening and Voice: Phenomenologies of Sound*, 2nd edn (Albany, NY: State University of New York Press, 2007), p. 20.

[15] *Dasein* ('existence') is a term that, for obvious reasons, does not lend itself easily to any strict definition. It can be characterized as 'the being for whom Being is an issue'. See *The Continental Philosophy Reader*, ed. Richard Kearney and Maria Rainwater (London and New York: Routledge, 1996), p. 24. Heidegger's *Being and Time* (1927) is an analysis

Stimmung has a broader range than 'mood.' Fear, for example, is a *Stimmung* for Heidegger, but it is clearly an affect not a mood. *Stimmung* seems to name any of the ways Dasein can be affected. Heidegger suggests that moods or attunements manifest the tone of being-there. As Heidegger uses the term, mood can refer to the *sensibility* of an age (such as romantic), the *culture* of a company (such as aggressive), the *temper* of the times (such as revolutionary), as well as the *mood* in a current situation (such as the eager mood in the classroom) and, of course, the mood of an individual.[16]

In Heidegger's framework, *Stimmung* is integral to individuals' experience of, and engagement with, the world. And concepts like 'tone' and 'attuned' reveal its inherent musicality, as Bowie also points out: 'The word for mood, '*Stimmung*', retains the sense of musical "mode" and "attunement" which has been lost in English.'[17] Nevertheless, Heidegger does not give music a prominent place in his work, and this is perplexing. In Bowie's words, '[i]t is not ... that Heidegger thinks that the forms of world-disclosure which he regards as allowing understanding of being in a non-objectifying manner must be inherently verbal': the world-constituting forms involve architecture, painting and literature, and 'there seems to be no reason why the same should not apply to music'.[18] One reason for the neglect of music may well be related to the general anti-Romantic sentiments of the 1920s, and Heidegger's 'suspicion of the "subjective" nature of emotions'.[19] Elsewhere, Bowie links the repression of music in Heidegger to 'his questioning in the 1930s of metaphysics and its relationship to subjectivity'.[20] So while *Stimmung* clearly has potential applicability to music, appreciation of this has been limited, and there remains considerable scope to explore the concept within musicology.

An important musical aspect of *Stimmung*, which is lost in the English translation as 'mood', is intimated by its root, *Stimme*: 'voice'.[21] From the same root, the verbal form is *stimmen*, meaning 'to be correct' or 'to be in tune' and therefore suggesting at the same time both a musical and a normative value. *Stimmen* furthermore suggests an active 'giving voice' to something: *einstimmen* also means to 'voice alongside' or 'sing along' and therefore to express agreement. In *Stimmung*, then, the voice is correct, in tune, and (recalling the connection to affect

---

of the various existential structures of *Dasein* – in other words, an investigation of the ways in which 'being-in-the-world' manifests itself and what (existential) meaning(s) this possesses.

[16] Hubert L. Dreyfus, *Being-in-the-world: A Commentary on Heidegger's* Being and Time, *Division I* (Cambridge, MA and London: MIT Press, 1991), p. 169.

[17] Bowie, *Music, Philosophy, and Modernity*, p. 68.

[18] Ibid., p. 75.

[19] Ibid., p. 76.

[20] Ibid., p. 290.

[21] As in Scandinavian languages, where *stemme* is the equivalent in meaning and usage, or in Dutch, where *stemming* is used for 'mood' as well as 'tuning' of an instrument.

and mood) powerful and atmospheric. And *Einstimmung* crucially straddles both individual and collective spheres, as an expression that variously describes a song for one voice, the act of 'joining in' and a unanimous agreement of several voices. Heidegger's existential phenomenology can thus be seen to convey a closeness not only between the individual and existence, but also between the individual and the collective, as well as between voice and being. In this framework, voice can be considered to be a powerful existential concept, and we can begin to ask ethical questions of musical works accordingly.

But what does the voice 'say', and – more importantly at this stage – *how* does it give expression to this? For the hermeneutic side of the argument, Heidegger's idea of silence as meaningful articulation is instructive. Here again (as with Dolar), we are dealing with the tension between the 'sayable' and the 'unsayable'. At the point where words fail us and we cannot speak (for example, in particularly emotional situations), we are not left with an empty void of meaninglessness. Rather, this silence is filled with the meaning of that which cannot be said. Summarizing Heidegger's view of Being as revealing itself in/as silence, Bowie associates this existential point with *listening*:

> Silence is the space into which meaningful articulation can emerge and it cannot be explained in terms of its opposite, because it is not just the lack of sound. It is linked in some important way to listening, rather than just hearing whatever sound there is, because this can just be a way of objectively registering something. Silence in these terms is not something that one judges to be present or that one brings about, but rather something that we can become aware of or open to.
>
> All this would seem to relate closely to music, in which silence can be as significant as the notes.[22]

As a form of articulation that is *not* language, music can be linked with silence, in that comprehension of the meaningfulness of both is dependent on whether the perceiver passively *hears* or actively *listens* (also recalling Abbate's active listener). For this listening to be effective, a directed and engaged awareness and openness is required (as we also discuss elsewhere in this book). Furthermore, the silent non-articulation of the voice is active: music (and language) shapes and carries out action as part of an inherently human practice, leading to opportunities for both expression and interpretation. While calling silence the 'space' of music, Don Ihde emphasizes its potency in a Heideggerian (existential) framework: 'Silence is nothingness but nothingness is sheer possibility.'[23]

So, we can restate that articulation (even if silent) is dynamic: music and language partake in and shape human action. The idea of silence as a potential

---

[22] Ibid., p. 70.
[23] Ihde, *Listening and Voice*, p. 223.

expressive mode can be related more precisely to *voice*. First, as Abbate would claim, a voice needs not be sung to be heard. Second, this encourages a sensitivity not just to what is being 'said', but also to *how* it is being said – including through silence. In terms of how something is being 'said', it is worth noting that laughter and crying are wordless human expressions understandable across the world, in any language, exemplifying powerful envoiced expressions not dependent on language. As for silence, certainly from a musical point of view, this can be articulate and highly expressive. In both cases, with its 'attuned correctness' – the inherent mixture of normativity and musicality – the voice contributes something of value, which can also be ethically relevant.

Another important angle provided by Heidegger on the world-disclosive properties of emotion is his attempted breaking down of the subject–object divide. Continuing with the issue of *Stimmung*, Bowie summarizes:

> Moods are not something we choose, they are what we *find* ourselves in, and they determine much of how we are. By suggesting that there is an inherent connectedness of inner and outer which is beyond the exercise of our will, [Heidegger] seeks to get away from the notion of the subject as an intending 'inside' which relates to an objective 'outside'.[24]

The consequence of this philosophical position for understanding the musical voice as an existentially and ethically powerful concept is twofold. First, the bridging of the subject–object gap opens up an opportunity to address the issue of intersubjectivity, the constant (hermeneutic) interplay within the shared space between self and other, which includes voice as a form of articulation. And, second, this framework helps to emphasize what the voice is already capable of doing and being, physically: it is necessarily at the same time 'inner' and 'outer', interior and transcendent, subjective and objective. Tied to the inner constitution of the subject, the voice constantly reaches out to its intersubjective surroundings.[25] Voice, as well as music, has the capacity to resist straightforward conceptual distinctions (like the one between subject and object), and show how we can reach beyond language and thought that is usually restricted by discursive categories.

In light of the previous discussion related to the philosophy of language and music, we now have a conceptual framework through which we can begin to consider musical ethics as a vocal ethics. While continuing Abbate's focus on the intersection between phenomenology and hermeneutics, other issues to pursue are those related to activity, agency, listening, the sayable and the unsayable, articulation, world-disclosive emotions (*Stimmung*), and silence. With regard to the tension between music and language, we have established that it is often not about *what* is being said, but *how* something is being said; this offers a possibility

---

[24] Bowie, *Music, Philosophy, and Modernity*, p. 69.

[25] For a related discussion of music, selfhood and intersubjectivity, see Katherine Higgins, *The Music of Our Lives* (Lanham, MD: Lexington Books, 2011), pp. 119–23.

for exploring the *musical* side to voice. Finally, the recognition of the importance of engagement and activity (rather than representation) is crucial for drawing out the ethical potential of the musical voice.

Case study: the ethics of voice in *Wozzeck*

> What I do consider my particular accomplishment is this. No one in the audience, no matter how aware he may be of the musical forms contained in the framework of the opera, of the precision and logic with which it has been worked out, no one, from the moment the curtain parts until it closes for the last time, pays any attention to the various fugues, inventions, suites, sonata movements, variations, and passacaglias about which so much has been written. No one gives heed to anything but the vast social implications of the work which by far transcend the personal destiny of Wozzeck. This, I believe, is my achievement.
>
> Alban Berg, 1927.[26]

For this chapter, as a 'way in' to thinking musical ethics as a vocal ethics, we remain in the early twentieth century and consider the example of Alban Berg's opera *Wozzeck* (first performed in 1925). The opera is in three acts and is written mainly in an atonal idiom, although scenes are also (famously) structured around strict forms taken from instrumental music (including a prelude and triple fugue and a passacaglia). The literary source was Georg Büchner's influential play *Woyzeck*, which tells a proto-expressionist tale of oppression of the working class by the medical and military professions. In Berg's opera, a soldier, Wozzeck, is forced to do menial jobs and to undergo various scientific experiments that take a toll on his physical and mental well-being. His common-law wife Marie (with whom he has a child) is frustrated by the hardship and Wozzeck's increasingly poor health and mental instability, and has an affair with the Drum Major. Wozzeck becomes jealous and eventually murders Marie. Under suspicion, he returns to the scene of the murder by a lake to retrieve the knife with which he stabbed her and accidentally drowns himself. The opera concludes somewhat ambiguously with the child being summoned by peers to observe his mother's corpse.

We cannot claim to cover here all of the many possible facets of voice and ethics in *Wozzeck*. Continuing the focus on intersubjectivity and musical 'moods', our (phenomenological) approach is limited to those ethical layers that may be detectable when we take the act of listening seriously. In particular, we explore what is revealed by the vocal lines when they may be seen to carry ethical implications that extend beyond the text. In addition to a musical elucidation based on the framework proposed above, we also investigate whether a work of

---

[26] From *Modern Music*, (November–December 1927), pp. 22ff. As reproduced in Douglas Jarman, *Alban Berg, Wozzeck* (Cambridge: Cambridge University Press, 1989), p. 153.

music (or art) can disclose something about the world that may, in one way or another, involve ethics. Here, given the multiplicity of potential ethical layers, a few words are in order about 'which' ethics we are dealing with. As a composer associated with a particular strand of modernism, Berg, like his contemporaries Schoenberg and Adorno, can be seen as having sought to establish an ethical as well as aesthetic response (one of opposition) to new currents of mass culture and expanding market forces in the interwar period. As Berg states in the quote above, the listener is expected to take away from his opera its social implications, which we can assume relate to the plight of the lower orders of an oppressive and unequal society. Our exploration of *Wozzeck*, broadly based on Levinasian ethics in discussing interactions between self and other, challenges ethical *ideals* in two ways. First, it responds to critical readings of this opera that claim its music embodies ideals related to humanity, redemption, and love. Our focus on voice reveals instead how more prosaic and perceivable intersubjective interactions in both plot and music challenge a striving for ideal or universal ethics, and maintain the opera's inherent ethical conflicts. And second, by focusing on the listener's experience of audible features, we point to an ethics coexistent with the ethics of a modernism that insists on a critical distance to the ordinary listener, to show how particular musical effects carry ethical implications for the audible perception of the opera. Crucially, it is through the music and especially through voice – in this case vocal lines in particular, but also lyricism as a signifier of subjectivity – that we broaden and rethink these ethical horizons. Thus confined to *Wozzeck*, but using a method applicable to other works, what emerges in this discussion is an ethics of voice for which listening is essential.

Ethical criticisms of *Wozzeck*

Writing in 1929, Adorno offered a reading of *Wozzeck* that has remained influential in scholarship on the opera. His interpretation is a clear example of ethical criticism. He claims that the opera's music, which contains 'truth' in 'its cells', reaches beyond the text and 'salvages a suffering that may have been intended in *Wozzeck*'s words but that the verbal drama no longer supports'.[27] For Adorno, *Wozzeck* 'adopts the stance of a *real humanity*'.[28] His explanation of how it does so draws primarily on a juxtaposition between subject and object.[29] He argues for an 'objective character' of the music that appears under the guise of musical subjectivism: Berg plays with both convention and perception by reaching back to traditional forms, while at the same time placing them within a sphere of psychological tensions. Conversely, the opera deals with psychological issues, but 'seizes' them (as Adorno puts it) through

---

[27] Theodor W. Adorno, 'The Opera *Wozzeck*', in *Essays on Music*, ed. Richard Leppert (Berkeley and Los Angles: University of California Press, 2002), pp. 619–26, at p. 619.

[28] Ibid., p. 620, emphasis in original.

[29] Ibid.

rigorous formal procedures.[30] Berg's approach is a dialectical one, and the opera should be seen neither strictly psychologically (Adorno points to a contrast here with Wagner and Debussy) nor simply as reviving old forms (*à la* neo-classicism). Rather, it presents a new development:

> If whatever truth there is in objective characters continues to exist in altered form even under the mantle of musical subjectivism, then a procedure is legitimized that cuts through the mantle and grasps anew the contents beneath it. This occurs in Berg's *Wozzeck*.[31]

In the aftermath of romanticism, Adorno clearly wishes to rescue the opera from any charges of subjectivism, despite its conspicuous psychological underpinning. His reference to the opera's involvement with childhood and psychoanalysis is significant here. For Adorno, Berg's music functions in a similar way to the psychoanalytic process in that it uncovers 'essential remnants of existence'.[32] This results in the construction of objective characters, rather than essentially individual and subjective ones. The subjectivity is avoided through the music taking rational control: 'The *construction* of *Wozzeck* ... is only the means of grasping this dream material before it dissolves into the atmosphere and drifts away in moods.'[33] The harking back to past forms and materials is a matter of recollection and re-imagining, and the images that the opera presents have similarly been excavated from the archaic realm, from childhood and dreams. With regard to the concept of *suffering* at the heart of his ethical interpretation, Adorno links this idea to the 'objective' characters; indeed, Wozzeck himself is compared indirectly to Christ by reference to the *Passion*, and thereby to universal suffering.

Given Adorno's critique of the 'illusory dream of romantic remoteness'[34] and the fact that expression is at the centre of his essay, it is curious that he does not mention the opera's Mahlerian D minor interlude, between scenes 4 and 5 in Act III. He is keen to stress that '*Wozzeck*'s expression has nothing whatsoever to do with *Tristan*'s', but has not taken account of the interlude, which obviously sets itself apart from the rest of the opera in being Romantic in tone and expression.[35] One way of explaining the omission is that for Adorno, the musical voice in *Wozzeck* is arguably that of the composer: he does not approach the opera from a listener's perspective, but focuses on the extent to which it succeeds in being 'objective' on its own (immanent) terms. In other words, he does not *listen* to the interlude as much as he seeks to support with analysis a positive reading of the opera's compositional logic, as well as its ethical import. So, for example, whereas he

---

[30] Ibid., p. 621.
[31] Ibid.
[32] Ibid.
[33] Ibid., p. 622, emphasis in original.
[34] Ibid., p. 621.
[35] Ibid., p. 623.

argues that the numerous songs in the opera (such as the 'Hunting Song', Marie's 'Lullaby', 'Ballad of the Gypsy' and the songs from the Tavern scene) do not 'conserve the recently departed romanticism', he appears to have underestimated the extent to which the D minor interlude *does* conserve this, through its recourse to tonality and Romantic *espressivo*.[36] Indeed, if the songs 'succeed' for Adorno due to their fearful *distortion* of tonality,[37] what does the interlude achieve by drawing directly on the expressive potential of a late Romantic idiom? Of course, if Adorno *had* discussed it, he might just have argued, along similar lines, that Berg takes the vestiges of a lost language (lyricism and tonality) and seizes them through rational, objective, compositional processes (he makes a similar argument in his work on Mahler).[38] And with regard to the listener, Adorno clearly (if indirectly) agrees with Berg's words above on how the musical construction is not supposed to be grasped, but that the key is their support for the drama and expression: the variations and fugues 'are saturated with expression; their purpose is to carry the expression coherently'.[39]

Even if (perhaps especially if) the music is not grasped in terms of its complex organization, it can be highly effective. It is notable that, despite Adorno's recognition of 'fear' as the dominant and fundamental emotion of the opera (thereby admitting that its emotional effects are not irrelevant), he does not engage in a deeper exploration of the role of the listener. In other words, he does not explore the space between subject and object, the intersubjective realm. Indeed, the objective, *distancing* effect of the music is imperative for his argument: 'the music does not suffer within the human being, does not itself participate in his actions and emotions. It suffers over him.'[40] Given the critical context and his particular aesthetic ideology, Adorno's approach to the opera is perhaps predictable, but the consequence is that he overlooks some crucial ethical aspects of the work. We argue below that on the level of *intersubjectivity*, through a focus on voice, we can offer an alternative to this particular modernist reading of the opera.

Further to Adorno and the topic of humanity and ethics, we can turn to Julian Johnson, who has offered an ethically relevant reading of both *Wozzeck* and *Lulu* that echoes some of Adorno's points.[41] Focusing on the musical portrayal of the relationship between the individual and society, Johnson brings out the issue of subjectivity and objectivity. His main concern is not plot or narrative, but rather

---

[36] Ibid.

[37] Ibid.

[38] See, for example, Adorno's 'Mahler Today' in *Essays on Music*, and the monograph *Mahler: A Musical Physiognomy*, trans. Edmund Jephcott (Chicago: University of Chicago Press, 1992).

[39] Adorno, 'The Opera *Wozzeck*', p. 623.

[40] Ibid., p. 625.

[41] Julian Johnson, 'Berg's Operas and the Politics of Subjectivity', in Nikolaus Bacht (ed.), *Music, Theatre, and Politics in Germany: 1848 to the Third Reich* (Aldershot: Ashgate, 2006), pp. 211–33.

the ways in which the music is able to contribute to the uncovering of political tensions.[42] In his argument, voice is indirectly combined with ethics, as can be seen in the following quote, the context for which is his clarification of *Wozzeck* and *Lulu*'s distance from the contemporary aesthetic trend of *Neue Sachlichkeit* ('New Objectivity'), despite their high level of realism which is normally associated with this trend.

> The music of these operas tells a different story and speaks with a different voice. At key moments, the music sets itself against the prevailing style of the words, using the orchestra to speak for a character, or calling forth a different, more inward voice from the characters themselves. Occasionally this takes the form of something resembling an aria; more often it is a brief but intense expression of reminiscence or desire, a lyrical protest against the prevailing unfeeling character of the world.[43]

Here, Johnson draws attention to some potent ethical tensions between individual and society – the (fragile) internal world of the subject and the (threatening) external sphere of social reality – and between music and language, where music is able to 'say' more than language can. It is in the music that he identifies a different 'teller', and – perhaps echoing Abbate's narrative 'disruptions' – he clarifies elsewhere that he is interested in the 'disjunctions' between the music and the staged drama.[44]

Further commentary on the musical voice in *Wozzeck* can add further insight to the ethical issues identified by Johnson. Intersubjectivity is clearly relevant to the ethical underpinnings of his argument, and at various points he emphasizes the complex and 'dialectical' nature of subjectivity and intersubjectivity, as in the following:

> The operas of Berg propose the category of subjectivity in a thoroughly dialectical way, not as some nostalgic lament for the condition of an earlier age. Subjectivity here arises from a *mediation* of individuality and collectivity, not their simple opposition, and both categories are reworked in the process.[45]

The term 'intersubjectivity' is, however, mentioned only once by Johnson, at which point it also becomes clear that there is potential for exploring in greater depth its music-ethical implications for *Wozzeck*:

---

[42] Ibid., p. 218.

[43] Ibid., p. 219.

[44] Ibid., p. 218. Also, 'at extreme moments, the orchestral voice appears disjunct or even oppositional to what takes place on stage' (p. 220). Johnson predominantly focuses on an instrumental, rather than vocal, voice.

[45] Ibid., p. 229, emphasis added.

> [Berg's music] does more than make a political objection to the individual's fate at the hands of an inhumane society; it offers the one element that is missing that might redeem that situation: care, tenderness, fragility, empathy, intersubjective understanding based on the richness of the subject, not its annihilation by a repressive notion of objectivity.[46]

This view offers a starting-point for the interpretation that follows in this chapter. Johnson has argued that the music acts as an ethical agent in *Wozzeck*: not only is music an element that offers an active response to a repressive objectivity; it also, crucially, attains a redemptive quality. For Johnson, this opportunity for redemption is present, above all, in the way in which *lyricism* signifies an expression of subjectivity, and the music (even if limited to the orchestra) sometimes both overcomes 'the bluntness of the opera's words' and acts as a supportive feature, offering resistance.[47] According to Johnson, the glimpse of this potential redemption is found in the D minor interlude:

> [The interlude's] lyrical tone is arresting precisely because of its antithetical stance to the prevailing tone of the rest of the opera. For some, it borders on a compositional miscalculation, introducing a Mahlerian *espressivo*, harmonically and melodically removed from the atonality and motivic density of the earlier music. This distance, of course, is precisely the condition of the interlude's power. The music is here both the breaking *out* of a lyrical impulse earlier repressed, and at the same time, something that breaks *in* to the work as if it were extraneous and foreign to its world. This twofold aspect accounts for the effect of the interlude as both catharsis and redemption – redemption in the sense that, amid all the horror of what takes place on stage, the music realizes a countervailing quality of care.[48]

But redemption for whom? At the end of the opera Wozzeck and Marie are dead, and the chilling final scene includes the announcement of this fact to their child. Johnson is not alone in associating the interlude with humanity in the opera, but not all commentary on this issue is equally positive, as he acknowledges in the quote above. Keeping in mind the question of who or what is 'redeemed', the ethical implications of other views prompt further reflection on this point; unlike Adorno and (to an extent) Johnson, the more negative responses to the effect of the interlude tend to focus on the experience of the audience.

Taruskin calls the interlude 'the great expressive climax in *Wozzeck*, where Berg made his most direct appeal to empathy', and identifies it as 'a catharsis

---

[46] Ibid., p. 230.
[47] Ibid., p. 220.
[48] Ibid., pp. 220–21.

to mark Wozzeck's death as tragic'.[49] But as Berg introduces this catharsis in an otherwise pessimistic environment, he eliminates some crucial musical effects that would be clearly recognized by the listener. This especially rests on the easily perceived juxtaposition between 'tonal' and 'atonal', and can be wholly tied to the effect on the audience. For Taruskin, ironic distance disappears with the interlude: because it is a uniquely tonal moment in this otherwise atonal opera, it turns assumptions of 'normal' and 'abnormal' upside down. In Abbatean terms, we can regard the interlude as a potent example of one of those narrative moments that 'disrupt the flow', and the result is a radical change in perception:

> [A]s soon as we respond as 'normal' listeners to the stimulus of the interlude's tonal catharsis, black and white are radically reversed. All the rest of the opera is now placed 'in quotes'. The distance of its special world from the 'normal' world of music becomes a part of the characterization, a metaphor for Wozzeck's crazed condition ... [The atonal music] consummately conveys the terror in Wozzeck; but to summon pity, the composer had to resort to an 'invention on a key'. In his very success with the atonal idiom ... Berg exposed its limitations.[50]

Certainly, by turning to tonality in this way, Berg can be seen to be 'letting down' his colleagues of the atonal school, for whom outdated expressive means and appeal to prevailing musical taste was a demonstration of aesthetic error (Stravinsky was also to lament *Wozzeck*'s popularity with audiences).[51] Taruskin's main point is that the compositional decision to resort to tonality diminishes and disrupts the effect of the atonal idiom: once the tonal idiom is laden with such emotive content, the atonality (wholly tied to Wozzeck's psychological state – that of terror) is shown to be incapable of engaging the audience's empathy. Taruskin and Johnson both identify a catharsis in the tonal language of the interlude, but their perception of its purpose and effect differs. For Johnson, the catharsis is a successful outlet of repressed feeling; for Taruskin, it makes apparent a stylistic incongruity while highlighting the lack of prior emphatic engagement. The former perception is tinged with hope and consolation, the latter with disappointment and confusion.

---

[49] Richard Taruskin, *The Oxford History of Western Music*, Vol. 4: *The Early Twentieth Century* (Oxford: Oxford University Press, 2005), p. 520.

[50] Ibid., pp. 520 and 522.

[51] Taruskin quotes Stravinsky's remark that 'what disturbs me about *Wozzeck*, a work that I love, is the level of its appeal to "ignorant" audiences' (ibid., p. 522). The quote is from Igor Stravinsky and Robert Craft, *Dialogues and a Diary* (Garden City, NY: Doubleday, 1963), p. 24. See also Jarman, *Alban Berg*, pp. 10–11, where he accounts for Berg's slight divergence from Schoenberg and Adorno. Although Berg shared their aesthetic positions (and, according to Adorno, was disappointed at the popular acclaim of *Wozzeck* at its premiere), he had, for example, a more positive attitude towards Brecht and Weill than his two peers.

We now return to the question of who, ultimately, is the recipient or beneficiary of this catharsis on the one hand, and the message of redemption, care, and humanity on the other: the composer, the audience, or the characters in the opera? If one ethically relevant weakness of the interlude can, according to Taruskin, be identified in Berg's adoption of a more tonal language to inspire empathy in his audience, Joseph Kerman has pointed out a not dissimilar deficiency in its effect on the relationship between the music and the drama. Kerman recognizes that the music of the interlude takes overwhelming emotional control: 'It is in the final interlude that one is first allowed leisure to feel what one has witnessed, here first that the enormity can be gauged in emotional terms.'[52] But an important gap is revealed once the effect of the interlude takes hold, in that the emotional response is solely a matter for the audience, not for the characters, who are all dead: 'it is not *of* the action, but *about* the action'.[53] This is problematic, especially from the ethical perspective we can read into Kerman, since the audience is invited to partake in 'self-pity', more than anything, because there has been no prior opportunity to link the characters with this overwhelming sympathy and depth of emotion:

> The emotion of the final interlude cannot properly adhere to [Wozzeck]; it is, rather, self-indulgence after the shattering experience to which the audience has found itself subjected. The basic rhythm is from terror to self-pity, away from the action.[54]

Finally, while it offers this moment of relief, it is arguably due to the magnitude of the interlude's emotional impact that the final scene of the opera has been viewed as particularly chilling: its unsentimental, childish unmusicality is juxtaposed, brutally and grotesquely, with the preceding events. Echoing Adorno's perception that the dominant emotion of the opera is fear, this leads Kerman to summarize that '[w]hat is genuine in this opera is the terror, not the pity'.[55]

As Taruskin aptly comments, in this opera 'the relationship between the humanizing music and the horrific subject is not at all direct'.[56] Underlying all the observations summarized above – and keeping in mind our account of musical discourse and agency in 'Discourse' (Chapter 2) – are ethically laden questions about whether the music has done full justice to the action and offered a suitable and convincing layer of humanity, care and empathy. The critical discourse certainly bears witness to a general perception of the opera's ethical effect. Although the work is not reducible to a simple 'communication model', as Johnson also

---

[52] Joseph Kerman, *Opera as Drama* (London: Oxford University Press, 1957), p. 231.
[53] Ibid.
[54] Ibid., p. 232.
[55] Ibid., pp. 233–34.
[56] Taruskin, *The Oxford History of Western Music*, Vol. 4, p. 508.

points out,[57] it is striking how the emotional impact of the interlude creates more dilemmas and unanswered questions. Finally, at the centre of all the discussions is what we can consider to be phenomenological concerns about the *effect* of the music, in terms of what we, as listeners, hear and how we are invited to respond.

Voice, intersubjectivity, and ethics

From the perspectives summarized above, it appears that the tonal idiom of the interlude provides catharsis for the audience rather than the characters of the opera. If Adorno and Johnson focus on the musical fabric in particular, both Taruskin and Kerman take the phenomenology of listening seriously in their ethical criticisms of *Wozzeck*. An important gap emerges here between 'the ideal' and 'the real': if the former approach is to an extent tied to a modernist ideal for music, the latter pertains to the actual experiences of audiences in the opera house. The question then becomes whether we might locate other ethically relevant moments in the opera, beyond the interlude. Given the focus of this chapter, we are particularly interested in how voice can contribute to the ethical discussion. Although voice is an aspect of Johnson's reading of *Wozzeck*, it appears that the *human* voice has been left out of accounts of relationships between music and humanity in the opera. The interlude is, of course, orchestral, and if there is indeed a gap between action and music (as Kerman suggests), the underlying argument could be that the characters have been granted very little self-expression – a lyricism which could attract the sympathy of the audience – and that this might have an impact on the overall perception of the opera's ethical message. In other words, if the music clearly delivers catharsis and a perception of redemption for the benefit of the audience through the interlude, what might the rest of the opera offer of 'care' in relation to the characters themselves? More specifically, what voices are they given that would articulate their experiences of subjectivity and intersubjectivity? Exploring moments of lyricism within the intersubjective space of 'Wozzeck and Marie', we challenge the argument that the music offers a redemptive capacity and consider additional ethical messages at work in the opera.

We can identify three intersubjective spaces shared by Wozzeck and Marie and in which ethical interaction takes place through the musical voice: their shared state of poverty, their relationship and their child. Drawing on the interpretative framework presented above, we focus first and foremost on the actual vocal articulations of the characters. In light of the intersections between phenomenology and hermeneutics, we examine Wozzeck's and Marie's articulation of their being-in-the-world via music and ask what this can tell us about redemption, humanity and catharsis in the opera. We focus in particular on two issues: vocal declamation and mood (*Stimmung*).

---

[57] Johnson, 'Berg's Operas', p. 230.

As Kerman has pointed out, *Wozzeck* 'depends on a highly individual kind of declamation. In a sung play, more than in any other operatic variety, declamation has to have a life of its own.'[58] He expands on this, referring to the independence of the vocal lines: 'Even these sung sections refuse to adhere to their accompaniment, for the most part; these vocal lines are too eccentric and the accompaniment is too dissonant.'[59] The sheer range of vocal styles in *Wozzeck* is one manifestation of this tendency. Berg blends spoken lines, *Sprechstimme* of different types, and fully sung phrases with different kinds of expression 'from fantastically chromatic and disjunct lines ... to an approximately Straussian, post-Wagnerian style of declamation'.[60]

We can add to this Johnson's comment that we can identify a lyricism or a lyrical tone in *Wozzeck* with a 'subjective interiority', which is not least discernible through its juxtaposition with music associated with the objective, collective world – for example, dance music or folk music.[61] Our questions here will relate to whether this lyricism can tell us anything about intersubjectivity; musical *interaction* between subject and object is the key. And, finally, in our search for links between intersubjectivity, voice and ethics, a focus on 'mood' is instructive. This point, which is made by Kerman, is particularly relevant for our endeavour to take the phenomenology of listening seriously:

> Much propaganda has been devoted to the musical organization of *Wozzeck*, so much that it is well to emphasize that the ultimate judge is the ear, not the eye, and that the work is destined for the opera house, not for the analyst's study. Berg's more complicated musical constructions are simply not perceived in the theatre, or rather, are perceived only to the extent of strong moods.[62]

Adorno's reading of *Wozzeck* referred to the successful compositional control of moods. Kerman suggests instead that moods are what the listener is able to perceive; he argues that each scene offers a distinct mood. It is in relation to these moods we can develop ethical insights with reference to Heidegger's notion of *Stimmung* and world-disclosive emotions. More specifically, we extend the notion of 'mood' and allow it to be understood in the broader sense of *Stimmung*, as integral to individuals' experience of, and engagement with, the world, the 'tone of being-there'. The music as well as the message of *Wozzeck* invites us to take such an approach.

---

[58] Kerman, *Opera as Drama*, p. 224.
[59] Ibid.
[60] Ibid.
[61] Johnson, 'Berg's Operas', p. 221.
[62] Kerman, *Opera as Drama*, pp. 225–26. The point about the non-perceivability of the musical complexity is also noted by Berg himself in 'A Word about "Wozzeck"', *Modern Music*, (November–December 1927), pp. 22ff. The essay is available in Jarman, *Alban Berg*, pp. 152–53.

'Wozzeck and Marie': poverty

The spaces of poverty and the child are both introduced via Wozzeck's voice in the very first scene. Having answered the Captain with only monotone responses, in particular with his repeated statement of unreflective agreement ('Jawohl, Herr Hauptmann'), the subject of conversation turns to morality and Wozzeck's illegitimate child. For the Captain, the child serves as evidence that Wozzeck is a 'good man' but has 'no moral sense'. As a response after the Captain has asked him to 'speak!' (b. 62), Wozzeck's voice finally breaks out of the monotone into a sudden burst of emotion (b. 127 ff.), and we are introduced to the most important motif of the opera, 'Wir arme Leut' (b. 136, Example 5.1), one which is highly relevant to the intersubjective space of poverty. Here, Wozzeck makes his first coherent, reflective utterance,[63] but the Captain fails to understand his intended meaning. The utterance contains, on the one hand, a statement about God and poverty and, on the other hand, a representation of Wozzeck himself in the music's lyricism. Johnson sees this as a 'protest of the conscripted subject',[64] but nevertheless both the fact of his poverty and the articulation of his subjectivity are lost on the Captain. Even though the Captain does not grasp the literal message of Wozzeck's outburst, however, it has a conspicuous effect on him. His immediate reaction is one of anger: he replies with a *fortissimo* shriek, 'What do you mean?' (b. 133), while 'jumping up in rage' (according to the stage direction). After Wozzeck's lengthy explanation, the Captain claims that he 'knows' that Wozzeck is a good man, but actually he remains confused. Musically, this second response is equally abrupt, if less angry (b. 153, marked 'somewhat nonplussed'), and it confirms that the message has still not been understood. The musical example below includes the 'Wir Arme Leut' motif, as well as a fragment of Wozzeck's explanation of poverty.[65] Further to the issue of voice, it is worth noting that the score gives specific indications of the appearances of the main motif, 'H' for Hauptstimme' (appearing in a principal voice) and 'N' for 'Nebenstimme' (in a secondary voice). In the passage here, 'Wir Arme Leut' is indicated by 'N', drawing attention to its appearance as a voice in the orchestral texture.

---

[63] Wozzeck briefly breaks his monotone 'Jawohl, Herr Hauptmann' with an exclamation of 'Wind!' (b. 72). This surprising utterance fits with the framework proposed by Johnson, which concerns the anxiety-infusing role of nature in *Wozzeck* and *Lulu*, internal as well as external. See Johnson, 'Berg's Operas', for example, p. 225.

[64] Ibid., p. 219.

[65] The full text of the passage is: 'Poor folk like us! You see, Captain, money, money! If one has none! Try bringing your fellow creature into the world in a moral sort of way! One has also flesh and blood! Now, if I were a gentleman, and had a hat, and a watch, and eye-glasses, and could speak politely, then I'd be virtuous too, It must be a fine thing to be virtuous, Captain. But I'm just a common fellow! Our kind is unlucky in this world and in the next too. I think if we got into heaven they'd make us help with the thunder!' Quoted from George Perle, *The Operas of Alban Berg*, Vol. 1: *Wozzeck* (Berkeley: University of California Press, 1980), p. 45.

Example 5.1   Alban Berg, *Wozzeck*, bars 136–142

All this is interesting from an ethical perspective because the music, and the voice in particular, carries meaning which is either twice misunderstood or not understood at all: Wozzeck's words, but also his non-verbal self-expression, are not properly grasped by the recipient. In other words, this lyrical expression of subjectivity and the intersubjective space of poverty are both 'above language', even in a moment at which he emphasizes language in a quote from the Bible ('The Lord spake'), establishing a connection to that ideal ethical sphere. The crux is that the ethical point that can be deduced from the musical material hinges on neither knowledge nor understanding. When heard (rather than listened to), Wozzeck's vocal articulation has a pronounced effect on the Captain and furthermore contains a message about poverty and morality that will stay with him throughout the opera, including a reference to the ideal ethics of 'God' that will return later with Marie. It is because of our perception as attentive listeners to the Captain's response that we can extract something meaningful, which can be seen to help articulate Wozzeck's subjectivity and its effect on another character.

Furthermore, the passage preceding the Captain's response to Wozzeck's biblical quote is introduced with a *Molto ritardando* slowing of the tempo and a pause on a dominant-seventh chord (b. 132), offering, in Taruskin's words, 'an unequivocally "tonal" moment of repose to coincide with, and underscore, a rare moment of unfeigned human warmth'.[66] What we have here is an example of music acting as an ethical agent in an interplay between phenomenology and hermeneutics, notably by resorting to tonality. This momentary glimpse of tonality functions, albeit on a micro-level, in a way not dissimilar to the interlude, helping to establish a link between tonality and catharsis early on in the opera.

Continuing with the point about 'redemption', the music in this early scene already does more than simply convey the repression of the subject (Wozzeck) by an oppressive object (the Captain, representing the 'normal' uncaring world); it potentially reveals a deeper level of ethics. Wozzeck's subjectivity, as well as the intersubjective space of poverty, is clearly introduced by the first strong, coherent vocal line in the opera; whereas the Captain wavers between cantabile and parlando, Wozzeck's voice is lyrical, coherent and unwavering. Since both articulation and reception are active components of the framework we propose, the Captain's vehement response is significant also because it shows that what Wozzeck has articulated *matters* as an expression of a strong subjectivity, even if it mainly reveals that the Captain is frustrated at not having understood the message. In other words, although a rare example in this opera of subjective expression, the music here serves as an ethical pillar of resilience, and through voice in particular.

'Wozzeck and Marie': the relationship

As our brief venture into the intersubjective space of poverty shows, one aspect of the humanity in *Wozzeck* can be found in the musical depiction of the idealized sphere of God, appearing in this brief moment of tonal 'human warmth'. Another important universal ethical value identified by scholarship on *Wozzeck* is that

---

[66] Taruskin, *The Oxford History of Western Music*, Vol. 4, p. 511.

of love.[67] Susan Greene, for example, reaches the following conclusion in her discussion of morality and free will in the opera:

> Berg stood *with* Wozzeck and Marie, looking inside them with the infinite understanding that grasped their sorrow and their dignity. This loving compassion touches in turn something nobler in each of us, the wellsprings of our own capacities for feeling. It is stirred by the genius of Berg's *Wozzeck*, which speaks his radical plea for a more honest morality, a morality in which the supreme virtue is love.[68]

From the argument presented in Greene's article, it is not clear, at least in terms of the opera's music, how this rather excessive conclusion can be reached. And as with the juxtaposition between the expressive intensity of the interlude and the cold brutality of the rest of the opera, it appears to present a conflict between 'the ideal' and 'the real'. How, if at all, is an ideal of love articulated by the music? This is an important question if we wish to understand adequately the qualities of redemption, empathy, humanity and care. If, as Kerman suggests, there is a noticeable gap between the drama and the music, then perhaps there is a similar distance between the music and any 'supreme virtue of love' that we might be inclined to associate with the relationship between Wozzeck and Marie. Certainly such a choice of distancing would tally with a portrayal of the characters' frustration and misery, but we would again need to explore the ethical implications, especially in light of the articulation of subjectivity through lyricism and the impact of the interlude on the audience. If love is a form of self-fulfilment (as for Hegel), the experience of the other, and self-reflection through love, can be regarded as being vital to individual subjectivity.[69] In the following, we unravel both subjective and intersubjective elements within the shared space of 'Wozzeck and Marie'.

What Wozzeck and Marie share can be regarded as unique to their relationship; there is no question in this case of deducing a tension between individual and society, but one of understanding a shared space between two individuals. Wozzeck and Marie share a space of poverty and 'meet' in 'Wir arme Leut'. In Act 1, scene 3, Marie quotes literally the crucial words from Wozzeck's earlier lyrical outburst

---

[67] For discussions of how love is central to the play, see, for example, David G. Richards, *Georg Büchner's* Woyzeck: *A History of its Criticism* (Rochester: Camden House, 2001): '[t]he love between Woyzeck and Marie ... is the subject of the play' (p. 18) and '[o]pposed to the pessimism and nihilism expressed in the play is the positive value of Woyzeck's suffering and of the love he feels for Marie and their child' (p. 45).

[68] Susan Greene, 'Wozzeck and Marie: Outcasts in Search of an Honest Morality', *Opera Quarterly* (1985), 3/3, pp. 75–86, at p. 86.

[69] Sandra Gorse, *Operatic Subjects: The Evolution of Self in Modern Opera* (London: Associated University Presses, 2000), suggests that '[u]sing Hegel, perhaps, one could begin the argument about how love (desire for the Other subject's reflective engagement) represents a core attribute of subjectivity' (p. 31).

(albeit with different music). Conversely, Wozzeck quotes (in Act 2, scene 5) the whole-tone scale of one of Marie's lines, 'Einer nach dem Andern'. This quotation can also be seen as a reference to poverty, because it works as a reminder of her self-defence (in Act 2, scene 3) as Wozzeck quizzes her about the Drum Major: since Marie's reason for having the affair is that she hopes it might bring her a better life, the link to poverty remains clear.[70] But if there is shared musical material for the intersubjective space of poverty, which continues to be a reference point through 'Wir arme Leut', one of the key motifs of the opera, a specific 'love motif' or 'love theme' does not appear in the score.

For our focus on intersubjectivity, it will be especially illuminating to draw out those moments in the score where emotional or sexual tension is played out between Wozzeck and Marie. Berg based his libretto on the faulty and incomplete Franzos and Landau versions of the play, omitted some scenes, and did not include the scenes in which Wozzeck and Marie visit a fairground and see a show in a tent ('Fairground scene' and 'In the Tent').[71] Although still functioning as social critique with their atmosphere of pessimism, these scenes portray the relationship of Marie and Wozzeck in a more positive light in that they give additional insight into their existence as a couple, and could have served to introduce a more intimate mood within the opera. Instead, the opera contains only two instances when Wozzeck and Marie are alone: Act 2, scene 3, after Marie has had her affair with the Drum Major, and Act 3, scene 2, when Wozzeck kills her.[72] What is striking in these scenes is not just the absence of love, but the prevalence of lust. Act 2, scene 3 is infused with sensuality and existentially complex, and it introduces an intersubjective space in which both interaction and attention to 'outside', non-psychological phenomena and being-in-the-world are crucial. As Wozzeck meets Marie outside her house, he begins rambling about visual perception: while staring at her, he says he sees nothing, and that 'one should see, one should grasp it firmly with one's fingers'. Having just been subjected to taunting by the Captain and the Doctor about the affair, he is looking for evidence of 'sin and shame', but sees only

---

[70] On the musical link between Marie's two wishes as presented in Act 1, scene 5 (the scene of the sexual encounter), Andrew Clements writes: '[t]he ritornello theme, related to the opening of the march, represents Marie's desire both for the soldier and for a new, better life' (Clements, '*Wozzeck*', in *The New Grove Dictionary of Opera*, ed. Stanley Sadie, Oxford Music Online, at: http://www.oxfordmusiconline.com/subscriber/article/grove/music/O005360 (accessed 19 December 2010).

[71] For a summary of the complexities of the genesis of the play and the libretto, see Perle, *The Operas of Alban Berg*, pp. 22–91, and Appendix II (pp. 207–21), which reproduces the Landau edition (1909) in its entirety (and thereby the Franzos edition as well, albeit with the scenes in a different order).

[72] The reverse symmetry of 2 and 3 is potentially significant and could bear witness to Berg's obsession with the number 23 (a fixation discussed in correspondence with Schoenberg around 1915 when he conceived the first act of *Wozzeck*). Berg 'used retrogrades to depict the working of fate'. See Geoffrey Poole, 'Alban Berg and the Fateful Number', *Tempo*, New Series, 179 (Dec., 1991), p. 7.

her 'rosy mouth' (Example 5.2).[73] Like the Captain and the Doctor, he focuses on the 'two red lips', but does not share their aim to establish whether there might be a hair left on her lips (from the Drum Major).[74] Instead, Wozzeck's attention appears directed primarily by his own attraction to Marie, and therefore he observes no fault. It is clear that a distinctive intersubjective space is opening up. Wozzeck considers Marie an object, in a way not dissimilar to his own objectification in the Doctor's experiments.

The perception of Marie as an object introduces further moral complexity. In light of our quest for humanity and empathy in this opera, how are we to understand this, in a context in which Berg supposedly (according to Greene) makes a plea for 'a morality in which the supreme virtue is love'? The objectification is an important aspect of the intersubjective space of 'Wozzeck and Marie'. As for the moral complexity, Martha Nussbaum is surely correct to argue that 'all types of objectification are not equally objectionable' and require 'careful evaluation of context and circumstance'.[75] In the context of the framework presented here, the ethical dimension of 'Wozzeck and Marie' can be seen in a new light, contrasting with the view that prevails in the criticism on the opera and the idea of humanity, empathy and 'ideal love' that has been proposed. We can argue that objectification challenges these ethical ideals for three reasons in particular, borrowing from Nussbaum's theory, which proposes seven ways in which a person can be treated as an object.[76] The first is the 'denial of autonomy', which is evident in Wozzeck's treatment of Marie as an object, as he tries to see what he believes the Drum Major has seen in her. Second, although not a tool for his own purposes,[77] Wozzeck *does* give the idea just before he kills her that he has 'ownership' of Marie, as we shall see below. And, third, Wozzeck is not inquisitive in terms of how Marie *feels*, so could, in this respect, also be seen to a 'denial of subjectivity'. None of these examples of objectification is *necessarily* morally wrong, but in this particular case – because they are not

---

[73] Marie's red lips arguably also signify objectification and desire (both sexual and material) in Act 2, scene 1, where she looks at herself in a broken piece of mirror, admires the earrings given to her by the Drum Major and exclaims 'with sudden intensity': 'I have surely as red a mouth, as the noble, rich ladies who have their mirrors from floor up to ceiling, and all their handsome lords who snatch up their hands and kiss them; yet I am always so poor and wretched!' (b. 70–80).

[74] It is worth noting that love is mentioned in the exchange, but it remains tied to pleasure (and is part of the 'experimental tenet' of the conversation). The Captain exclaims: 'Oh, I too have known the pleasure that love can bestow!' (b. 227–230).

[75] Martha C. Nussbaum, *Sex and Social Justice* (Oxford: Oxford University Press, 1999), p. 218.

[76] These are: Instrumentality; Denial of Autonomy; Inertness; Fungibility; Violability; Ownership; Denial of Subjectivity. The list is not exhaustive and is dependent on context. Ibid., p. 218.

[77] This would correspond to 'Instrumentality' in Nussbaum's theory.

explicitly presented as aspects of a more complex and even loving relationship – they do become morally problematic and can be considered instead to be on a par with the other subject–object relationships in the narrative, including the overall, unequal power-relationship between individual and society. Above all, unlike the virtuous morality proposed by Greene, the apparent lack of balance between love and (objectifying) lust calls into question the actual existence of the former in the opera. This all but eliminates any potential catharsis for the characters themselves, and diminishes the opportunity for audience empathy, in comparison with the interlude's powerful effect.

Continuing the focus on sensuality (and phenomenology), in addition to the sense of sight (including the objectifying gaze), the sense of touch is also highlighted in the heated engagement between the lovers. Wozzeck 'rushes at [Marie]' (b. 394), and she exclaims the fateful words that arguably plant the idea for her murder in his mind: 'Better a knife blade in my heart, than lay a hand on me' (b. 395–396).[78] Finally, the existential aspect emerges as Marie leaves and Wozzeck declares ('in a frightened whisper'), 'Ah! man is an abyss, it's giddy looking into his inner depths. I'm giddy' before going offstage. But if both seeing and touch are represented in this scene, what do we hear? The music is primarily a compilation of material from previous scenes, in particular the military march and the seduction scene with the Drum Major (from Act 1, scenes 3 and 5 respectively), so although Marie proclaims her innocence and pretends not to understand Wozzeck's allegations, the music reveals her guilt.[79] To that extent music (again) carries meaning over and above language. For our purposes here, it is instructive that the entire scene is written in Berg's special type of parlando, 'to be carried out in the manner of a rhythmical declamation'. Berg wrote extensive instructions for this vocal technique in the score, stating that 'the difference between ordinary speech and speech that can be used in music should be clear'. And he set down in no uncertain terms that there should be '[n]o singing under any circumstances! Still, the pitches are to be stated and held exactly as indicated by the notes, but *held with the tone* of the speaking voice.'[80]

In respect of the stipulation that no singing is allowed, one logical inference could be that Berg's intention was to focus attention on the words in these parlando passages, and have the text take precedence over the music. This, however, was not the case. In his instructions, he was careful to direct the performer to the origin of his approach, namely the *Sprechstimme* employed in Schoenberg's *Pierrot*

---

[78] The phenomenological–sensual angle is continued in Act 2, scene 4, where smell is also represented: the *Narr* smells blood as he interacts with Wozzeck, and thereby forebodingly points to what is about to happen.

[79] Douglas Jarman has pointed out this evidence of guilt. *Alban Berg*, p. 35.

[80] Alban Berg, 'The Preparation and Staging of "Wozzeck"' (1930), in Perle, *The Operas of Alban Berg*, vol. 1, p. 205. As reproduced in Jarman, *Alban Berg*, p. 88, emphasis added.

lunaire (1912).[81] Although the detailed requirements often leave performers more confused than enlightened, what is important here is that Berg's parlando technique can be considered to be inherently musical – that is, emanating *from* the music and not a means by which the text should be given a higher status.[82] That it is musical is particularly important because this allows us to consider the vocal lines in terms of their tone and 'attunement', as in Heidegger's concept of *Stimmung*.

What happens to subjectivity in this scene (Act 2, scene 3)? And does empathy find an outlet in the music, thus serving a redeeming or cathartic function for the characters? It is difficult to see how, and our exploration of intersubjectivity here instead confirms criticisms that the interlude leaves the rest of the opera 'in quotes', while it serves as catharsis for its audience. No contrary evidence is to be found in the vocal lines, which could have helped articulate and support a similarly strong ethical message on behalf of its downtrodden characters.

The voice in this scene is a musical voice, but a voice predominantly devoid of lyricism. Without lyricism, Marie and Wozzeck are not granted an opportunity for self-expression. Indeed, the scene shows subjectivity weakened and subdued. And *because of* the message that is carried across in the interlude, and the impression that catharsis depends on tonality and Romantic expression, it is within the opera's intersubjective space that this is most sorely lacking. This omission is relevant from an ethical viewpoint. Had some form of lyricism been given to Wozzeck and Marie (even while remaining within Berg's post-tonal idiom) there might have

---

[81] In the preface to the score, Berg writes: 'The performance of the speaking voice which is called for in certain scenes of the opera (Act I, Scene 2; Act II, scene 3; Act III, scene 1 and 4) is to be carried out in the manner of a
r h y t h m i c a l   d e c l a m a t i o n
The foreword to Arnold Schoenberg's "Pierrot Lunaire" should be consulted as well as the instructions given in the score of his "Glückliche Hand"' (Berg, *Wozzeck*, revised by H.E. Apostel (1955) according to the final corrections and amendments left by the composer. English translation by Eric Blackall and Vida Harford (Universal Edition), p. x).

On the issue of the relation between the music and the text, Schoenberg specifies in the Preface: 'It is never the task of performers to recreate the mood and character of the individual pieces on the basis of the meaning of the words, but rather solely on the basis of the music. The extent to which the tone-painting-like rendering of the events and emotions of the text was important to the author is already found in the music. Where the performer finds it lacking, he should abstain from presenting something that was not intended by the author. He would not be adding, but rather detracting' (Arnold Schoenberg, 'Preface', *Pierrot Lunaire*, op. 21 (Los Angeles, Belmont Music Publishers, 1990).

[82] Of course, this does not mean that anything should be detracted from the words either, and Berg emphasizes elsewhere that 'this melodically, dynamically and rhythmically determined way of speaking not only offers one of the best means of ensuring that the words are understood ...; it has also enriched opera with a valuable means of expression, created from the purest musical sources, which ranging from the pitchless whispered word to the true *bel parlare* of broad speech melodies – offers a welcome addition and an attractive contrast to the sung word' (Alban Berg, 'A Lecture on "Wozzeck"', in Jarman, *Alban Berg*, pp. 160–61).

existed a level of empathy and care involving the characters themselves, within the world of the opera. There is *one* brief instance of vocal lyricism in the scene, providing an aural glimpse of the lyrical redemptive quality of the music. This is in the passage where Wozzeck first says (in parlando) 'You are beautiful', then sings a biblical quote, 'as sin' (*'wie die Sünde'*), before returning to speech, which leads to the emotional climax of anger (agitato) (Example 5.2).

Example 5.2   Alban Berg, *Wozzeck*, bars 381–385

This brief lyrical moment takes the listener back to the first scene of the opera where Wozzeck sang about God and morality, and made his first strong statement of subjectivity. In this later instance, however, the moment remains weak, and Wozzeck quickly succumbs to the discursive disruptions of the parlando style. The effect on the listener of this very brief moment is threefold: it emphasizes Wozzeck's subjectivity (and morality); it alludes to the 'other' ethical ideal of the opera (religion); and because it brings attention to the lyricism which might have been, it also potentially emphasizes a lack of romantic love between Wozzeck and Marie (and thus a further articulation of subjectivity). In the same way that the interlude is capable of negating the bleak detachment of the rest of the opera, calling out for emotional involvement, this moment is oddly out of sync with the rest of the scene, its tone out of place.

The halting nature of parlando articulates well the tension experienced by Wozzeck and Marie as they deal with his suspicion of adultery. Julian Johnson suggests that the appearance of the same vocal style in the tavern scene (Act 2, scene 4) creates a distancing effect as Wozzeck, removed from the action, watches the Drum Major and Marie dance, in that it suggests an 'operatic speechlessness' that silences self-expression.[83] But in scene 3, coupled with the largely disjointed orchestral accompaniment, this vocal expression does more than represent anxiety, unease and a lack of subjectivity. Instead of an ideal love, the music is associated with mere physical attraction. While adding to the erotic theme which is already present in the text, it does this through *absence* in two ways: through the lack of a love theme or leitmotif by which romantic interest could have been expressed; and the denial of a lyrical expression of love in Wozzeck and Marie's vocal lines.

With regard to interaction, engagement and emotional articulation, it is interesting to note that Berg chose to give Wozzeck the only legato phrase in this scene (still in *Sprechstimme*) just before the only sung phrase: 'But see, you have such a rosy mouth, such a rosy mouth' (b. 381–382). Supported by a unison line involving a solo second violin (played pizzicato to offset the legato of the voice), piano or pianissimo dynamic markings in the other instruments, a temporary calando halting the flow and a swift espressivo figure in the first violin at the beginning, this phrase could potentially be articulated in performance with considerable tenderness, resulting in an audible expression of care. But instead of such a tone being realized in this passage, most performances opt for a hint of sarcasm and bitterness. The result is that the music (with the text) confirms 'Marie-as-object' and communicates Wozzeck's suspicion. To be sure, Berg has not left the performer with much space in which to convey care and empathy here, and it remains a very vague glimpse that is quickly and perhaps too easily passed by.

The only other scene where Wozzeck and Marie are alone is the scene of Marie's murder, Act 3, scene 2. Further to our 'quest for love' in *Wozzeck*, it is notable that the critic Andrew Clements suggests that in this scene, 'Wozzeck tells Marie that he loves her'.[84] But Wozzeck's vocal effusion appears instead to be a repeat of the lust (and frustration) from Act 2, again focusing on her lips: 'Ah! How your lips are sweet to touch, Marie! All Heaven I would give, and eternal bliss, if I still could sometimes kiss you so. But yet I may not!' (b. 86–94, Example 5.3). It is a passionate phrase, molto cantible for the first sentence and

---

[83] Johnson, *Berg's Operas*, p. 223. A related point is that the tavern scene can be seen to confirm further Wozzeck's objectification of Marie, as he continues to watch, describe and not interact.

[84] Clements, '*Wozzeck*'.

Example 5.3   Alban Berg, *Wozzeck*, bars 85–96

Example 5.3 (continued)

rubato for the second, and the score instruction is: 'he bends over her, in deadly earnest'. Nevertheless, Marie arguably remains here an object of erotic desire, and although Wozzeck alludes again to God by mentioning Heaven, there seems to be no redemption on offer for her. To put the point bluntly: without love, there is no forgiveness, and 'Marie-as-object' can be discarded. If Wozzeck cannot have her, nobody else should have her either, as he declares just before he kills her.[85] Despite the few glimpses that have served to remind us of what might have been, Berg's music effectively denies subjectivity to his unfortunate characters. Perhaps this is

---

[85] Incidentally, the way in which both the Drum Major and Wozzeck to an extent treat Marie as an object of exchange, as well as the link between her and religion in the opera brings to mind what Lacan said of 'the effective position of woman in feudal society. She is ... nothing more than a correlative of the functions of social exchange, the support of a certain number of goods and of symbols of power. She is essentially identified with a social function that leaves no room for her person or her own liberty, except with reference to her religious rights' (Jacques Lacan, *The Ethics of Psychoanalysis 1959–60*, ed. Jacques-Alain Miller, trans. Dennis Porter, vol. 7: *The Seminar of Jacques Lacan* (London: Routledge, 1992), p. 147).

one way in which he supports his socio-political point: namely that the 'poor folk' are unable to transcend the limitations of their existence and attain an articulate, lyrical form of self-expression.

A final, fateful misunderstanding in the exchange between the two characters serves as a fitting reminder of the Captain's failure to understand Wozzeck in Act 1, and this brings us full circle in our discussion of language and music. Wozzeck, noticing that Marie is shivering, whispers, 'You, who shiver will freeze no more in the cold morning dew'. 'What are you saying?' asks Marie, and Wozzeck replies 'Nix' ('Nothing') (b. 96). This is followed by a 'long silence' (marked in the score) before the horrible act that ensues. As a particularly potent example of 'silence as meaningful articulation', this musical silence indicates that words are no longer important. *Stimmung* takes over, and words from here on will fail. When Marie notices that Wozzeck is shivering and asks 'What now?', it is too late. He no longer answers her questions, but instead continues to reflect on how he cannot have her (a thought revealed by his vocal line), and subsequently enacts the deed that will prevent anyone else from having her, too. Finally, returning to the issue of tone, the *tone* of 'Nix' is arguably the same as that of 'Todt!', the single exclamation made by Wozzeck just after the murder (b. 106, Example 5.4). These words are uttered pianissimo and piano respectively, and although both are spoken to a single held note, they are given slightly different note lengths: 'Nix' two crochets tied together, opening up towards anticipation, silence and what will follow, 'Todt!' a quaver tied to a crotchet, and with an exclamation mark, thereby more conclusive. But their *tone* gives the same impression, of an absence of feeling, a void, nothingness. Both can be regarded as mere statements of facts, befitting a monotonous voice. It is apparent to the listener that Wozzeck's voice here becomes musically 'inarticulate': if the voice can be lyrical and vibrant, supporting subjectivity and humanity, it can equally – by omission or lack of these musical qualities – express a loss of self and a lack of care.

Example 5.4   Alban Berg, *Wozzeck*, bar 106

From our excursion into the intersubjective space of the relationship between Wozzeck and Marie, it appears that this is not the location for an expression of love in this opera, and certainly does not represent the ethical ideal of 'the supreme virtue' of love.[86] This section has also shed more light on the ethical repercussions of the interlude. While not entirely absent from the score, other moments of lyricism are very brief and remain weak in comparison; in the end they serve to confirm the lack of love, of care, and subjectivity on an intersubjective level.

'Wozzeck and Marie': the child

It is in the final intersubjective space of 'The Child' that we are offered a potential articulation of love, and thereby the possibility that the opera does not entirely negate redemption for the characters *within* the operatic world they inhabit. The child arguably binds Marie and Wozzeck together, but how strong is this connection and how strongly does this intersubjective space affect our perceptions of an expression of humanity? One relevant point is the child's actual parentage. Descriptions of the opera vary in their accounts of whether this really is Wozzeck's child: in the list of characters in the score, he is described as 'Marie's boy'; when together with Marie and Wozzeck he becomes 'the boy' or 'the child'; when alone with Marie she calls him 'my child'; and, in the first scene, the Captain refers to him as Wozzeck's child. Only once in the score, just after Marie's lullaby (b. 452), does Wozzeck call the child his own, but he does so ambiguously, as we shall see below. Scholars and critics are understandably confused by this uncertainty. Clements refers to 'the child' in connection with the moment after the lullaby, but for the final scene he makes reference to 'Marie's child' and 'her child'.[87] Both Johnson and Kerman call the boy 'Marie's child' or 'her child'; Taruskin writes 'their child' and 'Wozzeck's and Marie's little son';[88] and Jarman, in his interpretation of the ending of the opera, comments that 'the tragedy is about to be re-enacted with Wozzeck's child'.[89] Given that Georg Büchner specifies in the play that the boy (Christian) is Woyzeck's and Marie's, the lack of clarity on this point in Berg's opera is perplexing.

For our purposes here, the parentage of the child matters because if he is not Wozzeck's child and not perceived to be, then he has the potential to upset the intersubjective space of 'Wozzeck and Marie' and perhaps thereby deal a further blow to any ethical aim that the opera might support on the intersubjective level. The ambiguity can weaken their connection in two ways. First, it can cast doubt on

---

[86] The only noticeable instance of a 'lyrical Marie and Wozzeck moment' is so faint and brief that it has been called a 'lyrical apostrophe' by Johnson. It occurs in Act 1, scene 4 as Wozzeck calls out to Marie (who is not present): 'Ach! Ach, Marie' (b. 538–540). See Johnson, *Berg's Operas*, p. 228.

[87] Clements, '*Wozzeck*'.

[88] Taruskin, *The Oxford History of Western Music*, Vol. 4, pp. 513 and 517 respectively.

[89] Jarman, *Alban Berg*, p. 66.

Marie's moral credentials. Could *anyone* have fathered the child, even during the nearly three years that Wozzeck and Marie have been together? (The child's age remains unknown in both the opera and the play.) Kerman argues that Marie is a 'badly inconsistent character' in Berg's hands, and his description of the character is scathing: 'Shallow, unintelligent, sentimental, she has been living unmarried with Wozzeck for years, and makes a practice of sleeping with soldiers … How seriously can we possibly take her morning-after repentance?'[90] We may disagree, but the interpretation is certainly plausible, and not knowing for sure that the child is Wozzeck's does not encourage our empathy towards Marie.

The second way in which the ambiguity may weaken their relationship relates to the deeper connection between the child and love in the opera. Writing about the original play by Büchner, Greene has suggested that the child can be regarded as crucial for the love between Marie and Wozzeck:

> [Woyzeck] loves his younger, more sensual Marie deeply and passionately, a fact that is amplified by the invention of their child in the play.[91]

Apart from noting that the boy reminds Marie of her 'sinful liaison',[92] Greene does not explore the role of the child in the opera, and it is far from easy to extract from her account how the boy is an expression of love. It is when we turn to the music, however, that some support is offered. Johnson identifies in Marie's lullaby to the child (Act 1, scene 3) 'a utopian quality of calm and consolation', which is 'one of the very few expressions of love in the whole opera'.[93] Berg links Wozzeck, Marie and the child as a family in the sonata form of the orchestral introduction to Act 2, creating an entire scene in which the three are closely and, in his own words, 'organically related'.[94] If, in both examples, we encounter a family-oriented love, this could certainly be seen to add to the love potentially inherent in the intersubjective space of 'Wozzeck and Marie'. But the existence of this love depends to an extent on whether we consider the boy to be Wozzeck's child. It does not help, for example, that Berg again refers to 'Marie's child' in the lecture in which he explains the musical closeness between the three.[95] And Wozzeck is in a neurotic haze at the end of the scene with the lullaby – the only point in the opera when he says 'my child' – because he does so 'absently' and

---

[90] Kerman, *Opera as Drama*, pp. 228–29.
[91] Greene, 'Wozzeck and Marie', p. 76.
[92] Ibid. p. 82.
[93] Johnson, *Berg's Operas*, p. 222. Johnson points to a 'similar moment of lyricism' in the fifth of her seven of variations in Act 3, scene 1.
[94] Berg, 'A Lecture on *Wozzec*k', pp. 162–63. For an analytical exploration of some of the less audible discernible musical relations between Wozzeck and Marie, see also Janet Schmalfeldt, *Berg's Wozzeck: Harmonic Language and Dramatic Design* (New Haven, CT: Yale University Press, 1983).
[95] Berg, 'A Lecture on *Wozzeck*', for example p. 162: 'Marie, her child, and Wozzeck.'

'without looking at it' (according to the stage directions), and is merely echoing Marie who has just exclaimed 'Your child!' as she implores him not to ignore the boy. In other words, the lullaby's brief musical expression of warmth and love struggles in the already fragile intersubjective space of 'Wozzeck and Marie'.

The child is given minimal operatic voice, but this does not result in another instance of 'operatic speechlessness'. His voice may remain largely unsung, but it is not therefore unheard, because it is around him that pivotal ethical moments in the opera occur: Marie's 'Lullaby'; her song in Act 3, scene 1, in which she reads a passage from the Bible (about Mary Magdalen), expresses feelings of guilt as she looks at the boy, sings to him an ominous song about dead parents, and prays for forgiveness; and the final moment at the end of the opera, when the child receives the news of his mother's death (not, we note, of Wozzeck's). The first two of these three moments can be considered redemptive, because they add to ethical ideals about love and religion respectively, but we have seen how this redemption can be challenged by narrative inconsistencies or weaknesses.

As for the third moment, the child remains pivotal, but it is not clear exactly how the moment (and its music) will act in a redemptive capacity. For reasons already explored, scholars have tended to interpret the open-ended conclusion of the opera as a sign of further injustice to come: the child is left alone in an unkind world where the scenario of being poor and wretched is bound to repeat itself. As we have seen, the overwhelming emotion of the D minor interlude offers listeners a catharsis, but also risks leaving them perplexed, since the contrast of the final scene can seem shockingly detached. In Kerman's words:

> The epilogue following the interlude changes the mood strongly from the hysteria of the rest of the opera and the sentimentality of the interlude itself. Cold and entirely normal, it is the most naturalistic scene in the opera: children chanting a singing-game not in the disjunct chromatic style of Wozzeck's agony, but in the off-key tones of ordinary group unmusicality.[96]

When given the news of his mother's death by the other children (speaking), the boy does not reply, and instead carries on playing with his (imaginary) hobby horse, before joining the other children (who have left the stage before him) to see the dead body. On his way out, he chants 'Hopp Hopp' in a perfect fourth, to accompany his imaginary ride. From an ethical perspective, the child can be regarded as the 'ultimate alterity'. He is the 'other other' in the intersubjective space shared by Wozzeck and Marie, in which respect and responsibility for otherness are truly tested. The main weakness here is not the lack of voice, but an ambiguity with regard to love. The musical and dramatic blurring of family relations do not help establish a place for the child in any love shared by Wozzeck and Marie. If granted this crucial role as *their* child, the boy would become not only a key figure for pivotal moments in the opera, and thus a narrative voice or a

---

[96] Kerman, *Opera as Drama*, pp. 232–33.

teller offering a different story, but also a character providing life and hope beyond the end of the opera, as a potential symbol of justice to come.

Not all readings of the message of the opera are negative. In support of his claim about the redemptive qualities of the music, Johnson draws on the D minor interlude to suggest a more positive reading of the ethical substance of the opera, including the ending:

> Even the children are heartless in this world, as the closing lines of the opera underline. And, yet, for all that, the D minor interlude of Act III is also for them. The evocation of 'Wir arme Leut' in the orchestra is not a lament for Wozzeck and Marie alone but also for Andres, Margret, the apprentices, the drinkers and dancers in the tavern, the soldiers, and even the Captain and the Doctor. It is a lament for a world at odds with itself.[97]

In other words, echoing Adorno's view of the objective quality of the opera (including the characters and music), the redemptive function is for all the characters and the world that the opera portrays. Certainly, Berg's compositional treatment of the 'Wir Arme Leut' theme confirms this reading, since it functions as a latent voice throughout the work (including in the murder scene), coming to the fore in the interlude. However, unlike our venture into intersubjectivity in this chapter, Johnson's point (as well as Adorno's) remains tied to the idea of subjectivity as a protest against a collective:

> Through his music, Berg ... constructs subjectivity not simply as the victim of social conditions but as a force of resistance to them. The category itself is the strongest and most profound political gesture of Berg's operas.[98]

But, as the above discussion has shown, because of Berg's resort to tonality and Romantic expression in the interlude and the weak connections on intersubjective levels throughout the opera, it is possible to argue that the gesture of subjectivity remains a fragile one. This fragility is itself world-disclosive in that it exposes an ethical point pertinent to the interwar context, in which similar concerns emerged in the intellectual climate. For Heidegger, for example, in his aim to abolish the gap between subject and object (thereby participating in what was an essential goal of German Idealism, namely to reconcile the individual with the collective), he *subsumed* the individual under the collective; the everyday individual *Dasein* is always and necessarily lost in the 'they' (*das Man*).[99] To that extent, Berg's

---

[97] Johnson, 'Berg's Operas', p. 229.

[98] Ibid., p. 230.

[99] Martin Heidegger, *Being and Time*, trans. J. Macquarrie and E. Robinson (Oxford: Basil Blackwell, 1962). As Heidegger writes: '*Dasein*, as everyday Being-with-one-another, stands in subjection to Others. It itself is not; its Being has been taken away by the Others. *Dasein*'s everyday possibilities of Being are for the Others to dispose of as they please.

approach clearly offers 'objective truth' (Adorno) in terms of the modernist narrative, and thereby (at least implicitly) protest and resistance.

Conclusion

Our focus on ethics, intersubjectivity and voice has allowed a new narrative level of *Wozzeck* to emerge. In conclusion, we return to the impact of the interlude and its ethical ramifications. If the interlude works as a lament, it does so precisely because it draws on a Romantic idiom that would make this effect possible. But the interlude presents a challenge related to musical integrity: the humanity that is so obvious in the interlude is lacking from the rest of the opera (as both Taruskin and Kerman also argue, in different ways). So, would Berg's ethical point about social injustice not have been stronger had the atonal idiom been maintained without this Romantic interjection? As we saw above, Kerman's observation about the gap between the drama as perceived on- and offstage found further support in our analysis of the intersubjective space of 'Wozzeck and Marie'. Because the interlude is so overwhelming, the already weak intersubjective connections we unravelled via our focus on voice only become weaker. Furthermore, on this basis, the final scene of the opera arguably reveals most of all the obvious gap that Berg has at this stage succeeded in magnifying via the music, namely that between the (presumably) middle-class audience and the lower-class characters. The bluntness of the ending of the opera makes the contrast particularly clear. In the final analysis, the catharsis remains at a distance from the drama, and therefore *Wozzeck* could be said to offer brutal realism for its characters and cathartic romanticism for its audience. The effect is twofold: the characters are left to their fate, having not inspired empathy through their predominantly atonal idiom, while the audience is conversely granted a way out from the disturbing content and narrative. As the interlude provides listeners an opportunity for emotional release, it simultaneously deconstructs the ethical message of the opera. The communication of social injustice that Berg saw as his main achievement is neatly packaged, wrapped up in the velvet cloth of romanticized redemption and thus, in some way, may actually serve to neutralize opposition to forms of oppression in modern society and the desire to alleviate social inequality. Given our exploration here, it might be fair to suggest that had the conventionally expressive quality of the D minor interlude been omitted from the opera, Berg's message about 'the vast social implications of

---

These Others, moreover, are not *definite* others. On the contrary, any Other can represent them ... One belongs to the Others oneself and enhances their power. The Others whom one thus designates in order to cover up the fact of one's belonging to them essentially oneself, are those who proximally and for the most part "*are there*" in everyday Being-with-one-another. The "who" is not this one, not that one, not oneself, not some people, and not the sum of them all. The "who" is the neuter, the "*they*"' (p. 164).

the work' (with all the necessary frustration, fear, horror and lack of love) would be felt more directly and therefore more uncomfortably, leaving audiences (then and now) with further unresolved ethical questions to ponder.

Chapter 6
Engagement

Marcel Cobussen and Nanette Nielsen

> Thus experience of one's own body runs counter to the reflective procedure which detaches subject and object from each other, and which gives us only the thought about the body, or the body as an idea, and not the experience of the body or the body in reality.
>
> Maurice Merleau-Ponty, *Phenomenology of Perception*, p. 231.

Recapitulation

Some of the questions that recur most often throughout this book include: what is or what can be the significance of music with regard to ethical and moral issues? Is it possible to cast new light on ethics and morality through music? Can music *as music* – that is, primarily regarded as a sonic event, an audible process, rather than a fixed object – contribute to ethical positioning?

So far, we have explored several strategies by which to make plausible the idea of a musical contribution both to the discourse concerned with ethics and to concrete ethical behaviour. Music can teach us to listen more carefully; it can make us receptive and responsive to the voices of others and to the voice of otherness, to other voices and to the otherness of the voice, and thus not only to alternative messages, opinions and ideas, but also to subtle timbres, tonalities, *Stimmungen*, atmospheres and associations which might influence and regulate human action. Attentive listening means to allow otherness to enter us, to be able and willing to relinquish our usual defence mechanisms that all too often lead us to exclude that which appears strange to us.

When scholars attempt to offer ethical criticisms of music it becomes clear how music *resists* certain approaches, while inviting others. Discourse on music is saturated with ethical possibility: music can be deeply intertwined with the narrative of our moral lives, can inspire interaction and engagement; and the more we allow our various discourses to reflect its ethical multiplicity, the more justice we are able to do to various facets of music. While surpassing language and revealing the limitations of essentialist interpretation and logical argument, music also resists reduction to an ineffable object, and *demands* the responsible and responsive engagement of critical agents who commit themselves to explanation.

From the perspective of a musician, music might be the way to explore and develop certain kinds of interactions which perhaps are blocked in other parts of our lives. Especially in so-called free improvised music, the common tension between an individual and a collective responsibility for the well-being of the other is *aufgehoben*, sublated. Neither accepting an existentialistic solipsism nor resorting to predetermined agreements about how to act and live together, free improvisations are able to introduce forms of interaction that occupy a space between these two ethical philosophies. Furthermore, this music might lead us in a direction towards a more agonistic mode of hospitality which is conducive to a process of self-overcoming.

Although we must accept the fact that music is often used for controlling and disciplining bodies, for creating identity at the expense of susceptibility and openness to the other, even though the sound of music is potentially an instrument of power, regulation and violence, music can also contribute more positively to moral and ethical discourses. This is because music is able to challenge – explicitly and/or inexplicitly – the prevailing Western notion of a free and autonomous individual who is ultimately responsible for her or his own judgements and actions. Through music we gain insight into the *relational* subject, replacing the autonomous, authentic, rational subject that traditionally constitutes the necessary precondition for ethical claims. Ethics is not the result of subjective considerations, but comes into existence through continuous and complex intersubjective interactions between bodies, minds and environments.

Through voice, music provides a rich opportunity for clarifying and responding to particular ethical situations, challenging existing norms and offering further understanding of existing power structures. As it mediates between phenomenology and hermeneutics, the musical voice can be a specific way for individuals to articulate their being-in-the-world, thus also revealing music's world-disclosive properties. Again, by resisting privileging contexts (and concepts such as subject and object), the musical voice is able to express a demand for intersubjectivity because it tends to function as a form of mediation and communication. Once this is acknowledged, a powerful analytical tool presents itself for the ethical criticism of music.

Appassionata

As key ethical factors, we have pointed to the ability of music to encourage interaction and engagement, to prompt associations and memories, to invite moral reflection in complex ways, to reveal and shape the world anew, and to mould our subjectivities. An example from literature may cast further light on the way in which music can – on intuitive, non-intellectualized levels – challenge existing and embedded moral thinking, reorientate us after the decline of the 'grand narratives', and even reflect on geopolitical conflicts. In this concluding chapter, building on the approaches proposed in this book, we come full circle by reflecting again on listening as a central theme that has pervaded the pages from beginning to end.

In Eva Hoffman's novel *Appassionata* the principal character, Isabel Merton, a renowned concert pianist, falls victim to intense uncertainty with respect to the ethical values of classical music when she is carried away by the political ideology of her new boyfriend Anzor, a Chechen freedom fighter. After discovering that her lover is willing to use violence to achieve his aims and is plotting an attack, she breaks off the relationship. Her sensitive character, formed by a life dedicated to nineteenth-century Romantic music, cannot accept that their relationship has been used primarily as a cover for such objectionable activity. The seemingly autonomous and unassailable world of classical music, its alleged pristine beauty, is threatened by her encounter with political reality and moral zealotry. This becomes even more concrete when, several days after the love affair has abruptly ended, a bomb explodes in a Barcelonan venue during one of Merton's performances. Although it is not clear whether the Chechens are behind the attack, she begins to suffer from severe depression and no longer wishes to practise or perform. The attack has demonstrated to her that music no longer has any usefulness or urgency; performing classical music and attending concerts has become a snobbish pastime for people untouched by worldly abuses. Beauty cannot heal or hide injustice and amorality, and it is no alternative for the fight and right for freedom, food and self-determination. 'How could she have fallen for it, when what's going on outside is screaming pain and violence?'[1]

> She used to think that what mattered was the difference between piano and pianissimo, between a crescendo which ascends into triumph, and one which signals calm resolution. Instead, she should have been paying attention to the differences between a massacre and an act of war, mowing down people out of despair or out of conviction; mass killing perpetrated by deliberately marching armies, and carnage perpetrated in orgiastic mayhem. What use is her kind of knowledge, in the face of this? The exquisite nuances of Schubert, the hypertrophied involutions of Strauss, the whole super-subtle history of the soul? One thudding sound renders them null and void. Obsolete.[2]

Merton cancels the remainder of her European concert tour and locks herself up in a white-carpeted apartment in Marseille, without music, without any access to news events, without any desire for reflection.

And then, one evening, after months of darkness, ideas about the role music can play in human life return to her. Listening to Mozart's *Requiem* on a small radio, she slowly begins to realize that, compared to Mozart's effort 'to shape the energies which course through us and sometimes tear us apart',[3] the bomb attack was ineffectual and stupid. The strength of music, its contribution to ethics and morality, is in the 'molding of our forces till they are no longer brutal'.[4] Listening to music turns out to be Isabel Merton's access to tenderness:

---

[1] Eva Hoffman, *Appassionata* (New York: Other Press, 2009), p. 214.
[2] Ibid., p. 216–17.
[3] Ibid., p. 250.
[4] Ibid.

'What else is there to feel for the world, except tenderness? For its adventitious loveliness, its soft tissue, its utter fragility? It is what's left after the fear and rage are gone. Always justified rage, always unjustified tenderness.'[5]

Music, for Merton, honours the world not for its goodness, but for its Being. She listens again to Beethoven's late quartets and hears them as a form of defiance against the hard mercilessness of the world. Not solace, but antidote. 'Here's mercy which comes after anger, here's tenderness which transforms rage. Here is human force, contained in patterns so intricate and at the same time pure that they intimate a knowledge yet unknown':[6] this is how she interprets her listening experiences.

Isabel Merton's thoughts after her period of depression show some resemblance to Plato's observation that music's power to touch and move the human mind, soul and body should not be underestimated. But that which Plato warned against turns out to be the source of redemption for Merton: music's beauty forms a strong counterpart to the omnipresent violence, pain and suffering of daily life. Not as a refuge, as a comfortable place to withdraw from the cruel reality and to bury one's head in the sand (as Adorno would claim about particular bourgeois perceptions of music), but as a genuine alternative perspective on the world. Listening to music, for Merton, provides the opportunity to relate to everyday events, activities and things differently – that is, not indifferently (this is closely related to the view of Elaine Scarry, discussed in 'Listening'). These events, activities and things become something special, something worth living and caring for. In Merton's new musical experiences, in her newly engaged listening, and in her rediscovery of ethical values through music, Heidegger's ideas on art can be heard to echo: through art, things lose their ordinariness, and this 'discovery' obliges us to care.[7]

Towards an immanent ethics

If we find some insight, some truth even, in Merton's reflections, it may be the recognition that music offers no alternative within a sphere that is dominated and defined by moral doctrines, ethical ideals and political ideologies. Music seems to be most active and effective on another plane – often overlooked by Western logocentrism – which constantly traverses this domain.

Merton's renewed contact with music deconstructs an anthropocentric morality which has, as its consequence, a situation in which humans become objects in programmes and scripts, at the disposal of a higher logic (capital,

---

[5] Ibid., p. 253.

[6] Ibid., p. 260.

[7] See, for example, Martin Heidegger, 'The Origin of the Work of Art', trans. A. Hofstadter, in Heidegger, *Poetry, Language, Thought* (New York: Harper & Row, 1971), pp. 17–81.

state, community and so on). Instead she (re)discovers through music an ethics where being may be encountered, an openness, in Heidegger's words, towards the Being of beings. Through music, she realizes that 'man is not the lord of beings. Man is the shepherd of Being.'[8] Through music, she becomes attuned to Being and beings again and gets rid of pretensions to know how reality *really* works; these pretensions only impose a *certain* truth upon others as well as upon reality itself. Music teaches her that truth does not exist as a series of conclusive judgements; rather, through music, she understands that thought does not possess such a foundation, that we can never completely grasp the world. (Merton could be said to be in agreement with Taruskin's point which we recounted in 'Discourse': 'We'll never know all we need to know. But we must try not to believe all we need to believe.'[9]) The high-handed notion of 'knowledge is power' should therefore be exchanged for a more compassionate and tolerant contact with the world. Echoed in Merton's thoughts is Gianni Vattimo's *pensiero debole* ('weak thinking') – a thinking permeated by modesty, acknowledging 'a knowledge yet unknown'.

But perhaps even more important, experiencing music as it is discussed in *Appassionata* offers a perspective on an ethics 'beyond Good and Evil', namely an immanent ethics or an ethics without morality, as proposed by thinkers such as Spinoza, Nietzsche and Deleuze. In 'Listening' we saw that Alain Badiou starts his book *L'éthique* (*Ethics*) with the ancient Greek definition of ethics as the search for a good way of being or a wise course of action. However, precisely what this 'good' is remains unclear; it seems to be changing all the time, depending on particular situations and perspectives. Badiou therefore argues in favour of *an ethic* at work within singular processes. He rejects a morality defined as a set of universal rules that consist in judging and constraining actions and intentions by relating them to transcendent values. In that sense, Badiou seems to be following Nietzsche, who claimed in *Zur Genealogie der Moral* (*The Genealogy of Morals*) that 'we need a critique of moral values'.[10] Instead of transcendental principles, such as the opposition between Good and Evil, Nietzsche proposes a truly genetic and productive immanent ethics, in which our actions are repeatedly measured, tested and judged against one another. This idea is taken up by Deleuze, whose

---

[8] Martin Heidegger, *Martin Heidegger: Basic Writings*, trans. and ed. D. Farrell Krell (San Francisco, CA: Harper Collins, 1993), p. 221.

[9] Richard Taruskin, 'Material Gains: Assessing Susan McClary' (review), *Music & Letters*, 90/3 (2009), p. 461.

[10] Friedrich Nietzsche, *The Genealogy of Morals*, trans. H.B. Samuel (New York: Dover Publications, 2003), p. 5. Not surprisingly, Nietzsche's problem with morality, with this system of judgement, stems from his aversion to (institutionalized) religion. In Nietzsche's view, man is saddled with an infinite (and therefore unpayable) debt to the divine. It is this debtor–creditor relationship, comparable to the master–slave relationship, that lies at the origin of the traditional, transcendental ethico-moral realm and which condemns us to servitude without end.

other main source of inspiration is Spinoza. In *Qu'est-ce que la philosophie?* (*What is Philosophy?*), Deleuze and Guattari claim that:

> ... there is not the slightest reason for thinking that modes of existence need transcendent values by which they could be compared, selected, and judged relative to one another. On the contrary, there are only immanent criteria. A possibility of life is evaluated through itself in the movements it lays out and the intensities it creates on a plane of immanence: what is not laid out or created is rejected. A mode of existence is good or bad, noble or vulgar, complete or empty, independently of Good and Evil or any transcendent value: there are never any criteria other than the tenor of existence, the intensification of life.[11]

The potent danger of this immanent ethics is obvious: without transcendence or universal criteria, there is the threat of pure subjectivism or relativism. Or, as Daniel Smith summarizes, 'How can one evaluate modes of existence using criteria that are immanent to the mode itself without thereby abandoning any basis for comparative evaluation?'[12] To tackle this problem, Deleuze launches a three-pronged attack that takes as its standard 'the intensification of life' – that is, the possession and reinforcement of power.

The first stage is marked by the question of how a mode of existence, understood as a way of being or a lifestyle, determines how we act, think and feel. Deleuze, following Nietzsche and Spinoza, focuses primarily on the body and its potentialities. Bodies are composed as assemblages, aggregates of parts constituted by distinctive relations. They are defined by their capacity, their power to affect or be affected by other bodies. My power is augmented when a body encounters mine and enters into composition with it; conversely, my power diminishes when another body threatens my coherence or even destroys me. Hence the first question aims at gaining an insight into both the nourishing and the contaminating substances of a given being – that is, in the degrees of power and the different ways of affecting and being affected.[13]

The second stage deals with the question of how a mode of existence is evaluated. It is the question of knowing whether a mode of existence can deploy its power, whether it can increase its power of action to the point where it achieves maximum capability. Modes are evaluated in terms of their 'tenor of existence'. What an ethics of immanence will criticize, then, is anything that separates a mode of existence from its power of action.[14] This ethics favours affectivities with the

---

[11] Gilles Deleuze and Félix Guattari, *What is Philosophy?*, trans. H. Tomlinson and G. Burchell (New York: Columbia University Press, 1994), p. 74.

[12] Daniel W. Smith, 'The Place of Ethics in Deleuze's Philosophy', in Eleanor Kaufman and Kevin Jon Heller (eds), *Deleuze and Guattari: New Mappings in Politics, Philosophy, and Culture* (Minneapolis: University of Minnesota Press, 1998), p. 253.

[13] Ibid., p. 260.

[14] Ibid., p. 263.

potential to make a body pass from lesser to greater degrees of power, thereby better exercising its own propensities to affect and be affected.

The third stage poses the question if and how modes of existence are capable of affecting themselves in order to transform themselves. In other words, how are new modes produced?[15] Here, Deleuze is referring to loci of experimentation which one cannot know in advance; one can only be attentive to the unknown, to forms of resistance and destruction that are capable of creating new modes of existence.[16]

How, then, does this immanent ethics relate to music? Or, better, how is it that music can put us on the track of such an immanent ethics? Let's return to *Appassionata* and Isabel Merton's experiences once more. Under the spell of the Chechen freedom fighter Anzor, Merton tragically loses her contact with the music that once was so dear to her; the power to affect and be affected diminishes and even seems to vanish completely. Anzor's influence is the wrong medicine, poisoning her musical body. However, this love affair – working as both poison and cure – seemed also necessary to open the door for a recovery of music's ability to affect her. Merton (re)discovers an almost transpersonal intensity, a passage from one experiential state of her body to another, leading to an augmentation in her body's capacity to act, to act musically.[17] Her relationship with music has changed; she has learnt to listen to music differently. She regains music, but she and the music have entered a new relationship: music means something different to Merton now, and, consequently, this changes her too.

From immanence to engagement

Let us move now from Eva Hoffman's fiction to our own musical fantasies – 'fantasies', because a work is realized through our listening, 'not as a positivist ideal, but as a contingent interpretation', in the words of Salomé Voegelin.[18] In *Listening to Noise and Silence*, Voegelin, a sound artist and writer, argues that because sound unfolds over time, it cannot be examined as an artefact but only as a dynamic and continual construction. To listen means to share time and space with the sound source. Voegelin writes:

---

[15] In *What is Philosophy?*, Deleuze and Guattari give the example of believing in God. A new mode is not so much created by someone not believing in God any more, since he would still belong to the old plane as negative moment. Giving birth to a new mode or existence could, for example, be a belief in the possibilities of movements and intensities of the world. Deleuze and Guattari call this 'the empiricist conversion' (pp. 74–75).

[16] Smith, 'The Place of Ethics', p. 264.

[17] See also Gilles Deleuze and Félix Guattari, *A Thousand Plateaus*, trans. B. Massumi (Minneapolis: University of Minnesota Press, 1987), p. xvi.

[18] Salomé Voegelin, *Listening to Noise and Silence: Towards a Philosophy of Sound Art* (New York: Continuum, 2010), p. 17.

> ... [this production] involves the listener as intersubjectively constituted in perception, while producing the very thing he perceives, and both, the subject and the work, thus generated concomitantly, are as transitory as each other ... The auditory object does not precede listening; rather, it is generated in the listening practice.[19]

Thus – as we have encountered several times in this book – a thinking which takes listening as its starting-point immediately questions the notion of a transcendental, a priori subjectivity and objectivity: rather, the one constitutes the other. Listening produces music as a 'subjective objectivity'. Or, to relate it to the vocabulary used above, both the listening subject and the heard object or event at once affect and are affected by each other. And in Voegelin's words:

> Every sensory interaction relates back to us not the object/phenomenon perceived, but that object/phenomenon filtered, shaped and produced by the sense employed in its perception. At the same time this sense outlines and fills the perceiving body, which in its perception shapes and produces his sensory self. Whereby the senses employed are always already ideologically and aesthetically determined, bringing their own influence to perception, the perceptual object and the perceptual subject.[20]

What seems to be an ontological discussion about the existential differences between 'seeing' and 'hearing' – the first necessarily taking place at a distance, detached, from a meta-position, the second always relying on experiences, immersion and (therefore) the sublation of hierarchically ordered dualisms – also acquires an ethical dimension. Voegelin starts her book with a quote from Adorno: 'The point should not be to have absolutely correct, irrefutable, watertight conditions – for they inevitably boil down to tautologies, but insights which cause the question of their justness to judge itself.'[21] Instead of seeking after 'the Truth' (of music), both Voegelin and Adorno seem to advocate and affirm experience, strategies of engagement and efforts of interpretation. And putting the emphasis on experience is not only an existential 'choice', but also perhaps first and foremost an ethical call. Or perhaps both: to embrace a listening attitude which implies immersion and experience rather than the logic and rationality of a primary visual reality requires and leads to another way of relating to the world. In *À l'écoute* (*Listening*), Jean-Luc Nancy calls the visual tendentially mimetic, and the sonorous tendentially methexic – that is, having to do with participation, sharing, or contagion.[22]

---

[19] Ibid., pp. xii and 5.

[20] Ibid., p. xii.

[21] Theodor Adorno, *Minima Moralia. Reflections on a Damaged Life*, trans. E.F.N. Jephcott (London: Verso, 2005), p. 71.

[22] Jean-Luc Nancy, *Listening*, trans. C. Mandell (New York: Fordham University Press, 2007), p. 10.

Conversely, distance, which is necessary in order to engage visually with the world, necessitates a detachment and objectivity that presents itself as truth. The visual gap nourishes the idea of structural certainty and the notion that we can truly understand things. Listening, on the other hand, has no opposite: we are amidst sounds. Therefore, it cannot offer a meta-position; there is no place where I am not simultaneous with the heard. Consequently, listening means sharing time and space with the sound source.[23]

Listening has to do with engagement and sensibility: it is a method of exploration, working contingently and on a singular basis beyond the intentions of the composer and any stable ontology of the musical work. When regarded an activity before or beyond knowledge, judgement, or evaluation (which could involve, for example, relating a particular piece of music to a particular genre, category, function or historical context), listening is an essential prerequisite for an ethical approach. The fact that listening works beyond or 'in addition to' critical assessment does not make it inexact or less relevant, because it is, at least ideally, based on the rigour and responsibility of perception. And, as we have seen, a listener must be sensitively engaged if she/he is to enter into critical discourse in an ethically responsible way as an act of commitment to a 'demand that demands approval'. But the first step may be the realization that the sense produced by the act of listening comes out of sensation, out of an experiential sensing of the world as life-world.[24] Sense is sought in sound. Idea and representation are replaced by timbre and resonance; truth (that one understands) is substituted by sense (to which one listens).[25]

Cosmos

To listen *to* music: this is how the relation between a listener and music is generally described – as one-way traffic. For Nancy, however, listener and music are two resonating and vibrating bodies, related to one another in a perpetual movement of transmission and return. Consequently, listening means both to penetrate and to be penetrated. Listening means dynamic movement, coming and going, back and forth, to and fro. The transcendental subject of philosophy becomes the resonating subject of music.

To listen, to listen to music, is to enter a spatiality by which the listening subject pierces the sonic body and, simultaneously, is pierced by sounds, pierced by the auditory. Sound happens on bodies. Voegelin writes:

---

[23] Voegelin, *Listening to Noise and Silence*, p. xii.

[24] Ibid., p. 20.

[25] Kathleen Higgins writes that '[t]he structuralist interpretation of music has obscured the experiential basis for recognizing an ethical dimension to music' (*The Music of Our Lives* (Lanham, MD: Lexington Books, 2011), p. 137.

> It is the action of sound on the listening body, which triggers this body into the action of perception that produces the work and the body itself. This action is affective. Affection in this sense is the agency of perception, which is triggered by the affection of its object on the listener. Such affection does ... motivate behaviour, but not towards the ideal objectivity of the work, but towards its contingent production.[26]

An example of this experience of penetration and affect becomes manifest when listening to the CD *Tears* from Cosmos, a duo from Tokyo, comprising Sachiko M (sampler and contact microphones) and Ami Yoshida (voice). Sachiko M's short bursts of modulated sine waves in an extreme register and the scraping of the contact microphone are combined with the amplified ticking from Yoshida's windpipe and the splintered stream of her closely-miked rasps and gurgles. From the first seconds it becomes clear that structural listening is not appropriate as a means of contact with this soundworld. The squeaks, buzzes and ear-cleansing interjections enter the body not only through the ears; they also creep under one's skin and work directly on the brain and the nervous system, thereby undermining analytical distance, control and assimilation. This music requires experience, not analysis; sensibility, not reflection; immersion, not distance. *Tears* confronts us with the lack of distance between the listener and the heard.

The music of Cosmos can be regarded as a reconnection with the raw material of natural and synthetic sounds itself. However, based purely on the listening experience, the difference between synthetic and natural sounds can hardly be discerned. *Tears* is not primarily an interaction between two performers based on attentive listening, one using electronic equipment, the other the human voice; it is, rather, a complex network of almost tactile microscopic noises, rattles, hisses and drones, creating a genuine sonic jungle in which the dialectic between the mechanical and the organic is quickly sublated. Sachiko M's memory-free sampler and Ami Yoshida's abstract use of her voice dissolve any potential desire on the part of the listener to distinguish between the two musicians and their instruments. Instead, the listener becomes immersed in a sonic environment stripped of any reference to the extramusical, which thus opens this environment to a multitude of audible possibilities, to the plenitude of the heard, to a limitless imagination: no classification in an extrasonic catalogue, but a phenomenological journey emphasizing the practical experience of the music.

Nodes

Music is able to demand the responsive and responsible engagement of its listeners. It can demand an attitude of making a difference, of making a difference which

---

[26] Voegelin, *Listening to Noise and Silence*, p. 177.

makes a difference, to borrow a phrase from Gregory Bateson;[27] it can demand the rejection of indifferent action, without care, without attention.

This call or appeal of music can only be heard via the act of unconditional listening – that is, through immersion and unmediated experience, happening before or beyond rational and analytical reflections, interpretations and explanations.[28] In line with the ideas of Emmanuel Levinas and Zygmunt Bauman (see 'Listening') this ethicality might occur not so much in an endeavour to understand (music), but in an attempt to experience (music). As we have also shown, however, this kind of listening experience will nevertheless lead to a certain understanding (see 'Discourse' and 'Voice'). Music thus engages our intellectual, emotional and physical natures simultaneously.[29] If music's call has ethical overtones, those allow an immanent ethics to resonate, independent of any transcendental values, independent of absolute and universal ideas about Good and Evil, favouring instead intensities and affects. And music's affective character has ethical repercussions. This is the tenor of our thoughts thus far in this final chapter. It is time to bring these thoughts together in one final reflection.

Music takes us to an ethics of affinity and engagement evoked through aesthetic sensibility. And this aesthetic sensibility is first of all corporeal. Rather than falling back on a metaphysics of morals, music's call for an affective ethicality, resulting from a premediated contact with sounds, is dependent on bodily experiences and perception. Perception is triggered by the affectivity of its object on the listener. And such affectivity can motivate behaviour. Without this affective engagement we are running the risk of failing to experience, and only understanding a musical work as an object, at a distance, removed from our emotions and sensations.

What we are proposing is that ethics emerges in the space between listener and music, in the resonance of the listening and the sounding body, in the dynamic encounter of the listener and the sensory material. Instead of relying on predetermined principles, ethical values need to be worked out in an effort of engagement – that is, in a perceptual process of experiencing music. Ethical sensitivity depends on an appreciation of the unique, the typical, the singular.

---

[27] Gregory Bateson, *Steps to an Ecology of Mind* (Chicago: University of Chicago Press, 2000), p. 459.

[28] 'Beyond' and 'before' should not be understood as indications of time here. Rather, they refer to another plane of experiencing music. Nancy describes this plane as 'l'écoute de l'outre-sens', referring to a sense that operates outside signification, or, better, a sense that defers immediate signification. If listening can be regarded as a constant moving between the semantic and the corporeal, between concept and sonority, or between the grammatical (structure, meaning) and the acoustical, we are emphasizing the latter here, though not by trying to create a new opposition: the one is always already present in the other. See also Marcel Cobussen, *Thresholds: Rethinking Spirituality Through Music* (Aldershot: Ashgate, 2008), pp. 130–33.

[29] Higgins, *The Music of Our Lives*, p. xv.

The moral value or ethical dimension of one's perception cannot be measured in relation to culturally agreed, established moral principles, but is worked out in this moment of experiencing a particular piece of music.[30] According to Voegelin:

> ... the ethical dimension of art concerns the responsibility of the audience to engage in the work's affective production and to produce their own emotions that reveal to each listener his own ethicality. This clarifies that the ethical dimension of the work, played out in its affective perception, is not to do with what it might represent, but what it produces in terms of an aesthetic sensibility.[31]

On this view, music does not become ethical through ethical texts (libretto, song texts, programme notes, discursive contexts). Neither does it become ethical through a presentation in a context dominated by ethical ideas or moral principles. Nor is ethics an intrinsic quality of (certain) music or sounds. Instead, a musical ethics can only come into existence on the basis of a contact with a perceiver – that is, through the act of listening. Thus, ethical moments can only be understood as strategies of engagement, through receptive interpretation, affected and formed by both doubt and astonishment. Unravelling several nodes, which have emerged on previous pages, does not lead to a musical ethics that explains experience but to an ethics that is grounded on experience.

On the other side of a transcendental ethics which seeks to found a clear and unchanging conception of the difference between Good and Evil there glimmers an ethics which takes a body's capacity to affect and be affected as its criterion. And with regard to music this affectivity is realized through the act of listening.

Listening. That is where it begins, our contact with music. It is the only way to attend to music's call, the only way to experience music. That is why we began this book with a reflection on listening: listening as being hospitable to an otherness which escapes a logocentric dominance that has also determined many discourses on music. And that is also why this book ends with a meditation on listening. Only from this process of listening can the articulation of a musical ethics emerge.

---

[30] Voegelin, *Listening to Noise and Silence*, p. 181.
[31] Ibid., p. 182.

Bibliography

Abbate, Carolyn, *Unsung Voices: Opera and Musical Narrative in the Nineteenth Century* (Princeton, NJ: Princeton University Press, 1991).
Adorno, Theodor W., 'Bach Defended against his Devotees', in *Prisms*, trans. S. Weber and S. Weber (Cambridge, MA: MIT Press, 1981), pp. 133–46.
——, *Modern Music*, (November–December 1927), as reproduced in Douglas Jarman, *Alban Berg: Wozzeck* (Cambridge: Cambridge University Press, 1989), p. 153.
——, *Mahler: A Musical Physiognomy*, trans. Edmund Jephcott (Chicago: University of Chicago Press, 1992).
——, 'The Opera *Wozzeck*', in *Essays on Music*, ed. Richard Leppert (Berkeley and Los Angeles: University of California Press, 2002).
——, *Essays on Music*, ed. Richard Leppert (Berkeley and Los Angeles: University of California Press, 2002).
——, *Minima Moralia: Reflections on a Damaged Life*, trans. Edmund Jephcott (London: Verso, 2005).
——, *Philosophy of New Music*, trans. and ed. Robert Hullot-Kentor (Minneapolis: University of Minnesota Press, 2006).
Agamben, Giorgio, *Homo Sacer: Sovereign Power and Bare Life*, trans. D. Heller-Roazen (Stanford, CA: Stanford University Press, 1998).
Arendt, Hannah, *The Origins of Totalitarianism*, trans. L. Kohler (San Diego: Harcourt, Inc., 1994).
Aristotle, *The Nicomachean Ethics*, trans. H. Rackham (Ware: Wordsworth Editions, 1996).
Attali, Jacques, *Noise: The Political Economy of Music*, trans. B. Massumi (Minneapolis: University of Minnesota Press, 1985).
Augoyard, Jean-François and Henry Torgue, *Sonic Experience: A Guide to Everyday Sounds* (Montreal: McGill-Queen's University Press, 2005).
'Baby-eating Art Show Sparks Upset', *BBC News*, 3 January 2003, at: http://news.bbc.co.uk/2/hi/entertainment/2624797.stm.
Badiou, Alain, *Ethics: An Essay on the Understanding of Evil*, trans. P. Hallward (New York: Verso, 2001).
Bailey, Derek, *Improvisation: Its Nature and Practice in Music* (New York: Da Capo Press, 1992).
Barenboim, Daniel and Edward Said, *Parallels and Paradoxes* (New York: Vintage Books, 2002).
Bateson, Gregory, *Steps to an Ecology of Mind* (Chicago: University of Chicago Press, 2000).

Bauman, Zygmunt, *Postmodern Ethics* (Oxford: Blackwell, 1993).
Baur, Steven, Raymond Knapp and Jacqueline Warwick (eds), *Musicological Identities: Essays in Honor of Susan McClary* (Aldershot: Ashgate, 2008).
Becker, Howard S., *Art Worlds* (Berkeley: University of California Press, 1982).
Benjamin, Walter, 'Critique of Violence', in *Walter Benjamin: Selected Writings, Volume 1: 1913–1926*, ed. M. Bullock and M.W. Jennings (Belknap/Harvard University Press, 1999), pp. 277–300.
Benson, Bruce Ellis, *The Improvisation of Musical Dialogue: A Phenomenology of Music* (Cambridge: Cambridge University Press, 2003).
Berg, Alban, *Wozzeck*, revised by H.E. Apostel (1955) according to the final corrections and amendments left by the composer. English translation by Eric Blackall and Vida Harford (Universal Edition).
——, 'The Preparation and Staging of "Wozzeck"' (1930), in George Perle, *The Operas of Alban Berg*, Vol. 1: *Wozzeck* (Berkeley: University of California Press, 1980).
——, 'A Lecture on *Wozzeck*' in Douglas Jarman, *Alban Berg: Wozzeck* (Cambridge: Cambridge University Press, 1989), pp. 154–70.
Bergeron, Katherine, 'Prologue: Disciplining Music', in Kathleen Bergeron and Philip V. Bohlman, *Disciplining Music: Musicology and its Canons* (Chicago: Chicago University Press, 1992).
Berliner, Paul, *Thinking in Jazz: The Infinite Art of Improvisation* (Chicago: University of Chicago Press, 1994).
Borgo, David, *Sync or Swarm: Improvising Music in a Complex Age* (New York: Continuum, 2005).
Bowie, Andrew, 'Prolegomena to Any Future Ethics of Music' (typescript supplied by the author). Paper given at the Society for Music Analysis Winter Study Day on 'Music and Ethics', held at the University of East Anglia on 23 February 2002.
——, *Music, Philosophy, and Modernity* (Cambridge: Cambridge University Press, 2007).
Buber, Martin, *I and Thou*, trans. W. Kaufmann (London: Continuum, 2004).
Bull, Michael and Les Back (eds), *The Auditory Culture Reader* (Oxford: Berg, 2003).
Butler, Judith, 'Ethical Ambivalence', in Marjorie Garber, Beatrice Hanssen and Rebecca L. Walkowitz (eds), *The Turn to Ethics* (New York: Routledge, 2000), pp. 15–28.
Canetti, Elias, *The Human Province*, trans. J. Neugroschel (London: Pan Books, 1986).
Carroll, Noël, 'Moderate Moralism', *British Journal of Aesthetics*, 36 (1996), pp. 223–38.
——, 'Art, Narrative, and Moral Understanding', in Jerrold Levinson (ed.), *Aesthetics and Ethics. Essays at the Intersection* (Cambridge: Cambridge University Press, 2001), pp. 126–61.

––––, 'Narrative and the Ethical Life' in Garry Hagberg (ed.), *Art and Ethical Criticism* (Chichester: Wiley-Blackwell, 2010), pp. 35–63.

Chion, Michel, *Film, A Sound Art*, trans. Claudia Gorbman (New York: Columbia University Press, 2009).

Clements, Andrew, '*Wozzeck*', in *The New Grove Dictionary of Opera*, ed. Stanley Sadie, *Oxford Music Online*, at: http://www.oxfordmusiconline.com/subscriber/article/grove/music/O005360 (accessed 19 December 2010).

Cobussen, Marcel, 'Deconstruction in Music' (PhD dissertation, Erasmus University Rotterdam, 2002), at: http://www.cobussen.com.

––––, 'Ethics and/in/as Silence', *Ephemera* 3/4 (November, 2003), pp. 277–85.

––––, 'Noise and Ethics: On Evan Parker and Alain Badiou', *Culture, Theory and Critique*, 46/1 (April 2005), pp. 29–42.

––––, *Thresholds: Rethinking Spirituality Through Music* (Aldershot: Ashgate, 2008).

Cohen, Benjamin, at: https://plus.google.com/100441642353694045036/posts/WeQV18n3KVZ.

Connor, Steven, 'The Modern Auditory I', in Roy Porter (ed.), *Rewriting the Self: Histories From the Renaissance to the Present* (London and New York: Routledge, 1996), pp. 203–23.

Cooke, Mervyn, *A History of Film Music* (Cambridge: Cambridge University Press, 2008).

Critchley, Simon, *The Ethics of Deconstruction: Derrida and Levinas* (Oxford: Blackwell, 1992).

––––, *Infinitely Demanding: Ethics of Commitment, Politics of Resistance* (London, New York: Verso, 2007).

Cusick, Suzanne, '"You are in a Place That is Out of the World ...": Music in the Detention Camps of the "Global War on Terror"', *Journal of the Society for American Music*, 2/1 (2008), pp. 1–26.

Davies, Stephen, *Musical Meaning and Expression* (Ithaca, NY: Cornell University Press, 1994).

––––, 'Artistic Expression and the Hard Case of Pure Music', in Matthew Kieran (ed.), *Contemporary Debates in Aesthetics and the Philosophy of Art* (Malden, MA: Blackwell Publishing, 2006), pp. 179–91.

Deleuze, Gilles and Félix Guattari, *A Thousand Plateaus: Capitalism and Schizophrenia*, trans. B. Massumi (Minneapolis: University of Minnesota Press, 1987).

––––, *What is Philosophy?*, trans. H. Tomlinson and G. Burchell (New York: Columbia University Press, 1994).

DeNora, Tia, *Music in Everyday Life* (Cambridge: Cambridge University Press, 2000).

Derrida, Jacques, *Dissemination*, trans. B. Johnson (Chicago: University of Chicago Press, 1981),

––––, *Points. Interviews 1974–1994*, trans. P. Kamuf *et al.*, ed. E. Weber (Stanford, CA: Stanford University Press, 1995).

———, *Of Hospitality*, trans. R. Bowlby (Stanford, CA: Stanford University Press, 2000).

———, *On Cosmopolitanism and Forgiveness*, trans. M. Dooley and M. Hughes (London: Routledge, 2001).

Devereaux, Mary, 'Beauty and Evil: The Case of Leni Riefenstahl's *Triumph of the Will*, in Jerrold Levinson (ed.), *Ethics and Aesthetics: Essays at the Intersection* (Cambridge: Cambridge University Press, 1998), pp. 227–56.

Devisch, Ignaas, *Wij. Nancy en het vraagstuk van de gemeenschap in de hedendaagse wijsbegeerte* (Leuven: Peeters, 2003).

Dolar, Mladen, *A Voice and Nothing More* (Cambridge, MA: MIT Press, 2006).

Dreyfus, Hubert L., *Being-in-the-world: A Commentary on Heidegger's Being and Time, Division I* (Cambridge MA: London: MIT Press, 1991).

Duffy, Michelle, 'Inhabiting Soundscapes', *ASCA Conference Sonic Interventions: Pushing the Boundaries of Cultural Analysis*, Reader for Panel 4: *Soundscapes: Sound, Space, and the Body* (2005), pp. 51–57.

Dutch Journal of Music Theory (*Tijdschrift voor Muziektheorie*), 7/3 (November 2002).

Finn, Geraldine, *Why Althusser Killed His Wife: Essays on Discourse and Violence* (Atlantic Highlands, NJ: Humanities Press, 1996).

———, 'Giving Place – Making Space – For Truth – In Music' (unpublished paper, 2002).

Fischlin, Daniel and Ajay Heble, *The Other Side of Nowhere: Jazz, Improvisation, and Communities in Dialogue* (Middletown, CT: Wesleyan University Press, 2004).

Fiumara, Gemma Corradi, *The Other Side of Language* (London and New York: Routledge, 1990).

Foucault, Michel, *The History of Sexuality, Vol. I*, trans. Robert Hurley (New York: Vintage Books, 1990).

———, 'La naissance de la médecine sociale', in *Dits et écrits*, vol. 2 (Paris: Gallimard, 1994), pp. 207–28.

Fraser, Nancy, 'Recognition without Ethics?', in Marjorie Garber, Beatrice Hanssen and Rebecca Walkowitz (eds), *The Turn to Ethics* (New York: Routledge, 2000), pp. 95–126.

Frith, Simon, 'Music and Identity', in Stuart Hall and Paul du Gay (eds), *Questions of Cultural Identity* (London: Sage, 1996), pp. 108–27.

Gadamer, Hans-Georg, *Truth and Method*, trans. G. Barden and J. Cumming (London: Sheed and Ward, 1979).

Gaut, Berys, 'The Ethical Criticism of Art', in Jerrold Levinson (ed.), *Aesthetics and Ethics: Essays at the Intersection* (Cambridge: Cambridge University Press, 1998), pp. 182–203.

Goodman, Steve, *Sonic Warfare: Sound, Affect, and the Ecology of Fear* (Cambridge, MA: MIT Press, 2009).

Gorbman, Claudia, *Unheard Melodies: Narrative Film Music* (Bloomington: Indiana University Press, 1987).

Gorse, Sandra, *Operatic Subjects: The Evolution of Self in Modern Opera* (London: Associated University Presses, 2000).
Gracyk, Theodore, *Rhythm and Noise* (Durham, NC: Duke University Press, 1996).
Greene, Susan, 'Wozzeck and Marie: Outcasts in Search of an Honest Morality', *Opera Quarterly*, 3/3 (1985), pp. 75–86.
Hagberg, Garry (ed.), *Art and Ethical Criticism* (Oxford: Blackwell, 2008).
Hall, Patricia, *Berg's Wozzeck* (Oxford: Oxford University Press, 2011).
Hanshe, Rainer J., 'Agonistic Ethics: On the Hospitality of Warriors', paper presented at the East–West Passage Conference in Pécs, Hungary, 3–6 November 2010.
Hardt, Michael and Antonio Negri, *Empire* (Cambridge, MA: Harvard University Press, 2000).
Heidegger, Martin, *Being and Time*, trans. J. Macquarrie and E. Robinson (Oxford: Blackwell, 1962).
——, 'The Origin of the Work of Art', trans. A. Hofstadter, in *Poetry, Language, Thought* (New York: Harper & Row, 1971), pp. 17–81.
——, *Martin Heidegger: Basic Writings*, trans. and ed. D. Farrell Krell (San Francisco, CA: Harper Collins, 1993).
——, *Introduction to Metaphysics*, trans. G. Fried and R. Polt (New Haven, CT: Yale University Press, 2000).
Henriques, Julian, 'The Vibrations of Affect and their Propagation on a Night Out on Kingston's Dancehall Scene', *Body & Society*, 16/1 (2010), pp. 57–89.
Higgins, Kathleen, *The Music of Our Lives* (Lanham, MD: Lexington Books, 2011).
Hoffman, Eva, *Appassionata* (New York: Other Press, 2009).
Ihde, Don, *Listening and Voice: Phenomenologies of Sound*, 2nd edn (Albany: State University of New York Press, 2007).
Jarman, Douglas, *Alban Berg: Wozzeck* (Cambridge: Cambridge University Press, 1989).
Johnson, Bruce and Martin Cloonan, *Dark Side of the Tune: Popular Music and Violence* (Farnham: Ashgate, 2009).
Johnson, Julian, 'Berg's Operas and the Politics of Subjectivity', in Nikolaus Bacht (ed.), *Music, Theatre, and Politics in Germany: 1848 to the Third Reich* (Aldershot: Ashgate, 2006), pp. 211–33.
Kearney, Richard and Maria Rainwater (eds), *The Continental Philosophy Reader* (London and New York: Routledge, 1996).
Kerman, Joseph, *Opera as Drama* (London: Oxford University Press, 1957).
——, *Contemplating Music: Challenges to Musicology* (Cambridge, MA: Harvard University Press, 1985).
Kim-Cohen, Seth, *In the Blink of an Ear: Toward a Non-Cochlear Sonic Art* (New York: Continuum, 2009).
Kivy, Peter (ed.), *The Blackwell Guide to Aesthetics* (Oxford: Blackwell, 2004).

——, *Antithetical Arts: On the Ancient Quarrel between Literature and Music* (Oxford: Oxford University Press, 2009).
Klossowski, Pierre, *Nietzsche and the Vicious Circle*, trans. Daniel W. Smith (London: Continuum, 2005).
Kostelanetz, Richard, *The Theatre of Mixed Means* (London: Pitman, 1970).
Kozinn, Alann, 'Finally, a Fuss for Prokofiev', *The New York Times*, Tuesday, 18 December 2001, E1.
Kramer, Lawrence, *Classical Music and Postmodern Knowledge* (Berkeley: University of California Press, 1996).
Kreutziger-Herr, Annette, 'Das Andere und das Eigene. Zur Einführung', in *Das Andere. Eine Spurensuche in der Musikgeschichte des 19. und 20. Jahrhunderts* (Frankfurt am Main: Peter Lang, 1998), pp. 11–21.
——, *Das Andere. Eine Spurensuche in der Musikgeschichte des 19. und 20. Jahrhunderts* (Frankfurt am Main: Peter Lang, 1998).
Kristeva, Julia, *Revolution in Poetic Language*, trans. Margaret Waller (New York: Columbia University Press, 1984).
LaBelle, Brandon, *Acoustic Territories: Sound Culture and Everyday Life* (New York: Continuum, 2010).
Lacan, Jacques, *The Ethics of Psychoanalysis 1959–60*, ed. Jacques-Alain Miller, trans. Dennis Porter, vol. 7: *The Seminar of Jacques Lacan* (London: Routledge, 1992).
Leppert, Richard, *The Sight of Sound* (Berkeley: University of California Press, 1995).
Levinas, Emmanuel, *Totality and Infinity*, trans. A. Lingis (Pittsburgh, PA: Duquesne University Press, 1969).
——, *Collected Philosophical Papers*, trans. A. Lingis (The Hague: Martinus Nijhoff, 1987).
——, 'Reality and its Shadow', in Seán Hand, *The Levinas Reader* (Oxford: Blackwell Publishers, 1989), pp. 129–43.
Levinson, Jerrold, 'Music and Negative Emotions', in *Music, Art and Metaphysics: Essays in Philosophical Aesthetics* (Ithaca, NY: Cornell University Press, 1990), pp. 306–35.
—— (ed.), *Ethics and Aesthetics: Essays at the Intersection* (Cambridge: Cambridge University Press, 1998).
Lévy, Pierre, *Collective Intelligence: Mankind's Emerging World in Cyberspace*, trans. R. Bononno (Cambridge: Perseus Books, 1997).
Lyotard, Jean-François, *The Inhuman: Reflections on Time*, trans. G. Bennington and R. Bowlby (Cambridge: Polity Press, 1991).
McClary, Susan, *Feminine Endings: Music, Gender, and Sexuality* (Minnesota: University of Minnesota Press, 1991).
——, 'The World According to Taruskin', *Music & Letters*, 87/3 (2006). pp. 408–15.
——, *Reading Music: Selected Essays* (Aldershot: Ashgate, 2007).
MacIntyre, Alasdair, *Dependent Rational Animals: Why Human Beings Need Virtues* (Chicago: Open Court, 1999).

McQuiston, Kate, 'Value, Violence, and Music Recognized: A Clockwork Orange as Musicology', in Gary D. Rhodes (ed.), *Stanley Kubrick: Essays on his Films and Legacy* (Jefferson, NC, and London: McFarland & Company, Inc., 2008), pp. 105–22.

Massumi, Brian, *Parables for the Virtual: Movement, Affect, Sensation* (Durham, NC: Duke University Press, 2002).

Meelberg, Vincent, 'Sonic Strokes and Musical Gestures', in Jukka Louhivuori, Tuomas Eerola, Suvi Saarikallio, Tommi Himberg and Päivi-Sisko Eerola (eds), *Proceedings of the 7th Triennial Conference of the European Society for the Cognitive Sciences of Music (ESCOM)* (Jyväskylä: University of Jyväskylä, 2009), pp. 324–27.

——, *Kernthema's in het muziekonderzoek* (Den Haag: Boom Lemma, 2010).

Merleau-Ponty, Maurice, *Phenomenology of Perception*, trans. C. Smith (New York: Routledge and Kegan Paul, 1962).

Merriam, Alan, *The Anthropology of Music* (Evanston, IL: Northwestern University Press, 1964

Monson, Ingrid, *Saying Something: Jazz Improvisation and Interaction* (Chicago: Chicago University Press, 1996).

Nancy, Jean-Luc, *The Inoperative Community*, trans. P. Connor *et al.* (Minneapolis: University of Minnesota Press, 1991).

——, 'Responding for Existence', *Studies in Practical Philosophy*, 1/1 (1999), pp. 1–11.

——, *Being Singular Plural*, trans. R.D. Richardson and A.E. O'Byrne (Stanford, CA: Stanford University Press, 2000).

——, *The Genealogy of Morals*, trans. H.B. Samuel (New York: Dover Publications, 2003).

——, *Listening*, trans. C. Mandell (New York: Fordham University Press, 2007).

Nietzsche, Friedrich, *Kritische Studien Ausgaben*, 9, 11 [7].

Novalis, *Schriften. Die Werke Friedrich von Hardenbergs*, ed. Paul Kluckhohn and Richard Samuel (Stuttgart: Kohlhammer, 1960).

Nussbaum, Martha C., *Sex and Social Justice* (Oxford: Oxford University Press, 1999).

Oliveros, Pauline, *Deep Listening. A Composer's Sound Practice* (New York: iUniverse, Inc., 2005).

Passmore, John, 'The Dreariness of Aesthetics', *Mind*, 60/239 (1951), pp. 318–35.

Peek, Ella, 'Ethical Criticism of Art', *Internet Encyclopedia of Philosophy*, ed. James Fieser and Bradley Dowden, at: http://www.iep.utm.edu/art-eth/ (accessed 3 December 2011).

Peeva, Adela, *Whose is this Song?* [DVD] (Sofia: Adela Media, 2003).

Perle, George, *The Operas of Alban Berg*, Vol. 1: *Wozzeck* (Berkeley: University of California Press, 1980).

Peters, Gary, *The Philosophy of Improvisation* (Chicago: University of Chicago Press, 2009).

Plato, *Laws: The Discovery of Being*, trans. S. Benardete (Chicago: University of Chicago, 2000), pp. 284–312.

Plato, *The Republic*, Book III, trans. Benjamin Jowett (Charleston, S. C.: BiblioBazaar, 2007).

Poole, Geoffrey, 'Alban Berg and the Fateful Number', *Tempo*, New Series, 179 (1991), pp. 2–7.

Prévost, Edwin, *No Sound is Innocent* (Harlow: Copula, 1995).

Richards, David G., *Georg Büchner's* Woyzeck*: A History of its Criticism* (Rochester: Camden House, 2001).

Ridley, Aaron, *The Philosophy of Music: Themes and Variations* (Edinburgh: Edinburgh University Press, 2004).

Robinson, Dave and Chris Garrett, *Introducing Ethics* (Thriplow: Icon Books, 1996).

Robinson, Jenefer, *Deeper than Reason: Emotion and its Role in Literature, Music, and Art* (Oxford: Oxford University Press, 2007).

Rowe, Keith, 'Duos for Doris', liner notes (New York: Erstwhile Records, 2003).

Sacks, Oliver, *Musicophilia. Tales of Music and the Brain* (New York: Vintage Books, 2007).

Sandel, Michael J., 'The Procedural Republic and the Unencumbered Self', *Political Theory*, 12/1 (1984), pp. 81–96.

Scarry, Elaine, *On Beauty and Being Just* (London: Duckworth, 2006).

Schellekens, Elisabeth, *Aesthetics and Morality* (London: Continuum International Publishing Group, 2007).

Schmalfeldt, Janet, *Berg's Wozzeck: Harmonic Language and Dramatic Design* (New Haven, CT: Yale University Press, 1983)

Schnebel, Dieter, *Re-Visionen*, CD-booklet (Köln: Wergo/Harmonia Mundi, 1998).

Schoenberg, Arnold, 'Preface', *Pierrot Lunaire*, (Los Angeles: Belmont Music Publishers, 1990).

Selznick, Philip, *The Communitarian Persuasion* (Washington, DC: Woodrow Wilson Center Press, 2002)

Sloterdijk, Peter, *Im selben Boot. Versuch über die Hyperpolitik* (Frankfurt am Main: Suhrkamp, 1995).

——, *Sferen. Schuim*, trans. Hans Driessen (Amsterdam: Boom, 2009).

Smith, Chris, 'A Sense of the Possible: Miles Davis and the Semiotics of Improvisation', in Bruno Nettl (ed.), *In the Course of Performance: Studies in the World of Musical Improvisation* (Chicago: University of Chicago Press, 1998), pp. 261–89.

Smith, Daniel W., 'The Place of Ethics in Deleuze's Philosophy: Three Questions of Immanence', in Eleanor Kaufman and Kevin Jon Heller (eds), *Deleuze and Guattari: New Mappings in Politics, Philosophy, and Culture* (Minneapolis: University of Minnesota Press, 1998), pp. 251–69.

Spitzer, Michael (ed.), 'Special Issue: Music and Emotion', *Music Analysis*, 29/1–3 (March–October 2010).

Steiner, George, *In Bluebeard's Castle: Some Notes Towards the Redefinition of Culture* (New Haven, CT: Yale University Press, 1971)

Sterne, Jonathan, 'Urban Media and the Politics of Sound Space', in *OPEN 9 Sound: Sound in Art and Culture* (Rotterdam: NAi Publishers, 2005), no page numbers.

Storr, Anthony, *Music and the Mind* (New York: Ballantine Books, 1993).

Stravinsky, Igor and Robert Craft, *Dialogues and a Diary* (Garden City, NY: Doubleday, 1963).

Szendy, Peter, *Listen: A History of our Ears* (New York: Fordham University Press, 2008).

Taruskin, Richard, 'She do the Ring in different voices' (review), *Cambridge Opera Journal*, 4/2 (1992), pp. 187–97.

——, *The Oxford History of Western Music*, 5 vols (Oxford: Oxford University Press, 2005).

——, 'Music's Danger and the Case for Control', *The New York Times*, Sunday, 9 December 2001, AR1. Reprinted in *The Dangers of Music and Other Anti-Utopian Essays* (Berkeley: University of California Press, 2008), pp. 168–80.

——, 'Material Gains: Assessing Susan McClary' (review), *Music & Letters*, 90/3 (2009), pp. 453–67.

Taylor, Charles, *The Malaise of Modernity* (Concord: House of Anansi Press, 1991).

Taylor, Craig, 'Art and Moralism', *Philosophy* 84/3 (2009), pp. 341–53.

Taylor, Mark C., *Erring: A Postmodern A/Theology* (Chicago: University of Chicago Press, 1987).

'Tinkebell. My Dearest Cat Pinkeltje', at: http://looovetinkebell.com/pages/my-dearest-cat-pinkeltje.

Tonkiss, Fran, 'Aural Postcards. Sound, Memory and the City', in Michael Bull and Les Back (eds), *The Auditory Culture Reader* (Oxford: Berg, 2003), pp. 303–309.

Toop, David, *Haunted Weather: Music, Silence and Memory* (London: Serpent's Tail, 2004).

Ugresic, Dubravka, *The Culture of Lies*, trans. Celia Hawkesworth (London: Phoenix, 1996).

van Gerwen, Rob, 'Ethical Autonomism: The Work of Art as a Moral Agent', *Contemporary Aesthetics*, 2 (2004) (online) at: http://www.phil.uu.nl/~rob/PF_oud/s_inlcolleges/s_inlteksten/ea.pdf.

Voegelin, Salomé, *Listening to Noise and Silence: Towards a Philosophy of Sound Art* (New York: Continuum, 2010).

Williams, Bernard, *Ethics and the Limits of Philosophy* (London and New York: Routledge, 2006).

Winterson, Jeanette, *The Passion* (London: Bloomsbury, 1987).

Wolff, Janet, 'The Ideology of Autonomous Art', in Richard Leppert and Susan McClary (eds), *Music and Society: The Politics of Composition, Performance and Reception* (Cambridge: Cambridge University Press, 1987), pp. 1–12.

Yudkin, Jeremy, *Miles Davis, Miles Smiles and the Invention of Post Bop* (Bloomington: Indiana University Press, 2008).
Zappa, Frank, *Joe's Garage* (London: Zappa Records, 1979).

Index

Abbate, Carolyn 118–19, 123–4, 129, 131
Adams, John 14–15
Adorno, Theodor W. 29–31, 32, 79–80, 82–3, 93, 109n65, 126–7, 130–34, 151, 152, 158, 162
affect, affectivity 2, 7, 8, 23, 28, 40, 47, 49, 60, 65, 66, 67, 75, 79, 86, 87, 89, 91–4, 98n22, 99–102, 105–6, 110–15, 121–2, 148, 160–62, 164–6
Agamben, Giorgio 101
agency 6, 11, 50–51, 54–8, 105, 118, 124, 132, 164
Al-Qaeda 13
alterity 20, 23, 24, 65–6, 83, 87, 150; *see also* other(ness)
Aristotle 18n14, 39, 88n87, 101
Attali, Jacques 9n25, 31, 84, 100n30, 103
attentive listening 10, 12, 29–35, 64, 70, 155, 164
aural ethics 10, 11, 24, 27
autonomy, autonomism 5, 8, 11, 15–17, 38, 73, 75, 83, 87n77, 96, 100, 111–15, 117, 140n76, 156

Bach, Johann Sebastian 15, 29, 39, 41, 45, 47–9, 53, 103
Badiou, Alain 10, 16, 21, 22, 25–6, 30, 31, 55n59, 159
Barthes, Roland 30n47
Bateson, Gregory 165
Bauman, Zygmunt 10, 17–20, 21, 66–8, 71, 72, 75, 85, 165
Beethoven, Ludwig van 3, 31, 48, 103, 158
being-in-common 81–2, 87
being-in-the-world 102, 133, 139, 156
being with/for 18, 19, 67, 81–3, 85, 96, 151, 152n99
being-with-others 81–2
Berg, Alban 11, 117, 125–36, 138–52

Bergeron, Katharine 103–4
Berliner, Paul 63, 69n26, 71
body, corporeality 73, 82, 89, 100–108, 111–15, 155, 158, 160–66
Böhme, Gernot 102
Borgo, David 69
Bowie, Andrew 1, 3, 37, 42, 44, 120–24
Büchner, Georg 125, 149

Cage, John 3, 31
Canetti, Elias 13
care, carefulness 27–9, 33–5, 65, 87, 88n85, 92, 102, 105, 130–33, 138, 143–4, 147–8, 155, 158, 165
Carter, Ron 63–4, 88–9
censor(ship) 14, 17, 79, 103
collective ethics 11, 58, 72, 74–9, 83–90, 123, 151, 155
Coltrane, John (and Pharaoh Sanders) 73–4, 78, 85, 90
communitarianism 11, 74–84
Connor, Steven 115
control society 109
Cosmos (Sachiko M and Ami Yoshida) 163–4
Critchley, Simon 19n16, 21, 55–8

Davis, Miles (the Miles Davis Quintet) 63–5, 68n25, 73, 76, 78, 85–6, 88–90
deconstruction 21, 22, 25, 35, 89, 95, 152, 158
Deleuze, Gilles (and Félix Guattari) 21, 28n39, 109, 111, 115, 159–61
DeNora, Tia 93–4, 97n20
Derrida, Jacques 10, 19–21, 24, 25, 28, 30, 31, 35, 61, 82, 96, 105
discipline, disciplining 8, 11, 52, 76n48, 90, 101, 103–11, 115, 156
Dolar, Mladen 117–19, 123

duty 22, 59, 67, 75
Dylan, Bob 32–3

encounters (ethical) 10, 12, 22–3, 25–30, 33, 38, 59, 68, 81, 85, 100, 149, 157, 159–60, 165
emotion, emotional 14, 40–42, 46–50, 64, 79, 92–3, 95, 102, 105, 110n66, 111n68, 117, 121–2, 124, 128, 132–4, 139, 142n81, 143–4, 152, 165–6
empathy 15, 130–32, 138, 140–44, 149, 152
engagement 2, 5, 6, 10, 12, 28, 34, 37–8, 45, 46, 49, 50, 54, 57, 58, 117, 121–3, 125, 131, 134, 138n69, 141, 144, 155–6, 161–6
erotic, the, sensuous 14, 102, 139, 141, 144, 146, 149
essentialism 10, 23, 52–3, 55, 58
ethical atomism 76
ethical criticism 11, 37–9, 41–2, 44–58, 126, 133, 155–6
ethical experience 55–8
ethical listening 33
ethical suggestions 21
ethics of authenticity 74
ethos 19, 75, 100
Etzioni, Amitai 74

film music 45–50, 81
Fiumara, Gemma Corradi 34
football 11, 97–9, 111
formalism 2, 40, 43, 45n36
Foucault, Michel 101, 103–5
Fraser, Nancy 4n11, 97
freedom 5, 13, 14n2, 19, 34, 64, 67, 74, 77–80, 83–4, 86, 88, 157
Freud, Sigmund 16–17, 73
Frith, Simon 94–5

Gadamer, Hans-Georg 34
Gergiev, Valery 13
good, the (and evil) 3–5, 6, 16, 22, 26, 37, 39, 45, 55–7, 61, 75, 88–9, 92, 135, 158, 159, 160, 165–6
Goodman, Steve 8, 105nn48, 50; 107, 110n66

Greene, Susan 138, 140–41, 149

Hagberg, Garry 2n4, 38–9, 46n38, 61, 65n13, 71, 87n77
Hancock, Herbie 63–4, 85, 89
Hanslick, Eduard 14, 18, 40
Hardt, Michael (and Antonio Negri) 104, 109
(dis)harmony 1, 14, 41, 44, 78, 92, 93n4, 103
Haydn, Joseph 26
Heble, Ajay 69
Heidegger, Martin 23, 25, 28–9, 81–2, 121–4, 134, 142, 151, 158–9
   Stimmung 121–4, 133–4, 142, 147, 155
hermeneutics 11, 47, 52–4, 119–21, 123–4, 133, 137, 156
Higgins, Kathleen 1, 2, 34n60, 46, 64n11, 124n25, 163n25, 165n29
Hoffman, Eva (*Appassionata*) 12, 156–7, 161
hospitality 10, 16, 19–25, 27–8, 31, 33, 61, 68, 70, 88, 156, 166
hospitable listening 33
Hume, David 16–17

identity (individual and collective) 18, 48, 75, 77–8, 92–100, 106, 111–12, 156
Ihde, Don 121n14, 123
imagination, imaginative 10, 34, 45, 49–50, 68, 94, 164
immanent ethics, immanence 101, 115, 158–61, 165
improvisation, improvised music 11, 31, 58, 59, 61–4, 67–74, 76–81, 84–90, 155–6
individual/personal ethics 3, 8, 11, 16–19, 54, 58, 59, 65–6, 67–8, 71–80, 82–8, 90, 99, 100, 114–15, 122–3, 134, 138, 151, 155–6
intersubjective (relations, space, surroundings, interactions) 2, 4, 57, 97, 124, 126, 128, 130, 133, 135–40, 142, 148–52, 156, 162
intersubjectivity 11, 49, 57, 116, 124–5, 128–9, 133–4, 139, 142, 151–2, 156

jazz 51, 62–4, 70n31, 76, 79–81, 104n45
Johnson, Bruce (and Martin Cloonan) 8, 92, 95n14, 98, 106, 109nn62, 64
Johnson, Julian 128–35, 144, 148–9, 151
(in)justice 4n11, 10–11, 27, 31, 35, 37, 44, 49–55, 57–8, 61, 78, 132, 150–57

Kant, Immanuel 2, 14n2, 53, 56, 57
Karadzic, Radovan 95
Kerman, Joseph 50, 132–4, 138, 148–50, 152
Kim-Cohen, Seth 33
Kivy, Peter 6, 39–46, 49–50, 54, 57, 62
Kramer, Lawrence 3n10, 15, 22, 24n30
Kreutziger-Herr, Annette 24–5
Kristeva, Julia 100

language 10–11, 17, 19–20, 25, 31, 35, 40, 42, 70–71, 96n18, 100, 102n35, 118–24, 128–9, 131–2, 136–7, 141, 147, 155
Leppert, Richard 22n25, 24n30, 30n45, 79n54, 126n27
Levinas, Emmanuel 3, 10, 11, 18–21, 24, 25, 32, 61, 64–8, 71, 72, 82, 83, 85, 126, 165
Lévy, Pierre 63–4, 89–90
love 40, 45, 47–8, 59, 68, 91, 126, 138–41, 144, 146, 148–50, 153, 157, 161
lust 139, 141, 144
Lyotard, Jean-François 32–3n57

McClary, Susan 22–3, 50–55, 57–8, 159n9
MacIntyre, Alasdair 11, 74–5, 78, 85, 100, 114
Massumi, Brian 111–12n68, 115
meaning 7, 15, 19, 22–3, 42, 44, 47, 50, 55, 59, 70, 79, 81, 85, 92, 94, 95n12, 97, 98n22, 100n30, 102, 105–6, 110n65, 111, 113–14n74, 117–20, 122–3, 135–6, 141, 142n81, 165n28
Merleau-Ponty, Maurice 42, 73, 155
Monson, Ingrid 63, 69n26, 71
mood 40–41, 62n7, 107, 109, 121–5, 127, 133–4, 139, 142n81, 150
(a)morality, moralism 1, 3, 4–19, 21, 23, 26, 38–50, 52–8, 61, 65n13, 67–9, 73–5, 78, 88–93, 97, 102, 104, 107, 109–11, 114, 115, 135, 137–38, 140–43, 149, 155–9, 165–6
Mozart, W.A. 39, 41n19, 48, 93, 103, 157
Muzak (sonic branding) 8–9, 11, 108–11

Nancy, Jean-Luc 11, 33, 80–83, 87–8, 112–15, 162–3, 165n28
Nietzsche, Friedrich 3, 59, 77n30, 88, 105n49, 159, 160
non-listening 11, 59–61, 74, 76, 86–8
normalization 101, 104n47, 108, 111
Novalis 91
Nussbaum, Martha 140

obligation 51–4, 66, 75, 81
Oliveros, Pauline 30n47
open(ness) 3, 10, 20–21, 23–8, 30n47, 32–4, 70, 75n45, 78, 82–7, 89, 100n26, 111, 123, 156, 159, 164
other(ness) 10, 11, 18–22, 24–7, 31–5, 41, 55, 59–61, 65–8, 70–73, 76–7, 80–88, 94, 96–100, 103, 108, 112–13, 115, 124, 126, 132, 133, 143, 150–52, 155–6, 159, 165n28, 166; *see also* the same (the order of), sameness

Parker, Evan 25n31, 72–4, 78, 85, 90
Peeva, Adela 91–5
Peters, Gary 11, 69n26, 87–8n85
phenomenology, phenomenological 11, 42, 44, 46, 49, 55, 57, 119–21, 123–5, 133–4, 137, 141, 155–6, 164
philosophy 1, 3, 4, 11, 16, 19, 21, 25–6, 37, 54, 82, 84, 114, 117, 124, 160, 163
  analytical philosophy 2, 30, 37–9, 43
Plato 1, 2, 13, 14, 77n51, 92–3, 102, 158
playing-with 85–7
politics, political 13–14, 16, 94–5, 104, 107, 130
  biopolitics 101
(post)modernism, (post)modern ethics 17, 18, 24n30, 25, 33n57, 66, 96, 114, 126, 128, 133, 152
Prévost, Edwin 'Eddie' 69
properties 38, 40, 42, 46, 54, 116, 124, 156
proteophilia 68

psychoanalysis 73, 88, 117, 127

receptive, receptivity 29, 35, 55, 61, 70, 155, 166
redemption 126, 130, 132–3, 137–8, 143, 146, 148, 150–52, 158
relationality 11, 83, 113–15, 156
respect 28, 33, 58, 61, 65–6, 68, 70–71, 75, 78, 82, 88n85, 99, 150
(ir)responsibility 2, 6, 8, 11, 17, 18, 33, 34, 50–58, 59, 61, 65–77, 79–80, 82, 84–7, 90, 92, 96, 104, 109–10, 115, 150, 155–6, 163–4, 166
response, responsiveness 6, 7, 10, 27–8, 33, 34, 38, 42, 46–50, 58, 65, 69, 75, 87, 88n45, 92, 111, 126, 130, 132, 155, 164
Rowe, Keith (and John Tilbury) 11, 60–61, 74, 76, 78, 85–8, 90

Sacks, Oliver 104n47, 110n66, 113n74
Said, Edward 94
the same (the order of), sameness 11, 18, 21, 24–5, 26, 30, 32–3, 65, 70, 83, 86, 94, 96
Sandel, Michael 74
Scarry, Elaine 10, 27–9, 41, 61, 158
Schnebel, Dieter 31–2
Schoenberg, Arnold 26, 126, 131n51, 139n72, 141, 142n81
the self 11, 16–19, 25, 29, 55–6, 59, 61, 65–8, 73–5, 77, 82, 84–6, 94, 96–100, 102, 105, 111, 121–4, 126, 147, 152n99, 162, 164; *see also* identity; subjectivity
Selznick, Philip 74–8, 85
sensibility 2, 12, 27–9, 52, 59n1, 61, 69, 122, 163–6
sensitive listening 33
(ethical) sensitivity 27, 30n47, 32, 33, 65n13, 68, 88, 124, 163, 165
Simmel, Georg 83
silence 24, 34, 61, 103, 117, 121, 123–4, 146–7

Sloterdijk, Peter 80–81, 83–5, 86, 88, 96, 99n25, 102n38
sonic weapon (HAARP, the 'Scream', the 'Mosquito') 8, 102, 106–8, 111
Spinoza, Baruch de 159–60
Steiner, George 93
Sterne, Jonathan 108–9
Storr, Anthony 59
structural listening 30, 164
subjectivity 4, 53, 55–6, 117, 122, 126–7, 129–30, 135–40, 142–4, 146–8, 151, 162
Szendy, Peter 59

Taruskin, Richard 13–15, 22, 50–55, 57, 58, 118–20, 130–33, 137, 148, 152, 159
Taylor, Charles 74
Taylor, Craig 90n90
Taylor, Mark C. 96
Tonkiss, Fran 102

Ugresic, Dubravka 94–5
unethical 8, 9, 11, 46, 61, 65, 86, 92, 111, 115, 117

Vattimo, Gianni 159
violence 8, 25, 48, 65, 97–8, 103, 106, 111, 156–8
virtue 14, 16, 24n30, 67, 75–7, 92, 138, 140–41, 148
Voegelin, Salomé 34n59, 161–4, 166
voice 4, 11–12, 32–3, 40, 57, 61, 82, 115, 116–29, 133–7, 141–2, 144, 147, 150–52, 155–6, 165

Winterson, Jeanette 55
Wolff, Janet 22–3
world-disclosive 4, 37, 57, 121, 124, 134, 151, 156

Zappa, Frank 15n3
Zorn, John 70, 76, 80–81